# THE DAMASCUS COVENANT

An Interpretation of the
"Damascus Document"

PHILIP R. DAVIES

Journal for the Study of the Old Testament
Supplement Series, 25

Sheffield 1983

Copyright © 1982 JSOT Press
ISSN 0309-0787
ISBN 0 905774 50 7 (cloth)
ISBN 0 905774 51 5 (paper)


Published by
JSOT Press
Department of Biblical Studies
The University of Sheffield
Sheffield S10 2TN
England


Printed in Great Britain by Redwood Burn Ltd.,
Trowbridge, Wiltshire


British Library Cataloguing in Publication Data

Davies, Philip R.
    The Damascus Covenant: An Interpretation of
    the Damascus Document.- (Journal for the
    Study of the Old Testament. Supplement Series,
    ISSN 0309-0787; 25)
    1. Damascus Document 2. Zadokites
    I. Title                II. Series
    221.4 '4               BM175.23

JOURNAL FOR THE STUDY OF THE OLD TESTAMENT
SUPPLEMENT SERIES
*25*

Editors
David J A Clines
Philip R Davies
David M Gunn

Department of Biblical Studies
The University of Sheffield
Sheffield S10 2TN
England

# CONTENTS

# PREFACE

This imperfect study is possible, of course, only because of the labours of others before, to whom I have tried to do justice in the Introduction as well as the footnotes. The Bibliography includes works to which I have both referred and found helpful in preparing this book. I apologise to any scholars who feel they have been unjustly overlooked or misrepresented. Because of the nature of the argument of the book, and the rather extensive Introduction, I have not provided any indexes. I honestly do not feel they would have been helpful, and I can only crave the indulgence of reviewers and readers alike if they are obliged to work through the whole book in order to extract a valuable nugget.

I must offer especial thanks to the University of Sheffield, from whom I received grants in aid of the research involved; to Dr. M.A. Knibb for reading a fairly rough draft and offering helpful suggestions and criticisms, and to my colleagues who patiently endured enthusiastic monologues and expressed more interest than my obsession deserved. But I must reserve my deepest acknowledgement to Carol and Gareth, who endured the pains of domestic deprivation while I wrote, rewrote and finally typeset a rather long and frankly even tedious manuscript. To them the finished product is poor recompense, but they will never let me think so.

בין איש לאשתו ובין אב לבנו

(CD VII,8-9)

# INTRODUCTION

Why another study of the 'Damascus Document'? In 1970 Joseph Fitzmyer wrote:

> Future work on the Damascus Document will certainly be related to the studies of the Qumran fragments of this writing. Little can be done on this text that is of lasting value before the full publication of the Cave IV material.[1]

Although all this material has not yet been published,[2] there are two major reasons for the present work. The first reason is that Fitzmyer's comment coincided with a detailed treatment, in a series of articles, of this document by Jerome Murphy-O'Connor; and in 1971 appeared *Die Entstehung der Qumrangemeinde*, Hartmut Stegemann's 1965 Bonn dissertation, already taken into account to some extent by Murphy-O'Connor. This ambitious study included an important assessment of the evidence of CD concerning Qumran origins.

These two reconstructions have provoked considerable discussion, but very little advance has subsequently been made beyond them. To a large extent both scholars were in agreement: the starting point for any reconstruction of Qumran origins was the identity of the Wicked Priest, who must be the Hasmonean Jonathan; the 'Teacher of Righteousness' who apparently founded the Qumran sect was the (Zadokite) High Priest replaced by Jonathan. This much both scholars derived from the Qumran biblical commentaries. But while they agree that the Qumran community did not originate with this 'Teacher,' but had a prehistory, they disagree widely as to the scope and character of this earlier phase. Stegemann reaches the already widely - agreed conclusion that the roots of the community lie in the Hasidic movement of the Maccabean period, which split into Essenes (at Qumran) and Pharisees, whom the Scrolls criticise as apostates. Murphy-O'Connor, on the other hand, believes that the Essenes originated in Babylon, returned to Palestine during the Maccabean period and there met with opposition from the political and religious authorities. After a split in the movement, some of these Essenes withdrew to Qumran. But, as Josephus reminds us, very many lived elsewhere in Palestine. Indeed, accoprding to Murphy-O'Connor Essenes were also to be found in the Diaspora.

The issue rests substantially on the evidence of the *Damascus Document* (hereafter CD). Both scholars differ in their assessment of it; but equally, both have understood that it is primarily through critical analysis of the literary sources that the question of Qumran origins must be pursued, and have completely substantiated this assumption by the results of their work. They have in effect determined that subsequent work on the origins of the Qumran community can, and should; be pursued by means of renewed attention to the literary sources, which are chiefly CD and the Qumran *pesharim*. But while both these scholars accord priority to the evidence of the *pesharim*, I believe that the investigation of CD must have priority over that of the *pesharim*, and the present study therefore represents a new evaluation of Qumran origins. *Only* CD contains explicit historiographical statements about the origins of its community, a fact acknowledged by both Stegemann and Murphy-O'Connor, while it is also demonstrably more amenable to various literary-critical techniques of analysis than the *pesharim*, which pose much more difficult problems, and indeed still await an adequate source-critical, redaction-critical and traditio-historical analysis of their contents, including especially the apparent historical data they contain. It is no distortion to assert that research on the *pesharim* has concentrated either on its midrashic technique or on matching historical personages to its numerous ciphers. The relationship between this kind of midrash and historical data is one which has not been seriously explored, nor has any adequate investigation yet been undertaken into the history of transmission of the lemmata and their relationship to the biblical text at various stages of the evolution of the *pesharim*, if indeed such an evolution took place.

The second reason for the present project has emerged clearly only in retrospect. I had not anticipated at the outset the most important conclusion I should reach, namely that *the document as a whole is basically older than the Qumran community*, and that our available manuscripts (from Cairo and presumably also from the Qumran caves) represent a Qumranic recension. If this conclusion is correct, the Qumran fragments of CD can only attest the *post-redactional* history of the document. It now seems to me questionable whether a definitive Qumranic version of the document ever existed, so that the value of the fragments is likely to be mainly textual.[3]

## A brief survey of scholarship on CD

The following survey is certainly intended as no more than a sketch. Its purpose is to acknowledge the vast amount of effort and ingenuity which CD has attracted, and to signal the major problems of interpretation which have arisen. It will also illustrate the indebtedness of the present analysis to the insights and arguments of previous generations of scholarship, and as such, it is hoped, will compensate for the lack of voluminous annotation in the analysis itself.

In 1910 Solomon Schechter published *Fragments of a Zadokite Work*,[4] three fragments of two recensions of a document found in the genizah of a Qaraite synagogue in Old Cairo and acquired by the University of Cambridge. Although the manuscripts were mediaeval, their contents revealed a Jewish sect of conceivably greater antiquity. The name *Zadokite Fragments* derives from the title 'sons of Zadok' which the sect applied, among others, to itself. The more usual title nowadays used is *Damascus Document*, arising from the sect's claim to have been exiled in the 'land of Damascus.' The official siglum used to identify fragments of this document from Qumran is (Q)D, and by a process of adoption the Geniza manuscripts from Cairo are designated CD.

The two Cairo manuscripts were labelled by Schechter A and B, A containing 16 pages (I-XVI in Schechter's pagination) and B two pages (XIX-XX); the first fragment of ms. A (A1) breaks off on p. VIII and ms. B provides an alternative recension of A VII,5-VII,21 (= B XIX,1-34), continuing beyond the point where A1 breaks off (B XIX,35-XX,34). A2 comprises IX-XVI. The two fragments of ms. A correspond to two sections of the work; the first is generally called the *Admonition* (A1, B) and the second the *Laws* (A2), and the work as a whole contains three kinds of material valuable for reconstructing the history and identity of its authors. The hortatory *Admonition* includes historical summaries and some polemics; the *Laws* contain rules for a kind of community life.

For the contents of this document, I refer the unfamiliar reader to the translation at the end of the book. Briefly, they comprise the following: some reflections on the history of Israel, the punishment which it incurred, and the establishment of a new covenant community; a demonstration of the way in which Israel departs from the law, and an introduction to the laws of this remnant community, concluded by warnings against those outside the community, whoever would associate with them, and apostates who have left the community; finally, laws governing life in cities or in community settlements or 'camps.' Of especial interest are the references to figures such as a 'Teacher of Righteousness' (or 'Teacher'), a 'Spouter of Lies,' and an 'Interpreter of the Law,' together with statements about an exile from the 'land of Judah' into the 'land of Damascus.' Also important are statements regarding the Jerusalem temple, towards which the document expresses a cautious but not entirely negative attitude, and regarding proper times and seasons for religious festivals and holy days, which imply a special calendar observed by the community.

Finally, a word about editions of the text. Schechter published a transcription of the Hebrew text, a translation, and notes, but reproduced photographs of only two pages of the original (I and XX). A full set of photographs was not published until 1952 by Zeitlin; they are reasonably clear, but less so than the originals themselves. A good critical edition of the text was published by L. Rost in 1933,[5] in which the readings of previous scholars are amply collated, but the best available in English at present is that of C. Rabin.[6] However, it suffers from an attempt to conflate the readings of ms. A and B where they overlap, and although the texts of both are printed separately at the end, the result is most unsatisfactory. It is Rabin's text which I have used, however, although I have also been able to consult the originals at Cambridge.

Study of the *Damascus Document* falls into two periods, divided by the discovery of the Dead Sea Scrolls. As a generalisation, we may say that the problem for pre-Qumran commentators was that they had insufficient evidence regarding the identity of the sect, and numerous hypotheses were advanced. After the Qumran discoveries nearly every scholar thought that we now knew at least the identity of the community in question, and that interpretation of the document was to be undertaken in the light of what we could learn of this community from its own literature. Henceforth study of CD became a province of Qumran scholarship, and its peculiar problems were approached not in isolation, but within the context of the Dead Sea scrolls and also, to an extent, of Qumran archaeology. This new context, however, has raised new problems of its own. Two of these in particular will be discussed presently: the account of the origins of the sect in CD I, which mentions the capture of Jerusalem by Nebuchadnezzar, specific periods of time (390 years and 20 years), the appearance of a 'teacher of righteousness'—and the allusion to an exile in Damascus, which appeared, in the first phase of research, to be an invaluable clue in identifying the sect, but has now become problematic in that a visit to Damascus by the Qumran settlers cannot be fitted into what we seem to know of the history of the community at Qumran.

I
*Research in the 'Pre-Qumran' phase*

*Schechter, 1910*
The publication of the text by Schechter (see above) provoked a flurry of reaction and speculation, all of which was based on Schechter's own readings and corrections, since Schechter had forbidden inspection of the originals in the Cambridge University Library for five years after his edition. Schechter was nevertheless on the whole rather cautious about his conclusions, and certainly aware of the immense problems in identifying the sect from which the document originated. As to the document itself, he concluded:

> Apart from the defective state of the MS. owing to age, or the carelessness of the scribe, its whole contents, at least as they are represented by Text A, are in a very fragmentary state, leaving the impression that we are dealing with extracts from a larger work, put together together, however, in a haphazard way, with little regard to completeness or order. (p. X)

Schechter began his discussion of the history of the sect with the account in CD I, and particularly the figure of 390 years between the time of Nebuchadnezzar and the 'teacher of righteousness.' Of this figure he offered four alternative explanations, which it is worth recording since the problem tends to be overlooked in more recent discussion: (i) the figure is a reliable historical datum (and at one point Schechter himself seems to favour this[7]); (ii) a symbolic value is suggested by the occurrence of the figure 390 in Ezekiel 4,5; (iii) 390 is an error for 490, a typical apocalyptic calculation of the eschaton (as in Dan 9); (iv) the figure is an inaccurate guess, without any literal or symbolic value. This last perhaps comes closest to his own conclusion, for he comments:

I must, however, remark that I have my doubts about the integrity of the text relating to this date. For our calculation would necessitate the assumption that the author of our text knew more of the Persian chronology than either the great majority of the Jews or the Samaritans, which is not likely . . . we are practically left without any definite date. (pp. XXIIf.)

Schechter's reconstruction of the community's history was as follows: at the end of a 'period of wrath' which followed the destruction by Nebuchadnezzar, Israel was blindly groping its way under the erroneous teaching of a 'man of scoffing.' But God raised a 'bud' who became recognised as the 'Teacher of Righteousness,' also known as the 'Interpreter of the Law' and the 'Only Teacher.' He was one of the group who 'went out of the land of Judah.' This group was said to have walked in his precepts during the period after his death but before his second coming, an expectation which Schechter inferred from the phrase in VI,11: 'until one comes who will teach righteousness at the end of days.' This Teacher is also the Messiah of Israel and Aaron, rejected by the majority of the nation.

Doctrines such as this messianic expectation, and also the recognition of a different list of authoritative writings, a different calendar and a different halachah compelled the sect, under the leadership of the 'Star,' to withdraw from the bulk of the Jewish nation to Damascus, where the Teacher was presumed by Schechter to have died. After his death, there was some apostasy and backsliding, which occasioned rebuke and expulsion, but this did not threaten the continued existence of the sect which remained in Damascus, living in cities and camps, with one city set apart as the 'city of the Sanctuary.' The hostility of the sect was directed especially at the Pharisees, who in Schechter's view constituted the majority of Jews, and whom the document dubs 'builders of the wall'; the laws of the sect frequently show a 'strong divergence from the Pharisaic custom' (p. XVIII).

Observing that 'the annals of Jewish history contain no record of a Sect agreeing in all points with the one depicted' (p. XVIII), Schechter alluded to a certain Zadok who, according to the Qaraite al-Qirqisani (7th century CE), opposed the Rabbanites (*sc.* the Pharisees), and observed a solar calendar. Although the calendar of the sect in question is not described by al-Qirqisani, Schechter identified it with that of the book of Jubilees, referred to at XVI,3 as the 'book of divisions of the days.' Schechter's suggestion is that the 'Zadokites' are a group from which the Dositheans descended, a group into which this sect was finally absorbed. This speculation is one of the few elements in Schechter's work which, deservedly, has not borne fruit in subsequent research. But the following remark *is* to the point:

> ... one result which I am about to state seems to me to be beyond doubt. And this is that it is among the sects severed from the main body of Judaism in which we have to look for the origin of such Pseudepigraphic works as the Book of Jubilees, the Book of Enoch, the Testaments of the Twelve Patriarchs, and similar productions,—and *not* in Pharisaic Judaism. (p. XXVI)

### Lévi, 1911

In his French translation and commentary,[8] I. Lévi took issue with many of Schechter's conclusions. In the first place, his description of the work is 'a kind of sermon intended to warn members of a sect against the dangers of apostasy' (pp. 163f.). In the pursuit of this theme the author dwells on the historical punishments of Israel. As to the history and identity of the sect, too, Lévi offered different answers. He agreed that the 390 years of CD I cannot be taken seriously as an accurate figure, and he also doubts the relevance of Ezekiel 4,5, since it is difficult to see how this figure could apply to the Exile. Schechter's other suggestion that the figure of 390 might be an error for 490 is also dismissed since one would expect this figure to relate to the end of the Exile and the arrival of the Messiah, which, according to the document, had not yet taken place. Lévi introduced another possible calculation, derived from the chronology found in the *Seder Olam*,[9] which would lead to a date of 32 CE, into which no historical events such as described in this document could be fitted. Essentially, then, he shared Schechter's scepticism.

For his reconstruction of the rise of the sect, Lévi did not start from CD I, but from VI,11ff., which, as he interprets it, refers to those who have made an agreement not to enter the sanctuary to 'light the altar in vain.' According to Lévi, the sanctuary in question must be the Jerusalem Temple, and those involved must be priests. The sect is therefore priestly and originated while the Temple was still standing. This view permits a more precise dating than Schechter could achieve. From the rest of the passage, Lévi deduced that the priests concerned were deprived of their privileges by usurpers who had the support of the people. From elsewhere in the document we learn that under the leadership of the 'Interpreter of the Law,' these priests, 'shaking the dust of impious Judah from their feet' (as Lévi puts it), departed to Damascus where they awaited the arrival of the Teacher (*Maître de Justice*), the Messiah who would punish the wicked.

What known historical events could this sequence reflect? Lévi agreed with Schechter that the document attacks the Pharisees, and he mentioned three possible moments of Pharisaic triumph which might have provoked a departure from the land: the Hellenistic crisis of the early 2nd century BCE, the favour shown to Pharisees by Salome Alexandra in the 1st century BCE, and the events of 62 CE. The second of these did not affect the priestly privileges, and the third closely preceded the destruction of the Temple, of which CD gives no hint. Therefore, in Lévi's view, the events in question are those involving the usurpation of the Zadokite line during the period of Hellenistic reforms. In this act, Lévi sees the Hasidim (cf. I Macc. 2,42)—according to him the Pharisees—as accomplices. The sect itself, seen by Lévi as staunch supporters of the Zadokite line, 'sons of Zadok,' are identified by him as Sadducees, but not as that party is described in the late and distorted account of Flavius Josephus! Lévi's reasoning may not now appear sound, but if one identifies Hasidim with Pharisees, and divides the whole of 2nd century BCE Judaism into the major parties described by Josephus, there is little alternative choice available. Zealots are disqualified for chronological reasons, and the Essenes, though considered by Lévi, were not found suitable. His resulting identification of the sect with Sadducees was adopted, for similar reasons but with slight revisions, by Charles (see below) and also by R. Leszynsky in his *Die Sadduzäer*, Berlin, 1912, pp. 142-167.

*Margoliouth, 1911ff.*
In the same year as Lévi published his comments, Margoliouth began to write a series of articles in which he identified the sect as a group of Sadducean Christians.[10] He offered the tentative suggestion that the Teacher of Righteousness was Jesus Christ, the Messiah John the Baptist and the Spouter of Lies the apostle Paul. To achieve the required dating, he used the chronological data of CD I in a new way, although one anticipated by Lévi. He suggested that the figure 390 was an *a posteriori* calculation intended to place the destruction of the Temple, which had occurred in 70 CE, 490 years after the Exile. Such a calculation fitted with the reckoning of *bAb. Zar.* 8b-9a (cf. *Seder Olam* 30) in which only 52 years were attributed to the Persians. In

1951 J.L. Teicher revised Margoliouth's idea, and more recently still B.E. Thiering has presented a theory which shares some of these conclusions.[11]

## Charles, 1912

In his influential commentary,[12] R.H. Charles was apparently much influenced by the conclusions of Lévi, which he developed in certain respects. In particular, he assessed more positively the 390 years of CD I, which previous scholars had found problematic. He accepted the figure as an accurate calculation, thus allowing himself him to place the formation of the 'party' (as he preferred to call the 'Zadokites') between 196 and 176 BCE. Here he interpreted the 'root of planting' (Schechter's 'bud') as a group, a movement, and not a priestly individual as Schechter and Lévi had done. On his assumption that the calculation of 390 years is both literal and correct, the rise of this 'root of planting' coincides more or less with the period in which the Hasidim arose.

For these 'Zadokites,' Charles adopted the term 'reformed Sadducees'; these originated as the chief movers in a reformation which arose from a protest against hellenising High Priests and a consequent religious revival. The party which formed among the priesthood called itself the 'penitents of Israel' and apparently attempted a reform of the Temple cult. Failure led to a withdrawal to Damascus under the leadership of the Star (= the Lawgiver) 'possibly soon after 176,' and here the 'New Covenant' was established. On Charles' view, however, this party later returned from Damascus to the cities of Israel which they made the sphere of their missionary efforts (p. 785). For an unspecified period, until the coming of the Teacher of Righteousness, they were to obey faithfully the precepts handed down by the Lawgiver, and it was probably during this time in Judah that they came into violent conflict with the Pharisees, against whom most of the invective of CD is directed. After the death of the Teacher, whose activity is not described in the document, more than forty years elapsed before the date of the document itself, which was written in what was described as the 'end of days.' The imminent advent of the 'Messiah from Aaron and Israel' had to be, according to Charles, an offspring of Herod (Israel) and Mariamne (Aaron), which required a date of composition between 18 and 8 BCE, the lifespan of Herod the Great's male descendants.

While his speculation as to the date of the composition is best left unremarked, Charles' view that this party originated with the Hasidim has become dominant, partly because of the enormous influence and authority which Charles, and his *Apocrypha and Pseudepigrapha of the Old Testament* have always commanded in the English-speaking world, and partly because allusions in the Qumran biblical commentaries were later thought to point in the same direction. Yet Charles' use of the chronological data in CD I not only defied the objections of previous scholars[13] and his own concession that the figure was borrowed from Ezekiel 4,5, but also overrode a further objection of his own. For Charles' view is that the text of CD is incomplete, in disorder, and possibly based on earlier documents. In support of this last point, he observes that I,5 is a prose insertion in the midst of verse, and in his translation he encloses the line, which contains the chronological calculation of 390 years from the time of Nebuchadnezzar, within square brackets. Charles' recognition, if only by implication, that the original source contained no calculation, together with his dating of the document to the time of Herod the Great, a considerable time after the events supposedly described, should have led him in the steps of previous scholars who had placed less than total confidence in the reliability of the calculation.

## Lagrange, 1912

The commentary and translation of M.-J. Lagrange[14] offered yet another view of the date and identity of the Damascus sect. Founded by a High Priest named Zadok at a time of national catastrophe, the sect fled to Damascus as Judah was being punished by the 'chief of the kings of Yawan' (VIII,11). Some survivors of this catastrophe were penitent, welcomed the arrival of a 'Teacher of Righteousness' (who is also the 'Star,' the 'Staff' and the 'Interpreter of the Law') and awaited the coming of the Messiah, while others, under the leadership of a 'Man of the Lie' or 'Spouter,' continued to be rebellious, and were about to receive a new punishment.

Lagrange adopted a new method of dating the events. He understood the document to calculate sixty years—twenty years before the arrival of the Teacher (I,10) and forty after his death (XX,15)—between the initial catastrophe and the arrival of the Messiah. Neither sixty years after Antiochus nor sixty years after Pompey turns out to have provided a suitable occasion for a messianic arrival; however, an interval of sixty years after the destruction of Jerusalem and the Temple in 70 CE brings us to the revolt led by Bar Cochba.

Accordingly, argued Lagrange, the sect most probably arose in the time of Hadrian and is to be identified neither as Sadducees nor as Pharisees, but as a messianic group whose roots may nevertheless be as ancient as these other parties. For despite his relatively late dating of the emergence of this group, Lagrange acknowledged important similarities between CD and Jubilees, I Enoch and the Testaments of the Twelve Patriarchs. A similar calculation of the rise of the group was given by G.F. Moore, who also identified the catastrophe in question as the fall of Jerusalem in 70 CE and assigned the origin of the sect to the time of Titus.[15]

### Gressmann, 1912

In an interesting response to Schechter's publication of CD, H. Gressmann adopted a quite different interpretation of the document from those so far considered. In particular, he claimed that Schechter and many other scholars had failed to appreciate the function of biblical citations and allusions, and understood them too literally. For example, they saw in polemic expressed largely in biblical vocabulary and imagery a detailed description of a particular historical group, namely the Pharisees. In Gressmann's view this inference was invalid, and indeed he offered the view that the sect was basically *akin* to the Pharisees. He further maintained that CD contained no historical data whatever, but consisted entirely of an apocalyptic fantasy, orientated totally towards the eschaton and not towards events of the past. Statements purportedly about the past were to be read of the future. Apart from his tentative association of the sect with Pharisees, Gressmann's interpretation did not win much support, and was directly challenged by Meyer (see below). But a similar position in some respects was taken by Rost in 1933. In a brief introduction to his edition of the text,[16] he agreed that the data of CD I were useless for chronological purposes. Although disagreeing with Gressmann and numerous others in holding the *Admonition* to be a literary unity, Rost endorsed Gressmann's view of its character, declaring that I-VIII contained a work 'which is incomplete certainly at the beginning but also at the end, which sets the history of the sect in opposition to its enemies within an apocalyptic schema.' (p. 1).

### Meyer, 1919

R. Meyer vigorously defended a Seleucid date for the origin of the CD sect, against Gressmann's denial of any historical value in the text, and against Lagrange and others who had adopted substantially later dates.[17] In his view, CD, like I Enoch, Daniel, the Testaments of the Twelve Patriarchs and Jubilees, reflected the clash between tradition- alists and innovators during the Hellenistic crisis of the early 2nd century BCE. Following many previous scholars, Meyer regarded the chronological data of CD I as glosses, but in a procedure not dissimilar to that of Charles, found that they nevertheless pointed to the Maccabean period! The 'Spouter of Lies' who led Israel astray (CD I,14) was identified with the *huios paranomos* of I Macc. 1,11 who 'persuaded many, saying, "Let us go and make a covenant with the nations around us".' And in Meyer's words, 'there can be no doubt' that the figure is Jason (p. 31).

By 'Damascus' Meyer understood the populated oasis of culture of which the Syrian city was the centre. The formation of the community of CD, its departure from Jerusalem and the composition of the document all fall shortly before 170/169 BCE following the first entry of the Seleucid king Antiochus IV into Jerusalem. But while Meyer saw a probable connection between this community and the Hasidim, the two were not, in his view, to be identified as Charles had proposed. The text of CD, he argued, had subsequently been worked over and expanded, so that some portions of the text belonged to a later period, although no substantial change to the meaning of the original document had been effected.

### Ginzberg, 1911ff.

Louis Ginzberg's *Eine unbekannte jüdische Sekte* appeared in 1921, although the material was first published as articles between 1911 and 1914. A recent English translation contains material (chs. 8,9, and 10) which was not present in the original book, but which in the opinion of his son Eli Ginzberg must have been composed no later than the first World War.[18]

Ginzberg provided a wealth of linguistic and exegetical comment which it would be impossible to review here. His views regarding the history and identity of the sect were as follows. In the first place, it is not the origins of the sect which are reflected in the notorious first page of CD, for in Ginzberg's view that historical summary describes the pre-exilic history of Israel. The period of 390 years in Ezekiel 4,5 applied in its original context to the period of iniquity of the northern kingdom, and consequently the calculation in CD I which was based on it should be understood to terminate at 721 BCE when that kingdom ceased to exist. The 'root of planting' which followed it must therefore denote the kingdom of Judah which survived the fall of the northern kingdom, and the 20 years of groping like the blind describe the twenty kings of Judah from Saul (sic!) to Josiah. The Teacher of Righteousness was probably the High Priest under Josiah, namely Hilkiah.

To understand how the sect arose, Ginzberg started from the midrash on Ezekiel 44,15 (CD III,21ff.), concluding that the founders of the sect were priests who left Judaea to realise their ideal abroad and were 'joined' by new members. From VI,11 he deduced that this sect believed the Temple to be in impure, *Sadducee*, hands, and consequently swore to abandon it. For the same reason they had also to abandon observance of the holy days prescribed by the unclean priests. After their migration to Damascus, the Star, the 'Exegete of the Torah,' arose, and a new programme was devised. VI,19-VII,4 represents this new programme while VI,11ff. constitutes merely the Judaean programme previously in operation.

The halachah of this group, apart from distinct sectarian innovations, is consistent with what we know of the Pharisees' halachah, and the 'desolation of the land' mentioned in V,20 describes the warfare between Jannaeus and the Pharisees. According to *Meg. Ta'anith* this resulted in a flight of Pharisees to Syria. The death of Jannaeus raised problems for the group; some wished to return to Judaea, others preferred to terminate relations with their Judaean brethren and these formed a 'new covenant in the land of Damascus.' Members of this covenant became known as 'congregations of perfect holiness,' living according to the ideals of the 'Exegete of the Torah' who was also known as the 'Teacher.'

But the view that CD's halachah is consistent on the whole with Pharisaic halachah is not tenable, despite the later advocacy of Rabin.[19] There are also difficulties with Ginsberg's theory in innumerable points of detail. What deserves consideration, however, is the suggestion that CD shows us the emergence from a parent group of a movement wedded to the ideals of an individual 'teacher,' and that while the phrase 'new covenant' is applied to itself by this smaller *splinter group*, the migration to Damascus belongs to the *parent* group. Despite great differences on other matters, this particular conclusion is one which has also been reached in the analysis to follow, and although it was reached independently and on different grounds, the suggestion itself is to Ginzberg's credit.

*Büchler, 1913*

The view that the *Zadokite Fragments* and the sect which they reveal both originate in the mediaeval period was, as far as I can tell, first given prominence by A. Büchler.[20] There is, of course, no dispute that the Cairo manuscripts are mediaeval, nor that there are strong connections between its doctrines and those of the mediaeval Qaraites, as Schechter had himself fully realised and taken into account. Büchler argued, however, that both the halachoth and the language of the manuscripts were closely paralleled in Qaraite literature to the extent that they must be regarded as a Qaraite composition. This view was defended also by Marmorstein in 1918 and by Zeitlin from 1926 onwards.[21] Since the discovery of the Dead Sea Scrolls Zeitlin and other adherents of this view have been obliged to dismiss these as forgeries from the same period. We may note in passing that Zeitlin defended his late dating on the basis of the data in CD I as follows: according to Talmudic calculation, 490 years elapsed between the destructions of the Temple by Nebuchadnezzar and Titus (*bErub.* 12b; cf. *bShab.* 15a and see above for the use of the same data by Margoliouth). One hundred years earlier (i.e. 390 years) brings us to the arrival of Hillel, who is therefore to be identified as the 'Spouter' while Shammai must be the 'Teacher of Righteousness.' It is appropriate that this portion of our review should end with a reminder that internal indications of the date of CD and of the origin of the 'Damascus' community are scarce and, until the discovery of the Dead Sea Scrolls, were very much disputed.

## II
*Research in the post-Qumran period*

Following the publication of the Dead Sea Scrolls, correspondences with the *Zadokite Fragments* were quickly observed by several scholars. These correspondences included the figures of the 'Teacher of Righteousness' and the 'Spouter of Lies' (or 'man of the Lie') in the case of the *pesharim*, and a range of parallels—doctrinal, verbal and organisational—in the case of the Manual of Discipline or Community Rule (1QS).[22] CD has henceforth for all practical purposes been treated as one of the Scrolls, and included in virtually every edition of Qumran texts and translations. The appearance of fragments from this document at Qumran (see n.1) has been taken to justify this treatment. Yet the book of Jubilees, to which CD appears to refer, and which contains a great deal in common with CD, especially its calendar and its *Heilsgeschichten*, is not regarded as a Qumran text, although it is represented among the manuscript finds from the Dead Sea caves. Integrating the interpretation of CD with that of other Qumran texts has in fact created more problems than it has solved. My intention in this part of the survey is not simply to offer a review of an already well-reviewed field, but in so doing to support the assertion just made.[23]

The assumption that CD was written within the Qumran community has provoked several problems, notwithstanding similarities in doctrine and terminology with the Scrolls. Four important instances are the origin of the CD community, the location of 'Damascus,' the rôle of the 'Teacher of Righteousness' and the community organisation and rules.

*1. Origins.* Following discovery of the Scrolls, considerable attention was immediately devoted to the characters and events figuring in the biblical commentaries from Qumran, and especially the Habakkuk commentary (1QpHab). It was felt, and continues to be felt, that the often cryptic allusions this document contains refer to historical events attending the formation of the Qumran community by the 'Teacher of Righteousness.' In fact, it has been widely accepted that the key to decipherment of the personae lies in identifying the 'Wicked Priest,' who, following the influential treatment of G. Jeremias,[24] is now regarded by many scholars as a separate figure from the 'Man of the Lie,' and as a ruling High Priest. Since the archaeological evidence of the ruins of Qumran appears to place the settlement of a community there during the Hasmonean period, it remains only to identify the Hasmonean ruler who opposed the 'Teacher of Righteousness' and in whose reign the Qumran community was formed.

The methods and assumptions attending this process of reasoning are ill-founded and precarious, nor indeed can they be said to have produced any unaninimity. There remains disagreement whether or not the 'Wicked Priest' and the 'Man of the Lie' are in fact to be identified, and, consequently, dispute over the exact criteria to be used for identification.[25] Among those who have undertaken detailed analyses, Jeremias, Stegemann and Murphy-O'Connor agree that the Wicked Priest is the Hasmonean Jonathan, who assumed the High Priesthood in 152 BCE, and this identification may perhaps be described as presently the most widely-accepted of the alternatives. Among the significant voices of dissent are F.M. Cross, who favours

Simon, and A. Dupont-Sommer, who favours Hyrcanus II, placing the foundation of the Qumran community almost exactly a century later.

Consequently, the activity of the Teacher and the foundation of the community at Qumran are placed, in the opinion of a powerful majority of scholars which includes de Vaux, Vermes, Milik, Cross, Rowley, Jeremias, Stegemann and Murphy-O'Connor, in the mid-2nd century BCE. Indeed, if such a view is taken, the data of CD I can be interpreted in the more or less literal way initiated by Charles.

One finds, therefore, in post-1947 scholarship a recurrence of that ambiguity with regard to the data of CD I which we have noted in some earlier works. Many scholars, of course, have appreciated that the figure of 390 years at any rate cannot be taken seriously as evidence. Rowley in particular emphasised that he did not regard the figure as reliable, but did nevertheless regard it as accurate (even if by accident) because he could establish its accuracy *on other grounds*.[26] It is important to recognise, then, that the dating of the Teacher and of the origin of his community are in the case of virtually every scholar grounded on the evidence of the *pesharim* with CD I used *in support*. For all that the figure of 390 years has attracted attention, the majority of scholars recognise that it may be taken as correct only insofar as it can be confirmed by other evidence. It is not of itself a piece of independent evidence.

Yet Qumran research also inherited a tradition of interpretation, bequeathed by Lévi, Charles and Meyer of those we have earlier considered, which placed the rise of the community of CD in the Hellenistic crisis of the first half of the 2nd century BCE. It is nevertheless the case that the dating of the origin of the Qumran community, which has been almost universally identified as the CD community, is derived in current scholarship from the identification of the Wicked Priest. Yet this figure who figures so prominently in the Habakkuk commentary is totally absent from CD. It is important that this shift of evidential basis for the dating of the CD community is appreciated, for it is a symptom of the fact that the document has, since the discovery of the Scrolls, virtually surrendered its autonomy and become colonised as a Qumran document. Among other things, a Hasmonean context was read into CD where such a context was merely permitted rather than positively indicated. The origins of the CD community were not read out of the document, but imported *into* it.

2. *Damascus.* How does 'Damascus' in CD make sense in the new

Qumran context? We have seen that prior to the Qumran discoveries there was scarcely a doubt that this was to be taken literally. This unanimity has now been dispelled—by no new exegetical insight, but as a further result of the incorporation of CD into the Qumran problem as a literary product of the Dead Sea community. Nowadays, therefore, three kinds of answer to the identification of Damascus can be discerned. Two of them continue to uphold the literal meaning. According to the first, the Qumran community had sister communities in the region of Damascus, and it is to these related communities rather than the Qumran community itself that CD applies. This is the solution preferred by Milik and favoured also by Fitzmyer.[27] A second answer is the Qumran community may have come to the Dead Sea from Damascus, or sought refuge in Damascus between sojourns at Qumran.[28] A third answer, which is perhaps the most popular, abandons the literal interpretation and suggests that Damascus is a symbol for a place of refuge or of exile. Stegemann's version of this answer is that 'Damascus' need not indicate any particular geographical region, but may simply refer to the Judaean wilderness[29]; but the earlier and more widely embraced version is that of Cross, for whom 'Damascus' is a symbol for Qumran.[30] This last-mentioned view remains the most popular. Permutations of these views are possible and it has not been unknown for individual scholars to change their minds over this issue. Yet it is again worth noting that the problem of Damascus is largely addressed in terms of *Qumran archaeology, including the palaeography of the Qumran fragments of CD.* And this despite the fact that there is no allusion to Damascus in any of the documents whose Qumran origin is undisputed. The role of 'Damascus' is a problem peculiar to CD and calls in the first instance for an *exegetical* solution and, moreover, one within the context of the document in which it occurs.

3. *The 'teacher of righteousness.'* The rôle of this figure in CD also constitutes something of a problem. Much is currently made of his firm placement in CD I, since a literal reading of the chronological data there can be made to fit not too untidily (though not precisely, either) with archaeological data from Qumran. Yet we have earlier seen that many scholars from Schechter onwards declined to place much credence in them, while even the most literal interpreter of these data, R.H.Charles, implicitly demonstrated that they appeared to be glosses. If they are indeed not original to historical summary in which they are now embedded (and in the analysis to follow this will be

argued further), the chronological anchorage of the Teacher is uncertain. Indeed, even granted their integrity, a literal reading does not necessarily yield a Hasmonean dating for this figure, since scholars such as Rabinowitz and Jaubert (see below) have, not implausibly, placed him shortly after the Exile. Elsewhere in CD this figure appears only in ms. B, where he seems to play a very important rôle. Yet, outside of CD I he is absent from ms. A, even from its descriptions of the origins and history of the community. The situation is complicated by the fact that 'one who teaches righteousness' in VI,11 is clearly a figure expected in the future. Outside CD I, the only individual of the community's past who is mentioned in ms. A is the 'Interpreter of the Law.' Inevitably, he has been identified with the 'Teacher of Righteousness,' but this identification is unarguably a process of harmonisation rather than sound exegesis; it hardly eliminates the problem raised by the contrast between the presentation of the 'Teacher' in CD and in the *pesharim*.

4. *Organisation*. The most awkward question of all, in my opinion, emerges from the recognition that the community of CD is not in all respects identical to that of Qumran. For example, life in 'camps' is envisaged, marriage and children are legislated for, as well as private property. There is a general recognition among scholars that life at Qumran as reconstructed from archaeology and from 1QS does not fit the description of life in CD closely enough for the same community to be recognised in each case, although of course there are undoubtedly strong affinities, a fact which also requires to be explained. The solutions advanced in the face of this difficulty are, since CD refers to a 'Teacher of Righteousness,' who is understood from the *pesharim* to be the founder of the Qumran community, either that CD and 1QS refer to different periods of the same community's life at Qumran or that communities of the kind described in CD developed out of the Qumran community. The latter view is apparently supported by the descriptions of the Essenes from Josephus and Pliny, and the identification of this group with the Qumran community.[31] But while Pliny seems to have known of the Qumran settlement, Josephus does not; he states that 'they occupy no one city, but settle in large numbers in every town.' He also describes the Essenes as having a marrying order as well as a celibate one. Now, Josephus' information fits quite well with the suggestion that CD describes such Essene communities. But his description provides the impression that the Essenes are a numerous group; and indeed they are presented by Philo—who also

describes the Essenes as 'living in villages'—as numbering 'more than four thousand.'[32] However, on the view under discussion, that the 'marrying Essenes' and those in 'camps' developed from the Qumran community, certain historical questions are raised which have not hitherto been properly considered. Why should larger and more scattered groups be derived from a smaller one? And if this were the case, how did it happen? Are the differences between the the different régimes to be explained as the result of natural development or of doctrinal conflict? And, indeed, whence the 'Damascus' of these non-Qumran groups? If their origin indeed lay by the Dead Sea, is there any plausible alternative to regarding Qumran and 'Damascus' as one and the same, as the place where the community covenant was originally forged? Yet this equation is exegetically the weakest of all the alternative interpretations of 'Damascus' in CD, as will be argued in the following analysis.

For the real difficulties with the view of the relationship between CD and the Qumran community just described do not lie in the necessity of supposing that Qumran was not a closed community but during its lifespan spawned a nationwide movement. This is a conceivable, if not perhaps highly probable, development, and the silence of any sources on this point is not a decisive objection. The problem lies, as always, in the text of CD itself. Unlike the Qumran scrolls—and certainly the *pesharim*—CD actually describes the origins of the community, the foundation of the covenant and it expounds very distinctly the exilic ideology which undergirds both of these. It ascribes no place in the institution of its covenant to the Teacher, does not locate him at Damascus, knows (as I have said previously) of no 'Wicked Priest,' legislates for participation in the Temple cult—which the Qumran community of the Teacher is regarded by common consent of Qumran scholarship as having abandoned—and exhibits several other differences from the Qumran scrolls. These differences have been consistently devalued in Qumran research at the expense of the similarities. The real task, of course, is not to fabricate ingenious reconcilations of discrepant data, nor to distort the balance of agreement and disagreement between CD and the documents of the Qumran community, but to formulate an account of the literary evidence which is exegetically sound and which does justice to *both* similarities *and* differences between CD and the Qumran scrolls.

Yet scholarship on CD has not unanimously pursued the path of a Qumran synthesis. From my own perspective, I discern two divergent strands of research on Qumran origins. One adopted the solution just outlined, which identified the Qumran community with the Essenes, derived the Essenes from the Hasidim, and searched the *pesharim* for precise details of the events and persons which initiated the move to the Dead Sea. Representative of this strand are Cross, Vermes, Jeremias and Stegemann; despite the refinements of the last-named, his work may be seen as a summation of preceding research along such lines. The other strand is characterised by a focus on the text of CD itself, putting aside several of the problems raised by the Qumran literature as well as the prevalent hypotheses, and concerns itself with exegeting CD more or less in isolation, and certainly with attempting to define and solve problems largely within the context of CD itself. This strand is represented by the work of several scholars who do not necessarily share the same assumption nor attain the same conclusions, but whose work nevertheless presents us with some areas of consensus. It stands in sharp contrast to the first strand, exercising a centrifugal force to counter the tendency of the other strand.

The important contribution of Murphy-O'Connor is best seen, I think, not as representing a third strand, but as weaving together the other strands. I propose in the remainder of this Introduction to comment briefly on each of the two strands in order to put the present analysis into context and at the same time to re-emphasise the importance for Qumran origins of an appropriate exegesis of CD. The history of Qumran scholarship has been well enough charted, however, to make any further general survey unwelcome. By way of commenting on the first of these strands—that which pursues a synthesis of CD with the Qumran manuscripts and with Qumran archaeology—I shall therefore offer a critique of the work of Stegemann and indirectly of that of Jeremias on which it is greatly dependent. As yet there has been little attempt to confront the presuppositions and methodology of the approaches of these scholars. My description of the second strand covers a greater number of studies which have created less impact than have the Qumran syntheses on the under-standing of CD generally prevalent in current scholarship. Murphy-O'Connor's contribution, being more accessible than Stegemann's (which was privately published), is perhaps more familiar to many scholars, but its considerable impact on the present analysis necessitates a presentation of its main lines.

## III
### *'Pesher-based' reconstruction*

The first strand outlined above is well represented in Qumran scholarship, especially of the more popular kind which tends to be consulted most readily by non-specialists. But I shall focus here on the detailed and technical exposition of the Qumran-synthesis approach to the interpretation of CD undertaken in the monumental work on Qumran origins of H. Stegemann.

Methodology plays a large part in Stegemann's investigation and he devotes to it several pages of his *Die Entstehung der Qumrangemeinde*[33] to a discussion of the texts on which his reconstruction of the origins of the Qumran community is built. Before using the evidence of the texts, he requires that they must be confirmed as products of the community, not simply texts copied at Qumran; and that such texts must be of such a kind as to be able to provide genuine historical information, by which he means statements about the early community which utilise earlier traditions (p. 8). Then arises the question of how the sources thus chosen are to be used. Stegemann rejects the method of arriving at a picture of the original community by attempting to range the texts in chronological order and thence to compare characteristics of texts from the earliest period with those texts reflecting later developments. He also refuses to compile statements of different classes (*verschiedener Aussagebereiche*, p. 11) to fill out a complete picture of the history of Qumran origins, since different classes of statement are on the whole independent of each other, and any method of combination will be arbitrary.

Stegemann therefore opts for a method which concentrates on a single range (*Bereich*) of statements.[34] The framework erected from such statements can then be utilised in interpreting other Qumran texts containing historical references; this procedure affords better control over the material than one which integrates from the outset statements from different periods of origin. Once the basic framework has been constructed from a single range, the chronological sequence and historical points of reference of the various texts become easier to discern, and aspects of the *Theologiegeschichte* of Qumran can then be more adequately addressed.

Consequently, Stegemann proceeds to erect a framework using *statements about Jewish opponents of the Qumran community*. In effect, he places the entire weight of his investigation on the Qumran *pesharim.* He ends up, therefore, after an elaborate methodological preamble, with an argument very similar to that of Jeremias, but in addition to having expounded his methodology (unlike Jeremias), his use of texts is much less promiscuous and his exegesis more rigorous. Unlike Jeremias, he realises that such material can hardly be used as 'ready cash' (p. 13), for over the course of time the community must have met many different opponents, and one cannot attribute all statements about them to the period of the community's origins. But he is in no less doubt than Jeremias about the historicity or the transmission of *pesher* traditions. He remarks blandly that stereotyped statements about opponents, using uniform terminology, recur in texts which are different both in character and in date of origin, while individual personalities among the opponents are described with such distinct features that the conclusion that they refer to historical characters is inescapable.[35] Despite initial doubts among scholars, he remarks, this conclusion is now 'rightly accepted.' One cannot help remark at this juncture that such a statement forms a remarkable contrast with Stegemann's previous and commendable scepticism; although he acknowledges that the texts in question stand at some distance from the origins of the community, he appears to ignore the implications of that observation, the scope of which must be readily apparent to any NT scholar engaged in gospel research.

Briefly, then, Stegemann provides a defence of the kind of procedure which had long been working in Qumran studies, namely, an attempt to decipher the historical allusions thought to be present in the biblical commentaries, chiefly 1QpHab, 4QpNah and 4QpPss. The important difference in Stegemann's case is that evidence from other Qumran texts is not integrated simultaneously, but evaluated only when a consistent framework has been erected from the *pesharim* alone.[36]

After the *pesharim*, therefore, attention is directed to CD, or rather to statements in CD about opponents of the community. There is no attempt to understand the structure or history of the document, for this is regarded as an impossible requirement on the grounds that there are wide differences of opinion in previous research, and that the mediaeval date of the Cairo manuscripts makes conjecture about the history of the document precarious. However, Stegemann does acknowledge significant differences between CD and the *pesharim* and explains these as the result of CD's concern with the character of religious teaching of opponents rather than with historical distinctions between them. In accordance with the method adopted, statements in

CD about opponents of the Qumran community are reliable only insofar as they cohere with the framework built from the *pesharim*.

Other passages from the Qumran texts are subsequently discussed—parts of 1QS and of 1QH—but we may leave these aside and summarise Stegemann's exegetical conclusions and his historical interpretation of those results. From the Qumranic statements about Jewish opponents, Stegemann discerns two major groups, the community founded by the 'Man of the Lie' (which is also designated as 'Ephraim,' the 'Seekers of Smooth Things,' the 'Men of Scoffing in Jerusalem,' the 'House of Peleg' and the 'House of Absalom') and a group centred on the illegitimate High Priest, the Wicked Priest, in league with the ruling classes who are called 'Manasseh.'

Stegemann finds in CD only one of these two groups, that of the 'Man of the Lie,' which is called in the document the 'Congregation of Traitors,' the 'Builders of the Wall,' the 'Men of Scoffing,' and the 'House of Peleg.' This group, according to Stegemann's interpretation of CD, once belonged to the 'new covenant in the land of Damascus,' and appears as denying specific *halachoth* which were binding for the Qumran community and which distinguished it from the rest of Judaism. In laying the ground for these conclusions, Stegemann analyses the *Admonition*, and reaches the conclusion that the passages which refer to this group (I,13-18; IV,19f.; VIII,12f.-XIX,25f.; XX,13-15) *are all secondary expansions of the original text*. This conclusion, which is based on some of the most thorough exegesis yet undertaken on the passages in question, is of course potentially devastating to Stegemann's basic assumptions, especially of the reliability of the *pesharim*. In what remains as the original text, there is no direct allusion to the Man of the Lie, nor indeed to any of the other parties or titles recorded in the *pesher* traditions. Accordingly, the findings have to be explained away, and this is done by pleading that CD is interested in the *character* rather than the *origins* of the false doctrine which it counters. This 'explanation' is reinforced by the assertion that these secondary references to opponents in CD are nevertheless historically reliable; and why? Because they are consistent with the information in the *pesharim*! Here is perhaps the clearest example of methodological assumptions controlling evidence. When one is prepared to dismiss discrepancies between CD and the *pesharim*, can the similarities really be said to mean anything? Stegemann's method creaks here very audibly.[37]

CD does, however, provide for Stegemann some additional information regarding the enemies of the Qumran community. From V,20-VI,2 he deduces that the political ruling class is held responsible for the departure of the Jewish people from their traditions, and that it is this apostasy, as the authors see it, which occasioned the rise of the community (VI,2-11).

The historical evaluation of his exegetical conclusions is, like the textual basis itself, extremely narrow. Despite being absent outside the *pesharim*, the Wicked Priest provides that basis, a basis which itself rests on a single statement, that he 'ruled in Israel'(1QpHab VIII,9-10). Stegemann therefore searches for a ruling priest. He also establishes that the title הכהן ('*the* priest') in post-exilic Jewish literature always denotes the High Priest, and consequently the search is restricted to a Hasmonean. Now in fact the characteristics of the Wicked Priest in the *pesharim* can be taken to apply to all or nearly all of the Hasmoneans. Stegemann finds two exceptions: (i) during the time of this leader's rule the Temple treasures were immune from plunder by non-Jews; and (ii) his death took place outside Judah. Only Menelaus and Jonathan fulfil these conditions, and of the two Jonathan is better suited. This conclusion had already been established, and along similar lines, by Jeremias, who in turn confirmed what was already a widely-held opinion.[38]

In his treatment of the identity of the Teacher of Righteousness, however, Stegemann progresses beyond established conclusions, and specifically beyond those of Jeremias. The Teacher of Righteousness is also called הכהן and therefore must also also have been a High Priest. The Teacher and his arch-enemy were both holders of the same office; in Stegemann's view the Teacher must have been the High Priest deposed by the Wicked Priest himself.[39] None of the ancient sources refers to a predecessor of Jonathan, but according to Stegemann this is because either the sources had no interest in the figure (e.g. I Maccabees) or because they had no access to such knowledge (e.g. Josephus). Jonathan's usurpation explains his cipher 'Wicked Priest,' while the community in which the Teacher found a home was one which accepted him as the true (and therefore Zadokite) High Priest. Stegemann now utilises the historical sketch in CD I, and identifies the community to which the Teacher came as one of a number of related communities of a movement referred to as the 'plant root.' These lived in refuge from the Hellenising authorities and preserved the ancient traditional faith. Among these, the Teacher arrived as the only true representative of the covenant for which the communities stood. The communities are identified with congregations of the Hasidim (I Macc. 2,42 speaks of *a* congregation of Hasidim), and the places of refuge of these communities were collectively designated as the 'land of Damascus' or simply 'Damascus.'

The boycott of the Temple which we know the Qumran community to have observed is to be attributed to the Teacher, and was not in existence prior to his arrival; the 'Damascus' covenant was in fact scrupulously observant of the Temple cult (CD XI,18-20; XII,1ff.); in CD's reports, too, about the origin of the movement Stegemann finds no reference to a boycott of the Temple. But he does conclude that the Teacher, in his rôle as sole mediator of the covenant, required the Temple and its cult to be rejected. In this he met sharp opposition. Many would not accept his authority, and such opponents found a leader in the 'Man of the Lie.' The terms 'house of Absalom,' 'house of Peleg' and 'Ephraim,' which describe the followers of the Man of the Lie, reflect the separation which took place between the rival groups. Stegemann regards the Pharisees as originating with the community of the 'Man of the Lie.' Indeed, they acquired their name from their 'separation' from the Teacher,[40] although it seems quite preposterous that a derogatory title bestowed by a reclusive sect on what became a very influential and popular movement which grew in the midst of the Jewish people should become their regular designation.

Stegemann's investigation covers more ground and presents more detail than can be adequately summarised here. But I have intended primarily to convey his fundamental assumptions, methods and conclusions, especially those regarding CD. It will be clear both from remarks already made, and from my own analysis to follow, that I regard a good deal of his reconstruction as wrong, and seriously so. Stegemann has performed a valuable service in distinguishing within CD a pre-Qumran movement from which the Qumran community must be seen as a splinter. But his identification, dating and description of the 'Damascus' covenant is well off the mark because he has reached fundamental conclusions about these matters in advance of his analysis of CD. I think, too, that he has been insufficiently independent of received views, with the result that while his detailed argumentation is sometimes original, his conclusions emerge as not very much more than the refinement of a received consensus many of whose basic presuppositions remain unchallenged. But a detailed critique of what is a wide-ranging analysis is out of the question here,

while an alternative and more adequate reconstruction is still premature. My own reticence over drawing historical implications from
the following analysis of CD is partly a reaction against what I regard
as Stegemann's excess.

## IV
### *Alternative lines of approach*

The second strand of post-Qumran research on CD is less ambitious
and represented by a number of studies, all of which have in common
an attempt to grapple with problems outside the dominant interpretative
hypothesis of Qumran origins. If the consensus which culminates with
Stegemann's analysis represents a centripetal force, a gradual gathering
of divergent elements into a historical synthesis, these studies are
centrifugal, at least in their cumulative effect. Quite simply, in my
view, they show that the evidence cannot easily be marshalled in the
way Stegemann attempts.

### *Rabinowitz, 1954*
When the Hasmonean-Hasidic theory of the origins of the CD/Qumran
community had already become established, Isaac Rabinowitz wrote
what turned out to be an influential article, although its influence may
be attributable more to the fact that it broke a spell than to excellence
of scholarship.[41] Partly following the lead given by Ginzberg (see
earlier), Rabinowitz contended that CD I could not possibly be
speaking of 390 years after the Babylonian exile, as most scholars took
it, because the crucial Hebrew word לתיתו which follows the figure
must be translated '[390 years] as of His giving' (sic) and not '[390
years] after He gave.' Hence the 390 years may not be construed as
*following* Nebuchadnezzar's conquest but as *culminating* in it. Adopting
a fairly precise interpretation of Ezekiel 4,5 where the figure represents
the period of the sins of the Northern kingdom Israel, Rabinowitz
applied it to the divided monarchy from Rehoboam to Zedekiah. A
total of 393 years can be extracted from the biblical data, and the
excess of three years can, taking a clue from II Chron. 11,16-17, be
subtracted from the beginning of Rehoboam's reign.

Accordingly, CD I does not speak about the origin of a sect at all; it is
a summary of the history of Israel. The 'visitation' of God upon the
remnant was not a favourable act but one of punishment—the Exile—
and the 'root of planting' which followed was the post-exilic community

in Judah. The 'Teacher of Righteousness' is apparently Nehemiah.[42] At all events, the sojourn in Damascus must be understood as a reference to the Babylonian exile, prompted by Amos 5,26f. which refers to 'exile beyond Damascus.'

Rabinowitz also introduced or re-introduced the issue of the literary unity of the document. He found in CD three literary strata, a basic 'discourse of admonition,' of which there are parallel versions in mss. A and B, a second stratum consisting of glosses and comments, and a third stratum comprising the laws in IX-XVI.[43] The rationale for this literary analysis is nowhere spelt out; there is more than a hint of circularity about the whole procedure, and no evaluation of it is really required for our purposes. However, it signalled a literary-critical approach to CD which culminated in the analysis of Murphy-O'Connor.[44]

*Wiesenberg, 1955*
In an article published as a response to Rabinowitz,[45] E. Wiesenberg expressed a good deal of agreement, but nevertheless adopted a more sceptical attitude toward the chronological data of CD. On the question of the translation of לתיתו he finally agreed that it cannot signify 'after' (as held by the prevailing interpretation which Rabinowitz had challenged), but he interpreted the phrase and its immediate context as referring to the fall of the Northern kingdom, preferring the view of Ginzberg to that of Rabinowitz. The association of Nebuchadnezzar with this event is not on this view an anachronism, for it is the Nebuchadnezzar of legend and not of history who appears here. The 'remnant' which survives is the exilic community, and the 'root of planting' emerges from it. Yet since there is nowhere in CD any allusion to the restoration in Judah, this 'root' designates, in Wiesenberg's view, an unknown sect which came to birth 'possibly somewhere in the blank periods of the Persian or early Greek phase in the history of Palestine' (303-304). He also recognises that CD appears to claim that the sect originated in the exile, but regards this claim to 'hoary antiquity' as something to be taken *cum grano salis*:

> the three chronological data in the ZF yield, despite their apparent precision, as little historical information, in historians' exact sense of the term, as the less precise data in the DSS. The only sort of information obtainable from the ZF is the insight—as far as it goes—into the notions of an obscure sect. (p. 308)

*Jaubert, 1958*

Rabinowitz had argued that CD mentioned the Babylonian exile, though not as part of the sect's history, while Wiesenberg argued that CD referred it fictitiously to the history of the sect. A further contributor to this debate was A. Jaubert.[46] Her discussion is, in my opinion, a crucial one in the argument about CD and Qumran origins. She asked whether the exile in CD was the historical event of the 6th century BCE, as Rabinowitz supposed, or a more recent one in the history of the sect, as maintained by most scholars. One the one hand, she was well aware of the prominence of the Exile in much apocalyptic literature, and recognised that the sin-punishment-repentance sequence which recurs in CD figures prominently in the literature of the exilic period and continually thereafter. Jubilees, she pointed out, the 'plant of straightness' germinates in exile and is to be transported to Palestine, yielding a striking parallel to the 'root plant' which is to 'inherit His land' in CD I. On the other hand, Jaubert was aware of the typological value of the Exile in post-exilic literature, and saw the possibility that the community may have undergone an exile from Jerusalem which it presented typologically by the great Exile under Nebuchadnezzar.

Jaubert therefore raises directly the question whether the 'root' of CD I designates the Babylonian exiles (or part of them) or a movement which originated 390 years (or so) after the Exile began. In favour of the former, Jaubert observes that other historical summaries in CD III,10-IV,4 and V,15-VI,11 which also refer to the Exile contain no suggestion of a 390 year gap. The first of these other summaries also mentions a calendar revealed by God to the exiles, and here Jaubert's research on the solar calendar of Jubilees and the Scrolls is brought to bear; she had already concluded that such a calendar could be detected in the Priestly stratum of the Pentateuch and in Ezekiel, both products of the Exile. She concludes that the 390 years of CD I, as Rabinowitz had suggested, must be taken to culminate in the Exile and not to follow it; the 'root' is the exilic community in Babylon, not a community created centuries later.

Jaubert then exposes two further problems. First, all of the historical summaries in CD end with a reference to a 'time of wickedness,' which she takes to refer to the time of the writer(s) of CD. Yet if the exile to which these summaries refer is not exclusively typological, but also an historical event, the Babylonian captivity (as she maintains), it is not at all clear how the historical transition from the exilic starting point to the time of writing of the document is to be discerned in these summaries. Second,—and arising specifically from the first problem—what is the identity of the covenant referred to in CD? VI,18-19 refers to the 'new covenant in the land of Damascus.' This is surely the same covenant as that referred to in III,13, which is set during the Babylonian exile. Yet the reference in XIX,33-34 to 'those who entered the new covenant in the land of Damascus' includes also the Zadokites of the writer's own day. The problem, again, is one of transition. There seems to be on the one hand a typological correspondence between two events, but at the same time each event appears to have its own historical integrity; the one is not merely a shadow of the other. For Jaubert, the answer to these problems is as follows: Damascus has a *primary* reference to Babylon, as Rabinowitz contended. A Zadokite could not say 'Babylon' because it was a loathsome symbol of exile and of idolatry, so 'Damascus' was substituted. At the same time, Damascus could *also* refer to the place of exile *as it had become to the members of the community*, namely, Qumran.

The problem which Jaubert perceives here is critically important to understand the *Heilsgeschichten* of CD and hence the prehistory of the Qumran community. But her solution, that 'Damascus' has two meanings, creates problems with several specific passages in CD. For example, in CD VII,19 there is the phrase 'the Interpreter of the Law who came/comes/will come to Damascus.' The Hebrew participle is temporally ambiguous; does it refer to a visit to Babylon in the past, or a future visit to Qumran? To what time does this figure belong? In this particular instance, Jaubert decides that the verb has a future sense and that 'Damascus' means Qumran, because in 4QFl the 'Interpreter of the Law' is apparently an eschatological figure, possibly Elijah who will repatriate the Diaspora at the end of days. Another example of a problem raised by the ambivalence Jaubert invokes is the mention of the 'Liar' in I,13ff. This figure is brought into the text at a point where his historical context is not clear. Does he belong to the period preceding the Babylonian exile or to a relatively recent period from the point of view of CD's writer(s)? In this instance Jaubert opts for the past, that is, for the Babylonian exile and suggests that the Liar is Hananiah, the notorious opponent of Jeremiah. This engenders an interesting interpretation of the context. The 'last generation' in CD I,13 refers to the last *pre-exilic* generation; the Teacher of Righteousness had shown them, according to Jaubert's translation of CD I,11, what

God had done to their generation, and therefore this Teacher is a figure of the exilic or early post-exilic period; Jaubert prefers Ezra to Rabinowitz's Nehemiah. In CD XX,11-13, the reference to a 'covenant and an אמונה which they made in the land of Damascus' recalls the אמונה mentioned in Nehemiah 10,1, and Jaubert interprets accordingly. She argues, as we have noted, that 'it is surely unnecessary to take "Damascus" as a pure and simple equivalent for geographical Babylon' (p. 234); we have in CD a *'glissement'* of the term 'land of Damascus' towards a secondary meaning as the place where the covenant was made as well as the place of exile. In other words, Jaubert believes that there was historically a covenant made in Babylon, when the remnant was in exile. But the situation of the Qumran community, being members of a new *covenant* and also *in exile*, enabled them to use Damascus as a symbol also of Qumran.

This observation leads necessarily to the crucial question: are there, in fact, possible *historical* links between Babylon and Qumran, the two 'Damascuses'? Jaubert thinks this probable, citing the curious and certainly problematic 1 QM I,2-3, which refers to the 'exiles of the sons of light' in the 'desert of the peoples'—the place where according to Ezekiel 20,35 a new covenant was made. In this context, the reference cannot be to Qumran, for we have already met the 'exiles of the wilderness' as a different group, most probably the Qumran community itself. Could this, then, be a reference to Babylonian Jews? Another piece of evidence is the 4QPrNab fragment, an earlier version of the story in Daniel 4 which, it could plausibly be suggested, arose in Babylon.[47] In other words, Jaubert introduces the suggestion *that the roots of the Qumran community may lie in the Babylonian exile.*

Jaubert's essay raises a number of crucial problems in a commendably clear way and demonstrates an awareness of their complexity. It must be admitted that she falls well short of a solution, but her observations open the way to further research. In fact, as we shall presently see, a possible connection between Qumran and Babylon had already been suggested, on quite different grounds, by W.F. Albright, and was later to be seriously considered by other scholars, most fully by Murphy-O'Connor. A suggestion which Jaubert seems in fact to have offered as a way out of an exegetical dilemma has found a good deal of support on other grounds.

*Schwarz, 1966*
O. Schwarz's investigation of the first part of the *Damascus Document*,

published in 1966, examines the relationship of its components to the Old Testament.[48] She concludes from her examination of the contents that in its present form, the *Admonition*, far from presenting a connected or coherent account of the history of the sect, consists of several originally independent pieces, which require to be separately investigated. In all, she finds 26 such pieces in ms. A/1 and 20 in ms. B, whose relationship to the Old Testament she treats by dividing them into three kinds of material: A. narrative texts, dealing with history; B. exegetical texts; and C. legal texts.

Discussion of the narrative texts is concluded by a discussion of the chronological problems raised by the data of CD I, in which she illustrates the difficulty of arriving at even a probable reconstruction, concluding with Wiesenberg that the author of this passage was referring to a time which even for him already lay well in the past, and of which therefore he himself was uncertain (p. 88). Basically, she concludes, the history in the narrative texts is very close to that found in Ezra and Nehemiah, the important difference being that here the history is that of a sect, not of the nation as a whole.

Schwarz divides the exegetical texts into scriptural citation (*Schrift-bezug*) and *Damaskuspescher*, a term which is self-explanatory. There are six portions of *Damaskuspescher*, and their content permits Schwarz to draw some conclusions regarding the history of the community. She finds different periods of that history reflected in different portions of *Damaskuspescher*. This is found to be the case with reference to 'Damascus' (p. 122); in the third of them (VI,4c-11b), the 'land of Damascus' means the Babylonian exile, but in the fourth (VII,14b-21a) a spiritual exile. In thus finding more than one meaning for 'Damascus' Schwarz joins Jaubert. She suggests that three periods in the history of the sect reflected in this material, and preeminently in the Ezekiel midrash of IV,1ff. The 'priests,' 'levites' and 'sons of Zadok' in her view reflect three stages of development in the history of the community which represent respectively formation, development and the present situation. The formation and development take place in the context of exile in the 'land of Damascus'/'Damascus,' perhaps indicating an exile outside the land, and possibly the Babylonian Exile. But in the present situation the context, and the meaning of the symbol 'Damascus' is a self-imposed exile within Palestine itself, possibly at Qumran. The conclusion, then, is also similar to Jaubert's, but is based on an independent, and more detailed, analysis of the individual pieces. Schwarz carries the exegetical conclusions further, too, because she recognises their implication that a long period of historical development appears to lie behind the CD community.

Schwarz's comments regarding the history of the CD community are characterised on the whole by careful and restrained suggestion, with no hint of an urge towards speculative synthesis. This may well be due to the fact that she was not conducting an historical investigation, but studying the use of the OT in the document. What I would regard, therefore, as the significance of Schwarz's contribution—apart from its excellent coverage of scholarly discussion (to which I shall frequently be content to refer the reader)—is her presentation of the extent to which the OT lies behind the vocabulary and imagery of the document, and her demonstration that a relatively agnostic approach to the document, and an absorption with detail yields a spectrum of meaning. She has illuminated the nuances of this material which more superficial and harmonistic exegeses of this presumed 'Dead Sea Scroll' were unable to see or simply disregarded. On the debit side, Schwarz has carried through, however thoroughly, a very restricted programme. The document itself emerges from her study as still something of an enigma, and one is left to ponder whether her kind of historical conclusions can in the last analysis be most plausibly derived from what is basically an atomistic method of exegesis. Has Schwarz a convincing answer to offer Rabin, who in the introduction to his edition of the text of CD declared it to be essentially nothing more than a tissue of scriptural allusions from which nothing of historical value could be deduced? Rather more would seem to required by way of an explanation of the character of the document as a whole, and especially the function of the historiographical material, whether or not it is exegetically developed.

*Iwry, 1969*

A very important contribution to the debate about the meaning of 'Damascus' in CD was contained in a paper by S. Iwry in 1969.[49] This too was a direct response to Rabinowitz's article, and took issue with the thesis that 'Damascus' in CD should be understood symbolically, whether of Babylon or Qumran. Iwry rightly criticised the comparative neglect of the document compared with the detailed treatment accorded to the major Qumran documents, and deplored the lack of an adequate literary analysis of the document (he was apparently unaware of Jaubert's article). By taking a clear view of the *function* of the *Admonition* as a whole, he placed himself in a better position than most of his predecessors to draw valid conclusions about the history of the sect reflected in it. He described the document as a 'hortatory missionary work': 'It starts out with a kind of manifesto to the people, in which the author . . . seeks to introduce his group and its ideas to a new and wholly different environment' (p. 83). This group, in Iwry's view, were 'repatriates to Israel,' who brought with them from exile an esoteric message. In support of this, and refuting Ginzberg's description of CD's laws as broadly 'Pharisaic,' he emphasised the divergence between Pharisaic halachah and that of CD, endorsing Segal's view that the 'legislation was designed for a community living in a gentile environment . . . '

Iwry's arguments depend largely on his translation of the crucial phrase שבי ישראל, which the CD community apparently used as a self-designation. He criticises all those commentators who translate the phrase as 'penitents'; in his view such a translation is incorrect because (i) it is qualified by 'who went out of the land of Judah' which then becomes an obscure if not irrelevant datum; (ii) it fails to do justice to the Biblical echoes of the phrase; (iii) the phrase 'who went out from the land of Judah' idiomatically does not refer to a past act of departure, but to a place of origin (the Hebrew is היוצאים); (iv) with the meaning 'penitents,' the word שבי would have to be followed by a word expressing that of which they repented. If שוב means 'repent' here, the term שבי ישראל can only mean 'those who repented of (being) Israel.'

According to Iwry, the group compared itself with the early Israelites who entered the land after the covenant at Sinai and dispossessed the previous inhabitants, and also with the returnees under Nehemiah and Ezra. In particular, Iwry cites Ezra 2,1 (= Nehemiah 7,6):

> These were the people of the province who came up (immigrated) from the captivity (שבי) of those exiles whom Nebuchadnezzar king of Babylon had exiled to Babylonia, and they returned (ישובו) to Jerusalem and to Judah, each one to his city.

שבים, Iwry points out, is used 'all over Ezra and Nehemiah' to designate returnees. Moreover, the leading families were required at this time to present genealogical lists. Iwry points to CD IV,2 which reads, in his translation:

> Here are the Priests, the returnees to Israel who originate

> from the land of Judah and the Levites who joined them . . .
> Behold the exact statement of their names according to their
> genealogies, the time that they served in office, the viciss-
> itudes through which they have passed, and the years of their
> sojourn in exile.

Finally, Iwry asks, was Damascus a 'mere literary device' for
another place of exile? He rejects Rabinowitz's suggestion that
'Damascus' is a symbol for Babylon, although he is aware that it has
been supported by arguments of a different nature from W.F. Albright
(see below) that the beliefs and practices of the Essenes pointed to a
Babylonian origin, but finds no reason to doubt the literal sense. He
supports Segal's identification of this environment[50] with the Syrian
capital. The Jewish community in Damascus was, he observes, the
oldest outside Palestine. A return of some of these Jews to Palestine
during the restoration by the Maccabees is quite conceivable. But they
would have found conditions other than they had expected, with no
recognition given of their priestly status, with a non-Zadokite high-
priesthood in Jerusalem, a changed calendar and a very worldly
Hasmonean dynasty in power. Accordingly, they would have boycotted
the Temple, and, describing their era as the 'period of wrath,' adopted
the figure of Ezekiel 4,5 in calculating its length as 390 years. For
them, the exile had not ended, and so they parted company with their
fellow-Jews in Palestine, went to Qumran, and awaited the 'completion
of these years.'

Iwry's analysis has exerted a considerable influence on the thesis of
Murphy-O'Connor, most notably in its perception of the missionary
function of the document and of its community as Jews newly returned
from exile to Palestine. Its major weakness is the fact that the only
exile recorded in the historiographical passages of CD is that of
Nebuchadnezzar, a moment in history from which the origin of the
covenant of the community also appears to be dated. Now it is
conceivable that the great Babylonian deportation appears in CD as a
cipher for an exile, voluntary or otherwise, to Damascus. But it is
surely no less plausible to regard Damascus as a cipher for Babylon!
This alternative is indeed the one preferred by Murphy-O'Connor.

*Denis, 1967*
A.-M. Denis' account of the literary structure of the *Admonition* of

CD takes the form of an analysis of the theme of knowledge.[51] Initially, he finds, as scholars before him, three *monitions* marked by an introductory formula, at I,1, II,1 and II,14, which is similar in all three cases. These *monitions* are invitations to perceive and understand the works of God as about to be performed in the last days, a knowledge revealed only to those who 'know justice'—i.e. the sect. The purpose of the historical summaries which are contained in them is to reveal the works of God in the past and compare them with what is about to take place.

The first *monition* deals primarily with those whom God has led in the ways of his heart, the second with the behaviour of the wicked, and the third again with the wicked in history. In Denis' view, the common vocabulary of these three passages, strongly influenced by the book of Daniel, reveals them as a redactional unity. Next, Denis finds in IV,6-VI,11 a second section in which the wilderness wandering becomes a central point of comparison with the experience of the community. It was in the wilderness that the covenant was made, as the new covenant has now been made. Whereas in the *monitions* those who lived in former days were negatively presented, here they are described as virtuous. The writer lives in the time of the 'epoch of Belial' and just as in the wilderness Moses and Aaron were raised from among a faithless generation, so now God raises 'from Israel and Aaron' men of discernment. In this section, Denis sees reflected the consolidation of the community which is now concerned less with perception than with teaching and with understanding more fully its rôle vis-à-vis the remainder of the nation. It therefore derives from a later period than the *monitions*.

It can rightly be asked of this study, as in the case of Schwarz, whether an adequate basis has been found for the kind of historical conclusions offered. In a subsequent paper Denis offered a broader foundation for his view of the evolution of the community, but from this is became clear that he was operating with the assumption that the community of CD and the Qumran community of 1QS were virtually identical.[52] The value of his book, however, lies not in its contribution to the history of the community, but its clarification of the influence of wisdom terminology on the document. His study reminds us of the extent to which the 'Damascus covenant' was an *esoteric* one, whose members belonged by virtue not of obedience to manifest laws, but of insight into sectarian, 'hidden' interpretations of that law. The covenant community comprised those who 'understood,' and understood because God chose them. The saving 'knowledge' is a gift of divine grace. It is in this area that election operates. However, although there are parallels between the vocabulary of CD and Daniel, these have not been proved by Denis to be sufficiently striking to set the composition of the document in the Maccabean period or shortly afterwards, and despite a paucity of specific correlation with the Qumran literature, Denis may nonetheless be suspected of having already accepted in this study—as he did in his subequent work—that the community with which he was dealing was the Qumran community. Indeed, unless one attributes some such assumption on Denis' part, his historical conclusions appear somewhat forced.

### Albright, 1940-

The suggestion of Albright that the origin of the Essenes is to be sought in Babylon was first made as early as 1940,[53] and it was reached in the first instance not on exegetical grounds, nor indeed with the aid of any known 'Essene' material. Albright was struck by certain features of Essene life as described by Josephus, and only later found in the Qumran scrolls, which suggested a Babylonian provenance, such as interest in plants and stones, attention to divination and astrology, frequent lustrations (claimed to be hygienically necessary in Iraq, but not in Palestine; had he ever spent a day at Qumran?), prayer to God for sunrise before dawn and, finally, refusal to take part in sacrificial ritual—more easily explicable if the Essenes had long been distant from Jerusalem.

Albright's original suggestion was that the Essenes had migrated directly from Babylon to Palestine after the Maccabean victories. The discovery of the Scrolls brought to his attention the *Damascus Document*, a study of which provoked a revision of this itinerary, as well as of the Essenes' Zadokite lineage. A fuller account of the origins of the Essenes was offered in an essay by Albright and Mann in a collection published in 1969.[54] The authors express their fundamental conviction thus:

> No movement which involves the human mind or spirit appears suddenly without prior developments; still less do ideas and practices associated with any movement spring from nothing. In fixing the identity of the Qumran sect we must bear in mind the insistence of the sectarians that they alone were the 'returned of Israel.' From this their concentra-

tion on the legitimacy of their priests as 'sons of Zadok' is inseparable. To elucidate all this, it is necessary to go back somewhat in time.

The Babylonian exile, often described as the great watershed of Israel's history, may well have seen the first stirrings of classical Jewish sectarianism ... (p. 16)

Albright and Mann draw attention to the prominence of Zadokites in the Exilic and early post-exilic period, and especially in Ezekiel and Nehemiah. The reforms of Ezra are thought likely to have spread disaffection, especially among dispossessed 'sons of Zadok.' The argument, however, now moves to the Hellenistic crisis of the second century BCE, and using Ben Sira the authors suggest that the high-priesthood became a focus of national unity. The activities of the Hasmonean High Priest could have done nothing but provoke disunity. About 140 BCE, it is suggested, a group of Babylonian pietists found refuge in Damascus, a refuge in which the *Damascus Document* was composed. In its opening lines the period of uncertainty in Palestine, culminating in the persecution of the 'Right Guide' (Teacher of Righteousness) by the Hasmonean Simon, is depicted. The conquest of Samaria and Transjordan by Hyrcanus led to the settlement of part of this group at Qumran, where distinctive doctrines such as dualism and predeterminism, together with stringent regulations as found in 1QS—which are to be contrasted with those of CD—developed. The Essene order—for such this is—perhaps developed in two groups, one in which marriage was allowed, deriving its laws from a régime older than that of the 'Right Guide,' the other a more apocalyptic but also more stringently regulated group based at Qumran. Hence the description of two orders of Essenes by Josephus.

The authority of W.F. Albright was on the whole inadequate to secure very much respect for the suggestion that the Essenes originated from Babylon, and especially, perhaps, since his reconstruction became entangled with the more conventional theory which traced their origin back simply to the Hasidim. But Albright's hypothesis shows that the equation of Damascus and Babylon, suggested on various exegetical grounds, is not without independent support from a different set of considerations. Apart from Murphy-O'Connor, Albright's suggestion was also favourably regarded by W.D. Davies.[55]

All of the work so far reviewed has contributed in some important respect to the provocative synthesis of Murphy-O'Connor. But before reviewing his culminating interpretation, a number of other contributions to the problem of the historical and theological contexts of CD deserve mention. Although not all of them appeared subsequent to his researches, they can all be said to develop or suggest lines of interpretation beyond those pursued by Murphy-O'Connor.

In 1961 Morton Smith in a characteristically wide-ranging and stimulating paper threw a number of ideas into the melting pot.[56] Among the numerous suggestions with which he opens is that CD and 1QS, and especially CD, should be regarded as material for the training of novices, and he specifically uses the word *catechesis*, appealing to the 'marked homiletic elements... the edifying summaries of sectarian history... the comparatively elementary content of the legal material... the absence of information which goes beyond what novices might be expected to learn or could hardly be prevented from learning, etc.' After this significant observation, he moves to his main theme, an invitation to stop trying to fit the 'new material' (*sc.* the Dead Sea literature) into what we know of Judaism during the first centuries BCE and CE, and instead reconsider a longer period of Jewish history and see what this material contributes to our understanding of it. In his own words: 'what is, in fact, the general picture of Judaism to which this new material must be related?' (p. 349).

Smith regards sectarian conflict, with its 'righteous teachers' and 'wicked priests' as characteristic of virtually the whole of the OT, and mentions both Amos and Jeremiah. His comparison becomes more detailed in the early post-exilic period:

> ... the essentials of non-sacrificial worship—the worship of the synagogue, prayer and the ceremonial reading of the Law—are associated in our records with the return of Ezra, and it is likely to suppose that he brought them to Palestine from Babylonia. Now, the existence of this type of worship is of the greatest importance for the development of sects, because it facilitates the formation of small, private cult-groups which even the poor can afford to maintain... Membership in synagogues was therefore probably a first step towards the formation of sects, and this all the more so because these cult-groups were, from their inception, social groups, and especially groups of those who could eat together.

Some of the rules of purity could still be practised in Babylonia, and, so far as they were practised, they must have cut off those who observed them from those who did not. (pp. 351f.)

A closer analogy with the character of CD is drawn in the case of Nehemiah, which is presented by Smith as containing the basic covenant of a sect, the בני הגלה. Smith is especially—and rightly—concerned to establish that 'sectarian movements in Judaism began well before the Maccabean revolt' (p. 358). But his concern is not to 'clutter the subject with further identifications' but to show what sectarian Judaism reveals of the character of the Judaism from which it separates. The appearance of Jewish sects, concludes Smith, derives from the codification of tradition in a sacred law, and from the elevation of the learned teacher to the ultimate religious authority. This process cannot but lead to differences of opinion and this to the formation of sects when these differences are enshrined in covenants. It is the legal structure which constitutes the sect, and religious ideas, which may be borrowed from elsewhere and even discarded, remain non-essential.

As a profile of the *Damascus Document* Smith's remarks are fruitful; and although this may not have been the expressed purpose of the essay, it rightly reminds the exegete that his first task is to examine the character of *this* sect, its own understanding of its law, and its distinctive ideology, before attempting historical identifications, which can only have the effect of forcing the material into a mould. It is precisely the origin of the law of CD which raises acute problems for the currently fashionable—and, it must be said, rather uncritical—derivation of the community's essential characteristic from the Hellenistic crisis of the 2nd century BCE, since CD presents its covenant as a divine initiative taken well in the past, and its laws as hidden from Israel but enshrined for a long while in the community. The kind of analysis which Stegemann exemplifies does violence in the end to the presentation of law in the whole of CD, whose community introduces in this document a law which is said to be hidden from 'Israel' and therefore a revelation to any would-be novitiate. CD does *not* claim to be remaining faithful to laws until recently observed by Israel and only abrogated in the immediate past.

Attention may also be drawn, in this connection, to an recent and excellent essay on post-exilic Jewish sectarianism by J. Blenkinsopp[57] which focusses on *interpretation* as a key element in the development of a tendency which began with the Exile. He remarks: ' . . . an understanding of sectarianism in the Second Temple period has to start from the new situation after the exile, the potential for conflict which it contained and the actual conflicts of interpretation which it generated.' Blenkinsopp suggests, too, that the emergence of sectarian movements in the Maccabean period and later must be seen *as the end-result of a longer process*. Although earlier suggestions had already been offered in this direction, it is especially since the publication of Hanson's examination of the roots of apocalyptic[58]—regardless of one's assessment of its basic thesis—that the roots of 'intertestamental' Judaism have been widely ackowledged to be explicable only in terms of a much longer process, ultimately traceable to the Babylonian exile, and that this tracing back *involves sociological as well as theological description*. In addition, the Diaspora roots of the tales of Daniel, and possibly also the visions, have been strongly advocated.[59]

Another contribution towards the opening up of perspectives on CD was a study of atonement and salvation at Qumran by Paul Garnet,[60] although his thesis was hampered by the decision to treat the material according to the chronological order of the Scrolls established by Starcky.[61] The result is that CD is misplaced in the sequence. Nevertheless, Garnet discovered a fundamental theme of CD, even though he did not fully realise its centrality. He recognised the powerful influence of the *Holiness Code*, and especially Leviticus 26, on the Qumran community, and believed its character and purpose to be determined by what that Code required, namely Israel's penitence and, more importantly, its recognition that it had been righteously punished for its past sins. Such attitudes were a precondition for the restoration of Israel to its land. God's wrath was seen to be still upon Israel, and the task of averting it by prayer and penitence was taken upon itself by the community. But for Garnet the strong ideological ties between the community and priestly exilic literature and theology had no historical implications. The community's ideas arose from a reinterpretation of the original exilic condition in a new and later context of pollution of the land by Gentiles and apostate Israelites during the early 2nd century BCE.

Within this interpretative scheme, Garnet reserved his most explicit treatment for what he took as the earliest of the documents he studied, 4QDibHam. In its theology, he recognises, 'it is taken for granted that the prophecies of a Return had not yet been fulfilled and that the perspective was exilic; the "age of wrath" was inaugurated at the exile and had not yet been brought to a close'(p. 10). While this is certainly a valid interpretation of 4QDibHam, it can be applied equally well to CD itself. If Garnet had shed some crucial presuppositions, his description of 'exilic soteriology' would have embraced CD also. CD is indeed about law, as Smith asserts; but it is also about covenant and about exile. In Garnet's view, the community is still suffering the Babylonian exile brought about by the divine wrath which terminated the first covenant with Israel. From yet another perspective, then, the question returns: *is* the link with Babylon and the Exile necessarily typological? If the exile referred to in CD is the move to Qumran, is it seen as a repetition of the Babylonian exile or the continuation of it? Is 'Damascus' Babylon, the place of Israel's Exile and the birth of a new Israel, or a 'new Babylon' in which the community sees itself as re-exiled? An appeal to typological interpretation cannot be allowed to retreat from the challenge to spell out the typology with clarity.

## *Murphy-O'Connor, 1970-74*

A full evaluation of Murphy-O'Connor's exegesis of CD would have to commence with his earlier analysis of 1QS.[62] For this analysis not only reveals its author's deployment of the techniques of literary criticism, but also lays the foundation for his view of the history of the community at Qumran. He is able to attribute various stages of evolution in the history of the document to stages in the history of the Qumran community as evidenced by the archaeological data. The concern to match literature to (known or partly-known) historical context is a feature of his exegesis of CD. Another, and perhaps even more important characteristic of his exegesis is his concern to account for the Qumran documents as literary compilations. While he rigorously pursues source-critical and form-critical analysis to break up the documents, he is equally concerned to explain how the documents acquired their shape. In the case of 1QS, this shape is acquired not by haphazard accumulation, nor by the conscious redaction of an individual editor, but by growth around a core. Precisely the same view is subsequently taken of CD. This picture of development allows Murphy-O'Connor at times to relate later layers directly to earlier ones; the document at all times has a coherent shape, each successive stage growing from and adapting an earlier form, at the same time betraying its new circumstances. Murphy-O'Connor's literary criticism is, if elaborate, certainly elegant, and reflects the expertise of a trained biblical scholar, of whom Qumran studies have known too few.

While in this and in many other respects it is helpful to contrast the approach of Murphy-O'Connor with that of Stegemann, it must not be forgotten that in several fundamental respects the two are in agreement. Murphy-O'Connor accepts that Stegemann has satisfactorily shown the Wicked Priest to be Jonathan and the Teacher of Righteousness to be his predecessor in the High Priestly office. He accepts that the Qumran *pesharim* are the starting point for reconstructing the origins of the Qumran community itself. But while the developed view of Essene origins at which he finally arrives[63] is presented as a response to Stegemann, and brings together a number of diffferent strands of evidence, its foundation is laid in an exegesis of CD. While Stegemann and Murphy-O'Connor differ greatly in their reconstructions of Qumran prehistory, they also differ in their methodology, for while Stegemann, as we have seen, relegates CD to a secondary rôle behind the *pesharim*, Murphy-O'Connor takes more seriously the possibility that CD can provide an adequate basis from which Qumran prehistory can be reconstructed. One important difference between the two is in terminology: for Murphy-O'Connor the 'Essenes' are a group of ancient origin, from whom the Qumran sect emerged. For Stegemann and most other scholars, there are no Essenes before Qumran. Murphy-O'Connor's view that the Essenes originated outside Palestine naturally excludes the Hasidim from the Qumran family tree. This being said, there remain a few points at which what Murphy-O'Connor says of the Essenes in Palestine parallels quite closely what Stegemann says of the Hasidim.

The kernel of Murphy-O'Connor's interpretation of CD is a large central section, II,14–VI,1. He interprets this as a 'Missionary Document,' designed to win converts to the Essene cause.[64] In his exegesis of this, and all parts of CD, Murphy-O'Connor offers not a full exegesis, but a discussion of those features which either support or seem to contradict his basic thesis. The document opens by addressing itself to 'children,' a term taken to designate outsiders. Whether or not this observation is valid is not crucial, for the rhetoric of the entire composition is seen to betray a non-sectarian audience. The document purports to be about 'choice' and also to demonstrate the inevitability of punishment on those who choose their own desires. It emerges that the true choice involves recognition of a sectarian interpretation (revelation) of the law, and the group also seeks to substantiate its claims to be heard by publicising its genealogy. This genealogy, together with the title שבי ישראל and the reference to leaving the land of Judah suggest a returning group, and the parallel of the returning exiles with Ezra is invoked. This introduction to itself is immediately followed by an urgent call to join the commmunity before it is too late.

The document then attacks as a 'snare of Belial' what is apparently regarded by others as safe orthodoxy, and includes an attack on those who derided the 'laws of the covenant of God.' This attack implies a previous rejection by the 'establishment' of the community and its covenant. The audience of the 'Missionary Document' is confronted with a group which claims to preserve the authentic interpretation of God's will, and which is prepared to justify that claim by appeal to prophecy and the production of genealogical lists. Murphy-O'Connor's analysis of the rhetoric of the document, and the logic of his arguments, is generally impressive here; but for this very reason his decision to place the ending of the document at VI,1 is a most curious one. It breaks a sketch of the origins of the community which is paralleled elsewhere in the *Admonition*, and hence obscures the clear focus on the Babylonian Exile as their locus.

He also fails, I think, to do justice to I,1-II,14. This material he regards as comprising historical (I,1-II,1) and theological (II,2-14) introductions to the 'Missionary Document,' which attempt to re-apply it to insiders in danger of defection from the community. Opponents here are more directly and more bitterly attacked; the audience is addressed as 'you who know righteousness' and 'you who are in the covenant.' The historical summary in I,3ff., too, is more detailed than in the 'Missionary Document'; there is a period of confusion (twenty years of groping) and then the arrival of a Teacher. The 'Missionary Document,' it is argued, belongs within those twenty years, and for this reason contains no reference to the 'Teacher of Righteousness.' With the second introduction Murphy-O'Connor expresses perplexity; he suggests that it may be an attempt to explain how opposition to the will of God, even within a community, can exist. This line of interpretation is dubious especially in view of the intrinsic links of vocabulary and ideology with II,14ff.

In a second paper, Murphy-O'Connor analyses VI,11-VIII,3, which he calls a 'Memorandum.'[65] It consists of a series of 'precepts,' based directly or indirectly on the Holiness Code, and intended to remind readers of the laws they have undertaken to obey; the selection of precepts is governed by the conditions it serves, and stresses the selfish kinds of behaviour in which its hearers were especially lax. At the head is a statement about rejection of the Temple, from which it follows that the community addressed is negatively defined by opposition to the Temple cult, and positively by adherence to a special interpretation of the Law. This gives the clue to the *Sitz im Leben* of the 'Memorandum': a community withdrawn from the Temple and forced into a 'ghetto-like' existence leading to demoralisation and thus to defection. But 'nothing in the text suggests that this community is to be identified with that of Qumran' and here Murphy-O'Connor disagrees with Stegemann in holding that it was not rejection of the Temple which constituted the definitive claim of the Teacher; on the contrary, the Essenes already rejected the Temple. In fact, Murphy-O'Connor had previously deduced from his analysis of 1QS VIII,1ff. that it was the Teacher's decision to go to Qumran which led to the break with the rest of the Essenes. Accordingly, Murphy-O'Connor suggests that the 'ghetto-like existence' was solved by fleeing to more conservative, rural areas, and away from the cities. But although Stegemann had suggested a similar move on the part of his Hasidim, prior to the move to Qumran, Murphy-O'Connor does not follow him in identifying these places with the camps of CD IXff. for the legislation there implies a Gentile environment, to which, *ex hypothesi*, Hasidim or Essenes would not flee in order to be able to observe their laws without opposition. The *Laws* of CD, then, betray a Diaspora setting.

The 'Memorandum' has a epilogue in the form of an exhortation, a promise and a warning (VII,4-VIII,3), in which the A and B texts diverge. Here Ephraim designates the enemies of the sect and Judah the sect, and the *Sitz im Leben* which Murphy-O'Connor projects for this epilogue is the separation of a small (Judah) group from a large and powerful (Ephraim) group. The warning is able to fuse the historical outcome of the original separation (the Exile) with the future outcome of the present situation (God's judgment on the wicked).

The 'Memorandum' is preceded, according to Murphy-O'Connor, by a midrash which is self-contained. It is compared with the 'Missionary Document' and the 'Introductions' and associated with the latter because it has in common with them God's remembrance of the covenant as the motive for his favour to the remnant, while the 'Missionary Document' attributes the divine favour to the fidelity to the commands of God by the remnant itself. Also common to the 'Introductions' and the midrash is an individual figure—the Teacher on the one hand, the Interpreter of the Law on the other. The purpose of this midrash, it is suggested, is to provide a link between the 'Missionary Document' and the 'Memorandum,' and Murphy-O'Connor notes how very neatly it dovetails with the 'Missionary Document' in particular. However, he cannot assign it to the same source as the 'Missionary Document,' despite the excellent continuity between them, because to do so would contradict the contrast between them which he has tried—not very convincingly—to tease out. On the contrast, however, depends a good deal of his stratification and relative dating of the sources in the *Admonition*.

Murphy-O'Connor next analyses CD VIII,3-18 which he regards as criticising the ruling classes in Judah for their lack of support for the Essene cause. He entitles this document the 'Critique of the Princes of Judah.'[66] It reflects, in his view, a tone of bitterness, and belongs to the period in which the Essenes, having arrived in Palestine, were dismayed at the laxity of the law around them, and expected approval from the religious/political leaders, instead of which they encountered opposition. This document may be specifically dated to the High-Priesthood of Jonathan and has close contact with the language of the Teacher Hymns. But more of a problem than discovering the original *Sitz im Leben* is explaining why such a document has been preserved in CD. Murphy-O'Connor's conclusion is that it was adapted and reapplied against members of the Essene movement who had betrayed the Teacher.

Finally, Murphy-O'Connor considers XIX,33-XX,34, which consists of a *Grundschrift* criticising different sorts of community members; those who had left both spiritually and physically, those who were spiritually alienated from it, and those who remained faithful.[67] The first classification shows that not all who entered the covenant returned from Babylon, and that not all of those who did return remained within the community. The second classification is more significant in that it reveals a situation where disaffection needed to be countered by strong condemnation and prevented by vigorous exhortation. There is an interpolation in XX,1b-8a, however, which is remarkably similar to parts of 1QS, and exhibits a contrasting mood of calmness and discipline. This originated in the time of the Teacher, while the *Grundschrift* clearly reflects his recent death. Murphy-O'Connor finds a conclusion to the entire *Admonition* in XX,22c-34 in which its main themes are recapitulated.

The outlines of Murphy-O'Connor's view of the history of the

Esssenes have already emerged. Some further details draw on evidence outside the document. In the first generation after the return from 'Damascus' (Babylon), the Teacher was converted to the Essenes. A split was provoked by his arrival, and his proposal to move to Qumran led to outright opposition with the 'Man of the Lie,' known also as the 'Spouter.' Stegemann's view, as we have seen, was that the split was occasioned by the Teacher's claim to incarnate the covenant and also by the fact that the 'Man of the Lie' and his followers partially assimilated to conventional Judaism, and certainly resumed relations with the Temple—for Stegemann the crucial issue. In Murphy-O'Connor's view, however, the 'Spouter' and his group are accused only of rejecting the Teacher and not of cultic offences such as Stegemann envisages. He suggests that non-Qumran Essenes continued, and while differences of practice evolved, the crucial issue was confined to recognition of the Teacher.

Murphy-O'Connor's view offers, in my judgment, not only the best account yet of CD as a document, but also the best explanation of the condition of the Essene movement after the move to Qumran. But it is not without its weaknesses. One of them is the extent to which he accepts, with Stegemann, the historiographical value of the Qumran *pesharim* to the point where exegesis of CD is impaired. Another is his view that the Essenes rejected the Temple even before the Teacher — it is not substantiated from CD. The *Laws* of CD IXff. which apparently allow the Temple cult to be observed are dismissed by him as theoretical,[68] not because of any intrinsic evidence to that effect, but because his conclusions demand some such explanation of an awkward piece of evidence. Here the theory is allowed to distort the evidence.

A further, general criticism of Murphy-O'Connor's approach is that he has persisted in regarding CD as a Qumran compilation, and concluded that pre-Qumran material is present only as source-documents. The *Admonition* as a whole, in his view, must be explained in terms of the history of the Qumran community itself, and he is consequently obliged to lay great stress on supposed problems of defection within the community and the reapplication of original criticisms of outsiders to insiders. While his analysis of CD is generally soundest at the source-critical level and strong at the form-critical level, it is certainly weak at the redaction-critical level, although credit must be given for recognising this perspective.

A final criticism of Murphy-O'Connor's reconstruction of Essene history concerns his interpretation of the data of CD I. He accepts the chronological details given as literal (but nowhere defends this view), and yet finds it impossible to fit a period of twenty years between the arrival of the Essenes from Babylon at a plausible moment (he prefers the successes of Judas against Gentile neighbours) and the arrival of the 'Teacher of Righteousness.' He has, therefore, to interpret the figure of twenty years as intended to represent half a generation, and by calculating a generation as in reality twenty years, halve the value to ten years! There is much in CD to support the notion that its community saw themselves as returnees from exile, but we are in fact as yet some way from being able to decide when such a return from exile—if such took place—did occur, or indeed why. There remains an awkward mismatch between the statements of CD and the historical events with which it is usually associated. Even with the excellent work of Murphy-O'Connor, it seems that we have not entirely passed the stage where the solutions sometimes get in the way of the problem.

# I  STRUCTURE AND PLOT OF THE *ADMONITION*

*Structure*

It has become customary to divide CD into two parts, corresponding to A1/B (=I-VIII/XIX-XX) and A/2 (=IX-XVI). The nomenclature *Admonition* and *Laws* respectively is now commonplace. It has been the *Admonition*, especially recently, which has attracted nearly all of the attention, and understandably so. My interest is also in the *Admonition*, although I have attempted where possible to comment upon the *Laws* also.

The opinion of most scholars has been that the *Admonition* is a complex work; in Schechter's judgment it consists of 'extracts from a larger work, put together, however, in a haphazard way, with little regard to completeness or order.'[1] Among recent commentators, few follow Rost in taking the *Admonition* as a single and coherent composition,[2] yet there is little agreement as to the way in which it has been put together. Some consider it a fragment of a larger work (Dupont-Sommer), others as a collection of smaller units worked together (Maier), some as a number of coherent documents built up in a more or less systematic way around a core (Murphy-O'Connor) or a basic document heavily interpolated (Rabinowitz, and to a large extent Stegemann). Any attempt to explain the formation of CD as a whole, and the *Admonition* in particular, is confronted with the initial problem of the age of the manuscripts and the Qumran evidence. From the information given by Milik,[3] there seems to have been at Qumran additional material preceding p. I, between the *Admonition* and the *Laws*, and at the end of the *Laws*; furthermore, pp. XV-XVI preceded p. IX. But whether the Qumran evidence pertains to a more or less definitive Qumranic edition, or several editions, or different stages in the development of a Qumranic edition, we cannot know. It seems to me perfectly legitimate to consider the possibility that our document can be approached as a whole; the fact that it may have existed in different recensions does not mean that there did not exist an original compilation whose structure and plot can be discerned. As to the Cairo manuscripts, the Qumran fragments in any case confirm both the essential reliability of the A text in particular and also the basic sequence of its material. The additions at the beginning and end of A1 and the end of A2, which it is claimed the Qumran fragments reveal, do not constitute any significant disturbance of the structure of the document as the Cairo mansucripts represent it.

We are assisted in searching for the structure by the presence of introductory formulae in I,1; II,1 and II,14, but there is disagreement about whether these demarcate distinct sources or, on the contrary, demonstrate the unity of the material embraced by them. Nor is there agreement as to the extent of the material to be subsumed under the third of these formulae. Stegemann, in the absence of any more formulae, extends his *Grundschrift* from II,14 to the end of the *Admonition*, although he recognises numerous and substantial interpolations and expansions. Denis closes his first source, consisting of three 'monitions,' at IV,6a using as criteria vocabulary, doctrine and 'mood.' Murphy-O'Connor extends his 'Missionary Document' from II,14 to VI,1, on rhetorical and form-critical grounds. My own conclusion is that the formula of II,14 covers the material as far as IV,12 (see below).

Beyond this point it becomes more difficult to trace the boundaries of source-material or redactional sub-divisions in the *Admonition*, or to explain how it grew into its present form. The difficulty is compounded by several factors: the absence of explicit introductory or concluding formulae, the presence of so much midrashic material (e.g. at IV,13bff., VI,3b-11 and VII,10ff.), and the divergence between the two Cairo texts towards the end. Without any headings to demarcate the sections, it is only a redactor's train of thought which can guide us—assuming that there exists one to be discovered. Midrashic material can often obscure whatever basic train of thought is present, for it may frequently be read with equal plausibility as a development within an original source, which may by its very nature entail some element of digression, or as secondary expansion. In either case a midrash may also be seen either as an earlier and possibly self-contained unit or alternatively as a creation by the author of the material in which it is embedded or by the redactor responsible for its inclusion. The approach of Becker and Kuhn to this difficulty has been to separate midrash from discourse source-critically.[4] Rabinowitz's analysis of CD also separates midrash from discourse, although the methodological grounds for his analysis are on the whole difficult to discover. Schwarz has also separated narrative and exegetical materials and evaluated them separately. While this is justified to some extent by her programme, it does not lend itself to conclusions beyond those set by the programme. We cannot use midrashic form as a simple criterion of source-distinction. In the first place, there are several different kinds of scriptural usage which could loosely be called 'midrash.' In the second place, the use of scripture in CD is pervasive, and frequently sustains, or even provides, the train of thought. It plays an essential part in the 'plot' of the *Admonition*, as we shall see. In the following analysis, I shall use the word 'citation' when the biblical text is formally introduced as such, 'quotation' when a biblical text is rendered more or less accurately, and 'allusion' when I believe that a biblical text is being recalled to the reader's mind without citation or quotation. Obviously the third category is difficult to apply; readers may, depending on their familiarity with the Old Testament, find more or less allusion than I—or the original readers.

My first approach to this document presupposed a fairly heterogeneous compilation of material, much as it had struck Schechter. The longer I have worked with it, the more convinced I have become that, while undoubtedly compiled from existing literary sources, the *Admonition* is not at all a haphazard, or even topically arranged *anthology*, but the outcome of an extremely accomplished piece of redaction. The individual components and their sequence are secured not only by a clear and simple plot, but by numerous links of vocabulary, by means of which one passage comments on and develops what precedes. The integration is at times so complex that I have found myself wondering whether in fact CD is not substantially a free composition; but I have not found it possible to defend that view.

I suspect that the reason why the structure and organisation of CD has eluded scholars in the past is that its basic ideology has not been understood. Before the discovery of the Qumran texts, our horizons of intertestamental Judaism were restricted; after their discovery the endeavour to reconcile historical statements in CD with the Qumran *pesharim* led us in a wrong direction. Attempts to grapple with this document on its own terms, however, have produced insights without which the present analysis could not have been undertaken, as I have tried to show in the Introduction.

The structure of the *Admonition* of CD can be most adequately accounted in terms of a covenant formulary. Although the connection between CD and a covenant festival has been suggested from time to time,[5] it has been explored in detail only by Baltzer.[6] Working with the common assumption that CD could be included in the corpus of Qumran sectarian literature, he proposed the following comparison of CD with 1QS III,15-IV,26:

| I   | Dogmatic Section (Antecedent History) | I-VI,11      |
|-----|---------------------------------------|--------------|
| II  | Ethical Section                       | VI,11-VII,4  |
| III | Blessings and Curses                  | VII,4-6.7ff. |
|     | Corpus of Legal Stipulations          | IX,1-XVI,20  |

Compare Baltzer's analysis of 1QS II,15ff.:

| I   | Dogmatic Section     | III,15-IV,1   |
|-----|----------------------|---------------|
| II  | Ethical Section      | V,2-6.9-11    |
| III | Blessings and Curses | IV,6b-8.12-14 |

This section of 1QS is, of course, preceded by a description of a covenant ceremony in I,18-II,18, but I do not find Baltzer's analysis of the famous 'Discourse on the Two Spirits' persuasive. Its literary connection with the covenant ceremony is not in any case clear, for it is separated from the description of the liturgy by II,19ff. Its position in 1QS, its rubric, and its contents all lead one to classify it as catechesis, and there would be no reason to expect a covenant form here, even if one could be demonstrated, which I doubt. Certainly, the parallel with the *Admonition* of CD is somewhat forced.

Moreover, CD I-VI,11 is hardly well described as a 'Dogmatic Section'; Baltzer's subtitle 'Antecedent History' is much better (but has no parallel in 1QS). Yet there remains a valid comparison with the basic outline of the 'covenant formulary' as Baltzer has described it for the post-exilic period, namely[7]

> antecedent history
> statement of substance (general clause)
> stipulations of the covenant
> blessings and curses

The comparison highlights certain anomalies in the case of CD, however. The antecedent history in post-exilic Jewish literature tends to assume more and more the character of a confession; Neh. 9 is an excellent example, and 1QS I,21ff. also conforms. In CD there is no appreciable element of confession in the recital of antecedent history. The sins of the pre-exilic generations are described, but the author and his community do not explicitly identify themselves with them, referring always to the transgressors in the third person. Nor do they directly confess sins committed during the period *after* the exile. Rather, CD concentrates on the group with whom God restored the covenant, and who have been the objects of God's favours. The relationship to the past misdeeds of Israel is that of opposition and not identification. That is not to say, of course, that no penitential prayer was known to the CD community; there is a fragment of one at the end of the *Admonition* (XX,28bff.). But it is not intrinsically connected with the historical material, or with the establishment of the covenant, and its brief appearance highlights its absence elsewhere.

In Baltzer's analysis the blessings and curses in CD precede the corpus of laws, which provides another deviation from the *Bundesformular*. The solution to this difficulty may be to leave out of consideration the *Laws* and to regard VI,11-VII,9 as corresponding to the covenant stipulations in the covenant formulary. This recourse suggests an analysis which recognises the covenant formulary in the *Admonition* rather than in CD as a whole.

I accept the covenant-formulary as a model for the structure of the *Admonition*, but I would present it rather differently, as follows:

I,1-IV,12a    historical, describing the origins of the community, its nature and its purpose, and culminating in an appeal to join.

IV,12b-VII,9    legal, demonstrating first that those outside the community do not have the law but are straying. By contrast, the community is founded on law, a very stringent law, but one which offers salvation. A résumé of some of the community's laws is given, and a brief formula of promise and warning concludes.

VII,5-VIII,19    warnings, constituting a secondary expansion of the original Admonition, and comprising an extensive midrashic discourse and a critique of 'princes of Judah'; the purpose of this addition seems to have been to reinforce the claims of the community against contemporary Jewish religious authorities in the light of the respective fates awaiting them.

XIX,33-XX,34     A supplement to the original *Admonition*, betraying the presence of a new group, who have a Teacher, call themselves the 'new covenant' and bitterly condemn groups of apostates. This community is to be identified with the Qumran settlers. (The same group can also be held responsible for a few glosses and secondary expansions in the body of the original *Admonition*.)

Does this analysis provide us with any clue to the formation of the document? Baltzer recognises CD as, like 1QS, essentially a collection, in which the structure will be to some extent obscured by overlappings and repeated superscriptions.[8] A broad similarity between CD and the covenant formulary may in fact reflect no more than a possibly subconscious method of organisation used by the redactor; it certainly does not mean that CD was read or used as part of a covenant festival, especially at Qumran, for it does not read like a liturgy (compare 1QS I,18ff.). Nor is there any need to associate a covenant *Gattung*—if such a description of CD were correct—with a concrete *Sitz im Leben*. *Sitze im Leben* relate to forms, and not automatically to every document exhibiting that form.

Nevertheless, the document not only exhibits the general form of a covenant formulary, but is also *about* a covenant. This brings us to the question of plot.

### Plot

Following the recognition that the material as a whole conforms very well to a covenant formulary pattern, it is possible to discern a plot which all of this material serves, and which entails a function, to which I would give the name *catechetical*.[9] The three opening discourses themselves disclose elements of the covenant formulary, while their declared purpose is to reveal. What they reveal is a state of affairs between God and Israel described in covenant language as a 'covenant lawsuit,' a *rîb*. Part of this *rîb* is the election of a remnant to inherit the land that remains desolate and inhabited by those whom God has already rejected. Once the period of desolation of the land (which means also exile for the true Israel, the remnant) is accomplished, the land will be given to the true Israel and the wicked destroyed. The discourses offer to their audience not only a disclosure of this state of affairs but an invitation to become part of the true Israel. The fact that they partake of the form of a wisdom address, and contain words and ideas characteristic of OT wisdom literature also introduces us to an important feature of the 'Damascus covenant,' namely that unlike the Mosaic covenant, it demands not obedience to a 'revealed' law, but insight into a 'hidden' law. The covenant of this community is undoubtedly an esoteric one, in which the doctrine of election assumes a prominent rôle.

That the present age is one in which God has abandoned the old Israel (now represented by Judaism outside the CD covenant) is illustrated by showing that it fails to perform God's will. It has, in fact, been abandoned to Belial by God, and allowed to stray. It not only *does not*, but it *cannot* fulfil the covenant demands. It does not even obey the laws of the old, Mosaic covenant. Quite simply, it does not belong to the covenant; it is not the real Israel. At the same time, the real demands of God are shown to reside in the *halachah* of the covenant community, which 'received' them from God when he founded the present covenant with the remnant of the first covenant, after the 'desolation of the land' which ended the pre-exilic period. In VI,11ff. for the first time some of the main items of this *halachah* are set out, and followed by a promise to those who will keep them and a warning to those who reject them.

The warning is finally extended to those who enter the covenant and later abandon it; they shall be reckoned as those who had never joined. We have moved, then, from the initial proclamation of the *rîb* at the beginning of the *Admonition* to the warning against apostasy at the end, from the initial address to outsiders to the final warning given to those who have become insiders. We have seen, as it were, the audience progress from initial inquiry to final commitment. The fact that the final threats against actual apostates derive from a new community which has broken away from the original community does not destroy the plot of the *Admonition*, although it carries it beyond the level of catechesis.

Attention to the use of scripture in CD confirms the plot outlined above. Schwarz has demonstrated very fully what all commentators have recognised, namely that the *Admonition* is saturated with biblical allusions and references which extend from unconsidered reverberation of biblical phraseology to deliberate citation of texts whose biblical context supplies part of the meaning. Examples of this last category might be Ezek. 4,5 in I,5-6; Ezek. 20,11.13.21 (and Neh. 9,29) in II,16-17; Lev. 26,25 in XIX,13 and Deut. 32,33 in VIII,9. It can be shown, moreover, that whole passages of the Old Testament provide a conceptual framework for the *Admonition*, their influence unremarked by a reader who is not, like the author and his original audience, steeped in biblical language and literature and familiar with a tradition of interpretation of this literature. Biblical texts form part of the cultural heritage of the authors of CD, and have come to provide, as Lars Hartman puts it, 'a kind of warp on which the text is woven.'[10] Nevertheless, this state of affairs is misconceived if CD is dismissed as a mere 'mosaic of quotations' to which no evidential value may be attached.[11] There are certainly numerous examples of biblical phraseology which must be regarded as unconsidered and even as only part of the author's own biblically saturated vocabulary. But the cumulative force of the numerous quotations and allusions amounts to a statement that the 'plot' of CD can be read in the bible: the community, the time in which it lives, its laws, everything is anticipated, described, regulated in the bible. The conclusion is forced upon one that not only is the bible used by the community to present its appeal, but also that it was in the bible in the first place that the community found its identity.

The following analysis treats the *Admonition* in four sections, the titles of which indicate both the structure and the plot as I see them. The first three, *History*, *Laws* and *Warnings* reveal the covenant-formulary; the last, *The New Covenant* is, formally speaking, an extension of the preceding *Warnings*, but its importance ranges well beyond its formal role within the document.

## II  HISTORY: I,1-IV,12a

*Summary:* This section of the *Admonition* comprises three discourses introduced by similar formulae: I,1-II,1; II,2-14a; II,14b-IV,12a. Whether these are originally independent is difficult to say. Formally, they are identical; ideologically they are complementary, and disclose the present state of affairs between God and Israel. The first and third discourse describe the historical rejection of Israel by God and his gracious election of and covenant with a remnant, namely the community. The second describes the same predicament in predestinarian guise.

Are the three discourses which comprise this section originally independent compositions, or were they composed as a tripartite whole? They are introduced by very similar formulae:

| | | | |
|---|---|---|---|
| ובינו | כל יודעי צדק | שמעו | ועתה  I,1 |
| ואגלה | כל באי ברית | שמעו אלי | ועתה  II,1 |
| ואגלה | | שמעו אלי | ועתה בנים  II,14 |

| | |
|---|---|
| במעשי אל | |
| בדרכי רשעים | אזנכם |
| במעשי אל | אזנכם לראות ולהבין |

| | | | | |
|---|---|---|---|---|
| I,1 | And now | listen | all who know righteousness | and |
| II,1 | And now | listen | all who enter the covenant | and |
| II,14 | And now | listen to me | children | and |

| | |
|---|---|
| understand | the dealings of God |
| I shall open your ears to | the ways of the wicked |
| I shall open your eyes to see . . . . . | the dealings of God |

Do these opening formulae belong to the discourses or are they redactional? Do they address the same audience? No answer can be offered with any confidence to these connected questions. The repetition of identical or very similar formulae may or may not indicate different source-material, as can be illustrated from Proverbs or Ben Sira.[1] It is a tempting suggestion that 'all who know righteousness,' 'all who enter the covenant' and 'children' refer respectively to insiders, novitiates and outsiders,[2] but the variation may equally well be a rhetorical device.[3]

On the form-critical question, rather too little has been done. Denis simply describes the three passages as '*monitions (de révélation)*,' while Murphy-O'Connor describes the first two as 'Introductions' and the third as a 'Missionary Document'; only the last of these is conceivably a form-critical description, and the similarities between the three are not given any form-critical attention. There has always been more attention to content than form, which is perhaps partly explained by the historiographical importance they have been held to possess. Hence Jeremias refers to I,1-12 as a *Geschichtsaufriss* and Stegemann as a *Geschichtsabriss*, both of which are quite imprecise descriptions.

Now, as we shall presently see, this material owes much to the *Gattung* of 'covenant lawsuit' (*rîb*). But it is not itself a *rîb*; that is, it is not the announcement in the form of divine speech of a dispute which God has with Israel. Rather it is a *disclosure of an existing dispute*. It is not, that is, formally prophetic announcement but didactic instruction. This much the opening formulae make perfectly clear, and the distinction is vitally important for the understanding of the contents. These texts, as I shall argue, do not announce the onset of a divine *rîb* but *disclose an already existing one*. I have chosen to refer to these opening passages by the term 'discourse,' which may be as inadequate as any other, but at least conveys the form of the material as address and its content as instruction.

Let us consider the formal elements of this material more closely. Recently, Lars Hartman has undertaken a more developed form- and tradition-critical appraisal of CD I-II, in a monograph which focusses on I Enoch 1-5. Of the recent commentators on CD he cites only Denis, with whom he concurs in describing I,1-IV,6a as a 'coherent piece though tripartite.'[4] However, he limits his consideration to material delimited as I-II which is rather curious; possibly he means only I,1-II,14a, for certainly his observations pertain to the first two of the passages but not to the third. Hartman finds that, in common with many other pseudepigraphical and Qumranic texts, CD I-II exhibits nearly all of the typical features of a *rîb*-pattern or 'covenant lawsuit,'[5] namely:

| | |
|---|---|
| Scene of judgement | (I,2) [H's parentheses] |
| Call for attention or address | I,1; II,2 |
| God's righteousness | II,3f. |
| Charge | I,20f.; II,6.8 |
| Declaration of guilt | I,3.18ff. |
| Threats and/or condemnation | I,3f.17; II,5ff. |
| Bliss or rewards for righteous | I,7ff.; II,5.11 |
| Positive statement on covenant or admonition to obedience | I,4f. |

Further evidence of the connection between CD I-II and the theme of covenant is provided by the scriptural citations employed. Hartman furnishes the following:

| | |
|---|---|
| I,3 | Deut. 28,20; 31,17f.; 32,20 |
| I,4 | Lev. 26,25.45 |
| I,8 | Deut. 4,1; 30,5.18; 28,11 |
| I,10 | Deut. 4,29 |
| I,16 | Deut. 19,14; 27,17 |
| I,19 | Deut. 27,19 |
| II,1 | Deut. 29,19.26 |
| II,5 | Deut. 32,43 |

He concludes: 'Although the connections between the CD text and the individual passages of the OT are a bit loose, there can be no doubt that it is precisely the OT covenant blessings and curses that have influenced the contents of the CD passage.'

Finally, Hartman conducts a comparison of terms occurring in texts from the 'intertestamental' period which exhibit the '*rîb*-pattern.' He finds that CD I-II compares very closely with his primary text, I Enoch 1-5, the following elements occurring with the same (1) or similar (2) vocabulary:

| | | | |
|---|---|---|---|
| observe | (1) | turn away | (2) |
| know | (1) | transgress | (1) |
| (God's) works | (1) | great and hard words | |
| (man's) works | (1) | hard-hearted | (1) |
| change | | inherit the land | (1) |
| not do the commandments | (1) | | |

The conclusion drawn by Hartman is, not surprisingly, that behind the large number of *rîb*-patterned texts from the intertestamental period must lie some kind of common background. (He suggests a cultic frame of reference, and discusses celebrations at New Year, the Day of Atonement and Weeks.) We need not pursue this part of his thesis further. It is sufficient for us that he has not only demonstrated that CD I-II,14a is replete with covenant vocabulary and allusions, but at the same time reminded us how fruitful an examination of scriptural allusion and vocabulary can be for this kind of form-critical work. It is a method especially appropriate for texts of this period, and, as we shall see, especially for CD.

In the case of CD I-II,14, of course, Hartman's conclusions hardly require elaborate argumentation, since the word *rîb* occurs at the beginning of the first passage (I,2). Moreover, the covenant community is the main subject of all the discourses, and explicitly the first and third. It is also implicitly present in II,2-14a because in I,1ff., and indeed throughout CD, the theme of covenant is associated with two other themes, remnant and devastation of the land. In I,1-II,1 the starting point of the *Heilsgeschichte* of the CD community is the devastation of the land and the destruction of Israel which God brought about through Nebuchadnezzar. In II,2ff., where the treatment is neither historiographical nor narrative, the remnant is presented as a feature of every age, but, as we shall see, reference to it occurs, significantly, only after a clear allusion to the Exile.

Surely a *rîb* contains an announcement of divine punishment for covenant violation? Denis states that all three of these passages

> announce the imminent punishment of the wicked rebels, the heirs of all the apostates in history ... reveal ... to those who 'hold fast' to the covenant of the divine will, by virtue of which they can understand the malice of the wicked and, on the other hand, the perfect conduct to be observed in this time of judgement.

Stegemann[7] independently arrives at a similiar conclusion with regard to the eschatological and typological function of the passages, without committing himself to regarding all three as comprising a single source. Nor, as we have seen, does Murphy-O'Connor attend to the form-critical question of this material. It would seem from what we have just established that Denis and Stegemann, without using the term 'rîb-pattern,' have correctly described the meaning of the three discourses. But a careful reading of these passages raises a question mark against such a conclusion. In both I,1ff. and II,14ff. criticism of Israel, which in a rîb is directed at contemporaries, is here directed against *those of the pre-exilic period*; and the punishment which in a rîb is threatened as a future event, *has here already taken place*, namely the hiding of God's face from the land, and, implicitly, the Exile. But this act of punishment forms also the starting-point of the salvation of the remnant and their covenant with God, which persists up to the present time. There is no future punishment threatened in any of these passages.

The rîb is not announced, then, as a future event brought about by the wickedness of contemporary Israel, but as an ongoing one *resulting from the sins of pre-exilic Israel*. It is, simply, the state of the relationship between God and Israel ever since the abrogation of the first covenant. In the second discourse, II,2ff., where the theme is declared to be 'the ways of the wicked,' there is absolutely no mention of an imminent divine punishment of the wicked. Instead, the passage concludes by saying that God 'leads those whom he hates astray.' It is important to establish firmly the correct perspective of CD's rîb, since this constitutes a fundamental element of the ideology of the document. Concomitantly, the eschatological dimension of this ideology, which is certainly present, must be clarified by careful and detailed attention to the text, which neither Denis nor Stegemann can be said to have accomplished.

Let us now ask to what kind of audience, with what kind of presuppositions, is such a rîb being disclosed? The generally-accepted view has been that those addressed are members of the community being encouraged in their pursuit of perfection by the assurance of divine punishment for the wicked. Again, however, such a conclusion is reached on the assumption that CD originated within the Qumran community. It is of course possible, even probable, that members of the CD community needed to be reminded of the origins and the ideology of their community, even (as it will transpire) be faced anew with the decision to belong with the community and not the rest of Israel. But in order to be reminded, the members must have once upon a time been first instructed. What, in this document, suggests that its audience are in fact not being instructed for the first time? Indeed, whether or not this *Admonition* was recited regularly to community members, its argument is surely designed in the first place for converts. The importance of the history of Israel, here and in the whole of the *Admonition*, points towards an audience coming from outside the community, who hold a different view of God's 'dealings.' For them, God is with Israel, the land is occupied, the covenant is assured, the law is kept. They do not 'know' that God has long since abandoned them; they do not 'understand' that the true Israel is a remnant community, they do not 'perceive' that only this community possesses the divinely given law. It is a new perspective which the discourses 'reveal.' As noted earlier, the 'missionary' character of a substantial part of the *Admonition* has been argued persuasively and in detail by Murphy-O'Connor. The earlier suggestion of Iwry that all of the *Admonition* is to be seen in these terms is fully borne out by careful attention to the form, content and style of the material, and nowhere more clearly than in these three discourses. Let us now examine them individually and in detail.

### The first discourse: I,1-II,1

The discourse falls into two parts. After the introduction (1-2), there is an historical account running from the sins of pre-exilic Israel to the arrival of a 'teacher of righteousness'[8] who brings knowledge about God's deeds to a 'congregation of traitors' (3-12). The conclusion of this first part is marked by the verb עשׂה, referring back, as Stegemann observes, to the מעשׂי אל of 1-2. The second part, 13-II,1 describes the activities of the 'congregation of traitors' (עדת בוגדים) or the 'last generation,' mentioned at the end of line 12, and ends with what may perhaps be another allusion to 1-2 with the word מעשׂיהם. We shall consider these two parts separately.

I,1-12: It has been widely agreed that this first part is metrical, a feature which provides an ideal starting point for our exegesis. But one cannot accomplish any metrical reconstruction of this text without revealing a small but significant number of words and phrases which do not fit and which, given the general facility of a metrical reconstruction, strongly indicate secondary expansion. Their presence cannot be ignored nor the problem brushed aside, precisely because their retention or removal substantially affects the meaning of the whole passage.

These 'extra-metrical' words and phrases have been recognised as such from an early stage, and there is no excuse for recent scholars who have chosen to overlook their presence. Charles, who translated a good deal of the *Admonition* metrically, presented the whole first discourse in tristichs. Among the additions which emerge from his rendering is the phrase 'and in the age of wrath . . . He visited them' (ובקץ חרון . . . פקדם).[9] Rabinowitz, whose metrical arrangement is somewhat looser than Charles, dismisses a rather smaller portion, 'three hundred and ninety years . . . Babylon' as a gloss ('as many scholars agree'), and also identifies 'twenty years' as secondary.[10]

The scansion of Jeremias, however, affords the clearest demonstration of the metre and parallelism of this material. He presents five stanzas, four containing four lines and one containing six:[11]

i   (a¹)   (1)And now listen, all who know righteousness,
    (a²)   and understand the dealings of (2)God.
    (b¹)   For he has a dispute with all flesh,
    (b²)   and executes judgment with all who despise him.

ii  (a¹)   (3)For when they sinned in forsaking him,
    (b¹)   he hid his face from Israel [and from His sanctuary]
    (c¹)   (4)and delivered them to the sword.
    (a²)   But when he remembered the covenant of the fathers
    (b²)   he preserved a remnant (5)for Israel
    (c²)   and did not bring them to total destruction.

iii (a¹)   And in the period of wrath -- three hundred (6)and ninety
           years from delivering them into the hand of Nebuchadnezzar
           king of Babylon – (7)he visited them,
    (a²)   and he made a root for planting grow from Israel and from
           Aaron
    (b¹)   to occupy (8)his land
    (b²)   and to flourish on the goodness of his soil.

iv  (a¹)   And they recognised their iniquity
    (a²)   and knew that (9)they were guilty men,
    (b²)   and they were like the blind
    (b²)   and those who grope (their) way – (10)for twenty years.

v   (a¹)   But God understood their deeds,
    (b¹)   that they sought him with a perfect heart,
    (a²)   (11)and he raised for them a teacher of righteousness
    (b²)   to lead them in the way of his heart.

From this rendering one can identify several distortions of the metre, and especially the phrase 'three hundred and ninety years . . . Babylon.' But Jeremias mentions only a relatively minor phrase, 'and from his sanctuary' (וממקדשו), as a secondary expansion, and this on grounds not of metre but of parallelism between b¹ and b² in this stanza.[12] In view of the conclusions he draws, or fails to draw, it remains unclear why Jeremias undertook a metrical translation in the first place. Even more curiously, he cites in support of his deletion of וממקדשו—but without further comment—a rigorous metrical analysis of CD I offered by Soloff, which identifies several further expansions![13] Stegemann regards the reference to Nebuchadnezzar, 390 years and 20 years as secondary also, but Murphy-O'Connor treats the whole text as integral, and adopts the suspicious chronological data they contain without demur.[14]

The (highly probable) secondary addition of the phrases 'and from his sanctuary' and 'twenty years,' while not without significance,[15] has had a relatively minor effect on the meaning of the passage, compared with the substantial insertion which has (equally probably) taken place in lines 5-6, the first line of stanza iii. It is indicated in Jeremias' rendering by hyphens. The phrase 'period of wrath' is part of the original text which provides the basis for the subsequent expansion 'three hundred and ninety years from delivering them into the hand of Nebuchadnezzar king of Babylon.' It has been disputed whether the word לתיתו necessarily places the 'age of wrath' 390 years *after* Nebuchadnezzar or prescribes the length of time of the Exile, or even defines a period before the Exile.[16] For the present, however, the exact meaning and intention of the insertion is not important, for our immediate concern is with the passage in its original form. It may be remarked, nevertheless, that the glossator must have understood the divine punishment described in lines 3-4 as referring to the advent of Nebuchadnezzar. While this interpretation may seem self-evident, it is worth remarking at this juncture that no other divine punishment in history seems to be alluded to anywhere in the *Admonition*.

The notorious chronological data of this discourse, then, are to be regarded as secondary on metrical grounds. We cannot avoid asking now whether the reference to the 'teacher of righteousness' is also secondary. This question has not been previously (to my knowledge) raised, but there are legitimate grounds for its consideration. Slight evidence exists that expansion has taken place at this point also, although it amounts to a much less obvious distortion of the metre.

The answer cannot in any case be provided solely within the context of this discourse, but entails broader considerations regarding the redactional history of the *Admonition*. We shall revert to the problem at the conclusion of our analysis. Here can be advanced only the possibility of further expansion of the original discourse and the clues *in this passage* which prompt the question.

Jeremias' last stanza may, it seems to me, have been originally different, for his $a^2$ and $b^2$ are a little dubious. To begin with, Jeremias can find no place for 11b-12 in his reconstruction. Moreover, as the text presently stands, the subject of the verb ויודע in 11b is ambiguous. Although its proximity to the verb suggests that the phrase 'teacher of righteousness' may the subject, it is God who is the subject of virtually all the other verbs in this metrical passage, and several scholars translate with God as subject of ויודע also.[17] A further ground for suspicion is that the use of an infinitive construct (להדריכם) is unique. Finite verbs predominate as the first element in the preceding lines, as a glance at the metrical reconstruction shows. In the light of all these observations, one might suggest that the original $a^2$ of the last stanza read ויודע לדורות אחרונים and $b^2$ את אשר עשה בעדת בוגדים, and the words ויקם . . . לבו probably ought to be regarded as secondary.

Even if we leave open the question of this last possible expansion until further considerations can be applied, the removal of the other secondary material in the first part of this discourse leaves us with a text of a rather different complexion. The introductory formula (1-2) is a summons to 'all who know righteousness' to 'consider the dealings of God.' Does the use of צדק identify the audience as a sectarian one? This is by no means certain, for the initial phrase may be a quotation from Is. 51,7.[18] Surprisingly, perhaps significantly, צדק is hardly used in the *Admonition* until the final two pages which, it will be argued, derive not from the original community of CD but from the (Qumran) community of the 'new covenant,' where צדק can certainly be shown to have been favoured as a designation of the community's character.[19] But what of the similarity between יודעי צדק in line 1 and מורה צדק . . . ויודע in line 11? It is not easy to accept that this feature is accidental. Those being addressed are, it would seem, those who benefit from the activity of the 'teacher,' whose arrival is therefore a key item in the passage. Different evaluations are possible of this state of affairs. We may (i) suspect that כל יודעי צדק in line 1 has been secondarily retouched together with the addition of ויקם להם מורה צדק in line 11; or (ii) infer that the mention of the 'teacher' was inspired (wholly or partly) by the opening formula; or (iii) accept that the reference to the 'teacher' is an original part of the discourse. There is no point in attempting to decide between these alternatives at this stage. We cannot in any case attach weight to the opening phrase of this discourse; it can tell us only that the contents do not address committed opponents. I have already expressed my opinion, however, that the discourses were originally composed for converts and not established members of the community.

More important than the subject of 'understand' is the *object* of the understanding: the 'dealings of God.' These are defined in the following phrase introduced by the word כי (better translated 'that' than 'for'): God has a ריב and will execute or is executing justice on all who despise him. A second כי introduces the substance of the ריב, beginning with the sins of Israel, as the *rîb*-pattern requires. However, the sins referred to are those of pre-exilic Israel, and there follows a description of the punishment these sins incurred, the destruction of the land and the divine rejection, and then the history of the remnant which God preserved and has cared for. The meaning of the verb פקד is disputed. Most scholars take it in a benign sense, with the remnant as the object; Rabinowitz translates 'punish' with Israel as the object. The former seems more probable of the interpolated text, in which the punishment and the 'root for planting' are separated so widely. The parallelism shown in Jeremias' rendering also favours this alternative. But in the original text the latter seems preferable, since the 'period of wrath' can only be the duration of the divine anger, or, in other words, of the ריב. The meaning of פקד elsewhere in CD also favours Rabinowitz' suggestion.[20]

The remnant and the 'root,' then, are hardly distinguishable in the original form of the discourse. The remnant is designated as 'Israel' (or 'Israel and Aaron,' if the addition of 'Aaron' is not also secondary), and we are given no cause to recognise this 'root' as a particular group *within* the remnant, since elsewhere in CD the terms 'Aaron' and 'Israel' jointly designate the whole community.[21] In none of the other presentations of the origins of the covenant community in CD are we confronted with a distinction between the remnant and the CD community; the community is presented *as* the remnant, and not as a movement *within* it. However, in the expansion of this discourse which we have just described, it is clear that the remnant and the 'root' *are* presented as distinct, with the latter designating a new community originating a considerable time later than the original one, that is, the community to which CD originally, and still substantially, refers.[22]

The significance of this for the pre-history of the Qumran community may be set aside for the present. Our immediate concern is to understand that the historical review which our passage comprises is no more nor less than a *description of the* ריב, and not a prologue to it. The audience is being asked to understand that the 'dealings of God'— turning his face from the land, giving them up to Nebuchadnezzar, causing the remnant to remain, creating and enlightening a 'root' to return to the land—constitute a ריב; that is, an abrogation of the covenant by God as a result of Israel's transgressions. The sins and the punishment which constitute this ריב are not past and done with. The meaning of line 2b is not that a *future* divine punishment will come upon Israel for her present sins, but that punishment has been and is on Israel for having, as line 3 says, forsaken him. The ריב is a process which commences with God's turning his face from the land, and which describes the present state of affairs between God and 'all flesh.' ('All flesh' is taken from Jer. 25,31, and in the context of this discourse must be understood to apply to Israel; nowhere in CD is the question of God's dealings with other nations of concern.)

It is now clear what the discourse intends to teach its audience. As Denis observes, what is to be understood is a 'mystery,' in the sense that it is private knowledge mediated by 'instruction.' It will become clear that this 'mystery,' this perception of the real nature of the present state of affairs, is the content of all three of the discourses which open the *Admonition*. The divine *rib* is constituted, however, not only by a continuing punishment which is the perpetual 'desolation of the land' (and the perpetual Exile), but also by the existence of a remnant established by God under covenant to inherit the land. The most important part of the 'mystery' of God's dealings is that the community which utters this discourse is this saved remnant of the divine punishment, the sole possessors of the divine covenant.[23]

Denis' remark that 'what is to be understood is the eschatological activity of God, or at least its prelude'[24] and Stegemann's assertion that the *rib* is 'set within a specified period of time, that in which the Qumran community arose'[25] are both wide of the mark, since they misunderstand entirely the dimension of the *rib* and the place of the desolation of the land/Exile in it. The eschatological dimension in these passages, which is hardly prominent and almost entirely implicit, does not consist of an expectation of divine retribution for the present sins of Israel, but the culmination of the long-standing *rib*, in which the land will be restored to the remnant Israel, and (presumably, for it is not stated), those rejected by him will receive their final reckoning. It is in *this* perspective that the 'exile' of the community, which we shall encounter later as an important concept, is to be understood theologically; we cannot, with Stegemann, regard this exile as purely typological, for the making of the covenant with the remnant is placed historically in the context of the Babylonian Exile. The desolation of the land through Nebuchadnezzar is the occasion both of punishment and of covenant with the remnant. As noted earlier, Stegemann, like many other scholars, assigns the 'period of wrath,' the desolation of the land, the community covenant and the exile in the 'land of Damascus' to the Hellenistic crisis of the 2nd century BCE. It is a view which remains just possible on a reading of CD I,1-12 (even in its original form), although still conjectural and in any case ruled out by the evidence of the other historical summaries in the *Admonition*, where the desolation of the land, covenant and exile are indisputably those of the 6th century BCE. But at all events, Stegemann comments that in the present discourse, the desolation and exile are of no particular interest to the author of the text, whose concern is confined to the sequence of verbs in lines 7-11, which Stegemann interprets of the rise of the Qumran community. The suggestion is a feeble one; a heightening of interest is perhaps detectable in lines 7-11 as the sequence of verbs quickens towards the climax. But I can detect no grounds for distinguishing between the verbs of lines 3-6 and those of 7ff. On the contrary, the real break in the sequence is created by the presence of the phrase '390 years,' which drives a chronological wedge of some size between the Exile and the 'period of wrath.' With the phrase removed, the 'period of wrath' appears as nothing other than the period of the *rîb* itself, or, put another way, the period of the continuing Exile.[27] This interpretation, championed in recent times by Jaubert and Rabinowitz, corresponds perfectly with my interpretation of the *rîb*: the 'period of wrath' designates the period of punishment for Israel's sins. The motif of divine wrath in the *Admonition*, as we propose to interpret it, tends to support this interpretation; the definitive expression of that wrath is the *rîb* instituted in the 6th century BCE.

We must next consider the difficulty posed by the text of line 11b-12: ויודע לדורות אחרונים את אשר עשה בדור אחרון בעדת בוגדים, 'and he made known to the last generations that which he did to the last generation, the congregation of traitors.'[29] What is the relationship between the 'last generations' and the 'last generation'? If they are identical, why

does the author not use the same phrase or, better, a pronoun? Two
kinds of solution have been proposed: that the text is corrupt or that
the two phrases refer to different entities. Representing the former
alternative, Schechter proposed to emend אחרון to ראשון, 'previous.'
(Ginzberg's objection[30] that ראשון cannot bear this meaning has been
refuted by Rabin who cites a parallel from *bBer.* 35b.) Charles'
solution was to delete בדור אחרון as a dittograph; but this solves only
part of the problem, leaving us to discover what is the 'congregation of
traitors.' His proposal is similar to that of Stegemann, who regards
בדור אחרון as a gloss.

Representing the second alternative, Jeremias comments that the
phrase לדורות אחרונים is used in an inclusive sense, incorporating not
only the 'last generation' but those preceding it,[30] while Cothenet
paraphrases as follows: 'Il fit connaître aux futures générations ce qu'Il
ferait, lors de la génération suivante, à la congrégation de traîtres.'

The difficulties raised by the text are compounded by assumptions
about the מורה צדק. According to the Qumran *pesharim*, the Teacher
revealed the true meaning of the prophecies of Habakkuk which were
about the End (1QpHab VII,1ff.); also, the Teacher was a contemporary
of a 'Man of the Lie' or a 'Spouter of Lies' who is referred to in the
second part of our passage, lines 14f. Consequently, while the 'last
generations' are apparently contemporary with the Teacher, the 'last
generation' is contemporary with the 'Spouter,' who is also, according
to the *pesharim*, a contemporary of the 'Teacher of Righteousness.'
This line of argument leads inevitably to the conclusion that דור אחרון
and דורות אחרונים must mean the same thing. Consequently, the verb
עשה must be translated, with or without explicit emendation, as a
future tense, or read as a participle with a future sense.[31]

Without the influence of statements from the *pesharim*, other
interpretations have emerged. Jaubert translates עשה as a past tense:
'made known to the last generations— those after the Exile— what God
had done in an earlier generation— that of 587—to a congregation of
traitors— the traitors of the covenant who had brought about the ruin
of Jerusalem.'[32]

Several considerations lead me to suggest that Jaubert is, to a large
extent at any rate, correct, and that the divine activity disclosed either
by God or the teacher belongs to the *past* and not the *future*, or even the
present. In the first place, the verb without a pronoun or a noun reads
more naturally as a perfect than as a participle. Second, there is a
reference in line 21 to a past punishment of God, the victims of which

are referred to as a 'congregation,' and the verb in this case is unquestionably to be translated as a past tense—ויחר, 'was aroused.' Third, the 'dealings of God' which are the object of revelation in this passage have been seen to be events in the *past*. These 'dealings of God' cannot be future because no future dealings are actually revealed, and can therefore hardly be 'considered.' What *is* to be 'considered,' as has already been emphasised, is what God has done in the past, and the discourse is a disclosure of the meaning of these events, and not a warning of things to come.

The argument requires another step, for we should entertain seriously Stegemann's conclusion (see below) that I,13-18a is secondary. I would agree with him, too, that either דור אחרון or עדת בוגדים is probably part of the same process of interpolation.[33] If the reference to the 'man of scoffing who spouted . . . waters of falsehood' and who, according to the Qumran *pesharim*, is a contemporary of the Teacher of Righteousness, is not part of the original text, there is even less reason for equating the 'last generation' with the 'last generations.' Consequently, I would translate 'He made known to later generations what He had done to the congregation of traitors.' Their treason is surely the act of abandoning God mentioned in I,3; במועל אשר עזבוהו, and the concluding phrase of this first part of the discourse describes perfectly the function of all three discourses in CD, namely to reveal to contemporaries what in fact God has done, but what they could not hitherto see.

I,13-II,1: Schwarz has remarked that from the point of view of content, I,13b-II,1 could be seen as a comment on the 'last generation.'[34] But if the words 'last generation' are secondary, the comment upon them must be so also. Stegemann argues precisely this, that 13-18a is an expansion of the original text. Both formally and in content, he argues, it parallels 18b-II,1, and both cannot be original. Of the two 18b-II,1 is more probably original because it displays close affinities with 1-12, both verbal and stylistic. Verbally, משפט יעשה בכל מנאציו in I,2 and בעדת בוגדים [בדור אחרון] אשר עשה את in I,12 are taken up by ויחר אף אל בעדתם in I,21-II,1. (One could perhaps add מעשיהם in II,1 to these verbal links.) Stylistically, in 18-21 can be found a metrical pairing of verbs which parallels the metrical structure of I,7ff. Structurally, Stegemann suggests that at the end of the interpolation, in 18b, בעבור has replaced an original כי, while he also perceives a redactional link in line 12.[35]

Stegemann's arguments are plausible, although I would differ on some details; but by themselves they fall a little short of being conclusive. Murphy-O'Connor rejects the whole suggestion that there is a substantial body of secondary material here, dismissing stylistic criteria as being invalid for source-criticism.[36] However, he does concede that 'both I,17 and II,1 serve the same structural function' and deletes למען at the end of line 16. He describes the quotation of Hosea 4,16 as a 'punning gloss' and, reading יעבירו in line 20 as a deliberate change to a *hiphil* from the *qal* of Is 24,5 he identifies 'causing others to break the covenant' as the activity of the 'Man of the Lie.'[37] Stegemann's suggestions must nevertheless be seen in the light of other observations which lead him to the general conclusion that references to specific individual opponents of the Teacher in CD are all secondary, and we shall see in the course of this analysis that such a conclusion is coherent.[38]

Although I agree with Stegemann's view regarding the secondary nature of 13-18b, I retain some reservations with regard to the identity of the 'Man of Scoffing.' Although he is generally regarded, on the basis of the *pesharim*, as a sectarian opponent of the Teacher of Righteousness, his description is built out of citations (Is. 28,14; Prov. 29,8; Ps. 107,40), the criticisms made of him are not especially appropriate of a sectarian leader, and he is represented as a misleader of *Israel*, not of a sectarian group. I think that another possibility might be left open for further investigation: that 12b-18a is original, and that it refers to the pre-exilic generation, which is elsewhere characterised in CD (V,20ff) as having been led astray by false prophets. It is not impossible that the terms 'Man of Scoffing' and 'spout,' present in the original text of the *Admonition*, have been reinterpreted in the context of a Qumranic revision of this CD *Heilsgeschichte*. This suggestion leaves open the question whether any particular individual in the history of the Qumran community can be associated with the soubriquet, a problem yet to be seriously investigated. But, this suggestion aside, I believe, on balance and for a host of minor reasons, that Stegemann's conclusion offers a more satisfactory account of the text of CD at this point, at least for the present. However, I must also make it clear that agreement with Stegemann's conclusions at this point is not intrinsic to my view of the ideology of the discourse.

Let us now review the entire passage and comment further upon the secondary material. Stegemann's conclusion with regard to CD I,1-II,1 is that upon an originally eschatologically orientated *Grundschrift* which criticised a contemporary group and threatened them with punishment, a redactor has imposed a quite different aspect by the introduction of chronological data and the identification of the contemporary group with a specific community known to have been contemporary with the Teacher of Righteousness. He nevertheless accepts that the redactor's description of the Man of the Lie and his community is historically accurate. On the contrary, I find the *Grundschrift* to be orientated towards the past, referring explicitly to a specific act of divine punishment and also to the misdemeanours of Israel which led to it. I can find nothing in it which throws light directly on the origin of the *Qumran* community as it has been reconstructed from the *pesharim*. The only evidence for associating the *Grundschrift* with the Qumran community specifically is the mention of a מורה צדק, if the phrase is original to the *Grundschrift* and if it also refers to the person to whom the Qumran community ascribed its formation. At all events, the shifting of God's anger from the pre-exilic generation to a specific and more recent community, led by a 'Man of Scoffing,' probably belongs to a secondary stratum whose character Stegemann has exposed.

Finally, the incident referred to in I,21 has puzzled commentators. Charles—who also acknowledged that line 12 referred to a past event which 'belongs to some earlier date'—regards this reference as 'doubtful' while alluding to the foregoing misdeeds as persecutions of the Sadducees by Jannaeus or by the Pharisees. Dupont-Sommer, followed by Cothenet, identifies the event as the siege of Jerusalem by Pompey. The only previous reference to an act of divine punishment is the Babylonian devastation and deportation and I see no reason for doubting the view of Rabinowitz and Jaubert that this is what is referred to in both lines 12 and 21. If so, it seems that reflection on the deeds which brought about this punishment, which has not yet terminated, is an important part of the concern of these discourses. The pre-exilic Israel whose deeds brought about the Exile is always referred to in the third person, and those who speak in CD belong to the saved remnant, whose history begins only with the Exile, and who, as we shall see, alone possess the divine covenant. One of the central themes of CD as a whole is the presentation of the remnant group as the Israel with whom God is presently dealing. The rest of 'Israel' has been and is rejected, subject to the covenant vengeance of God. The *Admonition* will later attempt to confirm this thesis by showing that those outside the community have strayed (been led astray) from the will of God, proof that they have been abandoned by him.

### The second discourse: II,1-13

It has often been remarked that this discourse is different from those on either side of it. While this is undoubtedly true, the differences conceal fundamental similarities of ideology. Before discussing the form and content of this discourse, let us note some verbal links between it and the preceding passage. Apart from סררי דרך in I,13, which recurs in II,6 (perhaps offering a partial explanation for the form of the interpolation which this phrase introduces in I,13), we find that מתעבי חק echoes ויפירו חוק in I,20 while the lack of a remnant (שאירית ופליטה) for the wicked contrasts with the preservation of the remnant in the whole of the preceding passage (שאירית in I,4). ידע...מעשיהם...דורות and יסתר את פניו in lines 7f. also echo I,1ff., and פליטה לארץ in 11 may be compared with לירש את הארץ in I,7f. An equal if not greater number of verbal echoes exists with the following passage (see below), and perhaps can be seen to lend some support to the view that the three discourses form a single composition.

The identity of the audience addressed in this discourse depends on whether the phrase באי ברית means 'entering the covenant' or 'members of the covenant.'[39] Its stated theme is the 'ways of the wicked,' yet it deals as much, if not more, with the destiny of the righteous as with that of the wicked, presenting us with a dilemma similar to that of I,1ff., in which a *rîb* dealt as much with the election of a remnant as with the punishment of the wicked.

The discourse is strongly predestinarian in tone, and similarities in vocabulary and theology with the dualistic catechism of 1QS III,14ff. have been noted. The following is my own list:

| | |
|---|---|
| כי לא בחר אל בהם מקדם עלם | CD II,7 |
| כיא בם בחר אל לברית עולמים | 1QS IV,22 |
| ידע את                מעשיהם | CD II,7-8 |
| והואה ידע פעולת        מעשיהם | 1QS IV,25 |
| | |
| בטרם נוסדו | CD II,7 |
| ועליהון יסר כול מעשה | 1QS III,25 |
| | |
| ויתעב את דורות מרם | CD II,8 |
| אחת תעב סודה | 1QS IV,1 |

| | |
|---|---|
| מתעב כול גלולי נדה | IV,5 |
| וכן יתעב אמת | IV,24f. |
| | |
| ויסתר את פניו ...עד תומם | CD II,8 |
| להתם כול רוח עולה | 1QS IV,20 |
| | |
| וידע את שני מעמד...פרוש קציהם | CD II,9 |
| עם קצי שלומם | 1QS III,15 |
| לפי רזי אל עד קצו | III,23 |
| וכול קציהם לדורותם | IV,13 |
| לכול קצי עולמים עד קץ אחרון | IV,16 |
| | |
| לכול הוי עולמים | CD II,9f. |
| לכול קצי עולמים עד קץ אחרון | 1QS IV,16 |
| נתן קץ להיות עולה | IV,18 |
| עד קץ נחרשה...כול קצי [עולמי]ם | IV,25 |

These parallels, however, give little hint of the differences between the two passages. Both are concerned with predestination, but 1QS is dualistic. The wickedness of man is caused by the spirit (angel) of darkness in 1QS, but in CD by God. In CD the role of angels is only as agents of God's appointed destruction. Another difference lies in the eschatological emphasis in 1QS and the absence there of any allusion to the history of Israel or even of the Qumran community, in the 1QS passage. Our passage is not entirely bereft of historical allusion. In 8-9 the phrase 'He hid His face from the land' undoubtedly describes a specific act. Its interpretation is rendered difficult by the following words מי עד תומם.[40] A definitive solution may have to await the discovery of a Qumran fragment of this passage, but at all events we may translate עד תומם as 'until their destruction' or 'until their completion.' This phrase is then susceptible of two interpretations. Since the context is of past events, it may indicate a period which has been completed, marked by an historical event; it may on the other hand refer to the future. In either case we encounter a period of time during which God has hidden his face from the land. The initial act of hiding is not difficult to interpret, for it is a reference to the Babylonian destruction (cf. Ezek. 29,23 and CD I,4). It is difficult to imagine what event in the past might have constituted the תום, other than the extinction of the pre-exilic generations themselves. But in fact, the question of the deeds of the wicked remains a contemporary issue; had the wicked all been destroyed, the point of the present predestinarian discourse would be lost. Therefore we must understand the face of God as *remaining hidden from the land*; the punishment continues, and the תום remains to be accomplished. This interpretation is corroborated by the phrase 'in order to leave a remnant for the land' in line 11.

After mentioning the definitive act of God's hiding his face from the land, the passage ceases to be concerned exclusively with the wicked, and concentrates on the righteous. In this respect we encounter the same descriptive sequence as in the previous discourse: before the devastation of the land, all is wicked; after it emphasis is all on the graciously preserved remnant, who live during the time in which the devastation and Exile is prolonged. It is to this period, which comprises the horizon of history from CD's point of view (as is the case with the book of Daniel), that 9bff. applies. It is in the light of this interpretation, therefore, that we read (11) 'in all of them (sc. epochs of years of eternity) God raised for himself men of name to leave a remnant for the land and to fill the face of the world with their seed.' The context makes it clear that the 'epochs of eternity' do not extend back beyond the hiding of God's face from the land, i.e. the Babylonian devastation. I translate ארץ as 'land' and not, as Dupont-Sommer, 'earth' because nowhere else in the *Admonition* does ארץ mean this; because Dupont-Sommer's translation of תבל as 'universe' does not make sense; and because the association of remnant with land is present in CD I,7-8. תבל must, then, be translated 'world.' In fact, the 'men of name' raised in every epoch fulfil two goals: they remain to inherit the land, and also to populate the earth. It is tempting to develop a remark of Schwarz[41] and suggest that here is a claim on behalf of the Jewish diaspora to be fulfilling while in Exile the earliest commandment of God to man (Gen. 1,28). But the absence of any supportive evidence elsewhere in CD must be acknowledged, and perhaps the allusion is rather to the Noachic covenant. There is another possible allusion to the Deluge and to Noah here in the phrase אנשי שם and in פלימה. Such allusions would furnish a link with the beginning of the next passage (see below).

A further point of resemblance between this passage and the other discourses is that when God has raised up this remnant he teaches them, ויודיעם.[42] It is a consistent feature of the remnant in CD that they are not only preserved, and preserved to inherit the land, but also made to *understand*. This understanding is given ביד משיחו רוח קדשו וחוזי אמת,

which must refer, I think, to the prophets.[43] In VI,1 משיחו הקרש certainly refers to the prophets, who appear alongside Moses, rejection of whose teaching led to the desolation of the land. In I,11 the teaching comes through the מורה צדק. The contrast between the true prophecy, which enlightens the remnant, and false prophecy, by which in large measure Israel was led astray in the past (e.g. I,13ff.), is another *leitmotif* not only of these initial discourses, but of the entire *Admonition*.

There are also detailed and significant points of contact with the following discourse in II,14ff., especially in line 13. פרוש + שם recurs in IV,4-5 (פרוש שמותיהם), as does קריאי שם as a description of the remnant. In IV,6 there originally stood a list of names and details, probably in genealogical form. The word פרוש in IV,4 is therefore to be translated 'list,' as Schiffmann has demonstrated.[44] The function served by that genealogy, it will be argued, is to emphasise the continuity of the remnant, to show not only that it has antiquity, but also that it continues and indeed is still open for other Jews to join. The continuity of the remnant, and implicitly therefore its constitution in the present moment, are asserted in this passage also. One important difference between the two passages is that II,2-14 displays no interest in what one may call an 'eschatological timetable,' while one of the further functions of the genealogy of IV,6 is to reinforce the message that there is a *prescribed period* after which association with the remnant will no longer be possible and, implicitly, that the period will shortly close.

Despite superficial differences between this discourse and the other two, we have now discovered extensive agreement between the terminology and ideology of all three, and shown that they form a much more coherent body than has usually been appreciated. Because of their mutual coherence, the ideology which informs each of them is able to emerge more clearly and to be identified with greater confidence. The major difference between this and the first discourse is, of course, the predestinarian account of God's dealings. This predestinarian account is surely to be seen as a preparation for the challenge which the third discourse is about to make to the audience. The community seems to believe that while it must recruit new members from outside, these will join because they have been predestined to do so (and hence, perhaps, the phrase כל יודעי צדק at the opening of the first discourse). Those being addressed are not simply being invited to 'join the remnant'; they are being invited to understand. If they understand, this understanding will be seen as proof of their divine election. (This aspect of sectarian mentality and ideology can, of course, be extensively documented in Jewish literature of the Second Temple period, and the entire history of Christian sectarianism.)

## The third discourse: II,14-IV,12b

The superscription addresses the audience simply as 'children,' and the stated purpose of this discourse is to 'open your eyes and see and understand the dealings of God, to choose what he favours and reject what he hates.' If these two elements are to be taken together, we have a purpose which is slightly different from that of the first discourse. There it was revealed that God's dealings with men were to be discerned as a *rîb*. In both the first two discourses the stage, as it were, is set; the character of the first is historically descriptive, the second theologically descriptive. This third combines elements of both kinds of description, but proceeds beyond description to summons. The fruit of such knowledge—itself a product of election?—is the ability to *choose* between what God loves and what he hates; in effect, to choose between the ways of the remnant whom God has rescued and enlightened, and the wicked, whom God is punishing and has caused to stray. This movement from description to challenge is, in my opinion, no accidental outcome of the juxtaposition of source-material, but a deliberate step in the argument of the whole *Admonition*, by which the hearer or reader is first told something, then told the significance of it, and finally challenged to act on it.

Stegemann's view is that this discourse is directed towards members of the community in danger of apostasy. If one is obliged to postulate its origin within a closed community such as Qumran, this is one of the few conclusions possible. But there are really no positive indications that apostasy is recognised as a danger in this discourse. Murphy-O'Connor, as we have explained, has argued that II,14-VI,1 is directed towards non-members of the Essene community. Whether or not the use of the neutral address 'children' supports this view, as he claims, his analysis demonstrates that the argument of this discourse justifies the description 'Missionary Document.' This seems to me the most plausible account yet offered of the original function of this discourse. As to the possibility that it was later used to remind community members (as Murphy-O'Connor suggests), the absence should be noted of any indication that the audience are being reminded of what they know already. Nor are those addressed reprimanded or threatened. In short, there are no internal indications that this material has been redirected from its original audience and towards community members. The heading of the previous discourse באי ברית is most probably to be taken to mean that the second and third discourses at least are directed to *initiates in the process of making their choice*. In this respect, 'Missionary Document' may not be an entirely correct title. It seems to me preferable to think of the function of the discourses as catechetical rather than apologetic, and that indeed is my view of the original *Admonition* as a whole. If there is any implication that they are addressed as outsiders—which is to me not clear—no more than a rhetorical device may be in question.

What is the extent of this discourse? Over what material does the opening rubric extend? Stegemann regards all the material to the end of the *Admonition* as governed by it; and indeed the rubric is general enough to serve for the *Admonition* as whole. However, it is quite possible that the rubrics of the three discourses are original and not redactional, in which case we must use source-critical criteria to determine the extent of the material to which they apply, and not assume that the redactor of the *Admonition* intended these rubrics to govern the whole of his own composition.

Let us briefly review the material before us. We are first given a survey of the history of Israel before the Exile, summed up in III,10-12 where the whole pre-exilic world is described as having been given over to the sword because it forsook the covenant and pursued its own desires. Then we are told of the remnant, its origin and its members throughout history. Those who follow after them will also receive God's pardon, but when the period comes to an end, there will be no further opportunity to enrol in the community of the covenant.

This leads into a description (IV,12bff.) of the practices of those outside the community, intended to prove that they have been abandoned to the devices of Belial, and to anticipate the introduction of some of the community's halachic principles, which are given in VI,11ff.; intervening, however, is another historical summary, whose purpose, in my opinion, is to contrast the community with those who under the influence of Belial do not (and cannot) keep the law, to explain the origin of the halachah and the importance of observing it. There is such a logical coherence between all the elements that to distinguish individual sources seems invidious. However, the criticism of practices outside the community, from IV,12-V,15a is certainly composed of originally independent elements, and linked to the following section by a redactional passage in V,15b-16. This following passage itself is both in form and content rather similar to the account of the origins of the covenant community in III,12bff., and is therefore unlikely to have belonged to the same original source.[45] I have suggested IV,12a as the end of the discourse, therefore, for no single compelling reason, but for a number of rather minor reasons, the most telling of which is that I cannot find any other plausible termination. IV,12a does offer a very appropriate ending to the discourse, with the climactic statement that the choice is not simply a matter of reflection, but an urgent challenge. On my 'covenant-formulary'-derived reading of the 'plot' of the *Admonition*, IV,12a marks the end of the theme of history, while IV,12b introduces the theme of law. In any case, however, the remarkable cohesion within the document between the various sources makes source-division frequently a matter of relatively little importance.

The many verbal similarities between this and the first discourse have frequently been noted; e.g. I,1/II,14; I,3/III,11; I,4/III,10; I,4/III,13; I,4/IV,9; I,8/III,18; II,1/III,8-9. The similarity of form is also quite evident; in Cothenet's words, both these discourses are 'méditations sur les leçons de l'histoire,' but there is a difference, for while I,1ff. was purely descriptive, here the audience are being told what they can do. In the discourse as I have defined its limits, there is no criticism of others except of the pre-exilic Israel, an observation which also holds for I,1ff. The use of examples from the pre-exilic period suggest an audience which is both Jewish and still in a sense outside the community, a suggestion reinforced by the emphasis on the antiquity and continuity of the community's covenant and on the possibility of following those who first entered into it, as well as by the absence of any threat or denunciation of those outside.

We see in this discourse, as in the previous two, that the destruction of the land and the exile into Babylonia forms the watershed of Israel's history. The pre-exilic period can, in fact, be written off as if a single episode, as it is in I,1ff. Nevertheless, by using several episodes from the history of pre-exilic Israel, the author is able to repeat several key terms and phrases. By identifying these, we can understand what points he is especially concerned to make:

| | |
|---|---|
| to choose what God likes and to reject what he hates | II,14-16 |
| for many have gone astray . . . . . from long ago | II,17 |
| the Watchers *walked in the stubbornness of their hearts* | |
| and fell **because they did not keep the commandments of God** | II,18 |
| and their **CHILDREN** | II,19 |

| | |
|---|---|
| all flesh on dry land perished | |
| *THROUGH DOING AS THEY WANTED* | |
| **and not keeping the commandment of their maker** | II,21 |
| UNTIL HIS ANGER WAS AROUSED AGAINST THEM | II,21 |
| and Noah's **CHILDREN** | III,1 |

| | |
|---|---|
| Abraham **kept the commandments of God** *AND DID NOT CHOOSE WHAT HE HIMSELF WANTED* | III,2-3 |
| and he passed them down to Isaac and Jacob who kept them and were in covenant for ever | III,3-4 |
| their **CHILDREN** went astray | III,4 |

| | |
|---|---|
| those in Egypt | |
| *walked in the stubbornness of their hearts* | III,5 |

| | |
|---|---|
| and took counsel **against the commandments of God** *AND DID WHAT WAS RIGHT IN THEIR OWN EYES* | III,5-6 |
| at Kadesh *THEY CHOSE THE DESIRE OF THEIR OWN SPIRIT* and listened not to the commandments of their teacher | III,7-8 |
| THE ANGER OF GOD WAS AROUSED AGAINST THEIR GENERATION | III,8-9 |
| their **CHILDREN** perished through it | III,9 |

| | |
|---|---|
| the land became desolate, the first covenant members were destroyed *BECAUSE THEY CHOSE THEIR OWN DESIRE* | III,11 |
| *and walked in the stubbornness of their hearts* | III,11f. |
| but **those who held fast to the commandments of God** were saved | III,12-13 |

The key motifs of this summary emerge as follows:

1. **keeping the commandments of God**
2. *not walking in stubbornness of heart*
3. *NOT FOLLOWING ONE'S OWN DESIRES*
   (language less stereotyped)
4. THE ANGER OF GOD BEING AROUSED
5. the succession of rebellion through **CHILDREN,**
   which ends every episode.

The whole pre-exilic period is characterised by repeated rebellion, repeated punishment, and repeated renewal of rebellion by the 'children.' This repetition is brought to an end by the definitive act of punishment which resulted in loss of the land, and destruction of the pre-exilic world—and its children, for that pre-exilic world did not survive. But because of the fidelity of some children who did not rebel and follow their own desires, a new line of succession was begun through the survivors of that generation. These are characterised as holding fast to the commandments (and what this means is to be spelled out later in the *Admonition*), and by *continuing fidelity*; continuity from one generation to the next within this remnant after the Exile balances the cycle of rebellion and punishment and rebellion of children in the pre-exilic period. Previously, those who came after the sinners also sinned, despite punishment; those who come after the first members of the covenant will join an everlasting covenant, foreshadowed by the patriarchs who were באי ברית for ever. For while the author contrasts the pre-exilic covenant with the post-exilic covenant, he is anxious not to break the link with Israel's sacred past completely. The covenant of the community is not presented as without precedent, nor its members as a new breed; they are the remnant of the first covenant. This appeal to continuity in some sense with the previous covenant, and also with the patriarchs, is evidence, I believe, that the document addresses those who retain some allegiance to the old 'Israel,' represented by Judaism outside the community. Nevertheless, the second covenant which God 'established' (הקים) is on a different footing from the first. There is ambiguity between the *Heilsgeschichten* in CD on the identity of this covenant with that of the 'first ones,' which is not, I think, of historical or theological significance; it is the nature of the argument being pursued at this juncture which determines the attitude taken towards the former covenant. We must not lose sight of the fact that we are dealing with a *rhetorical* text, whose meaning can only be apprehended when the gist of the argument is perceived and the context of each step in it is taken into account. At this point, the author is ready to introduce his audience to the fact that the new covenant has a character of its own, with its own halachah, which is indeed the only halachah, just as the community possesses the only covenant. This contrast between the old and the new Israel will be drawn in an even blunter manner later in the *Admonition* by labelling the two respectively 'Ephraim' and 'Judah.'[46]

Genealogy, then, links the whole survey together; the children of the sinners, the children of Abraham and, in IV,6, the genealogy of the covenant community. The choice between doing God's will and one's own, the subject of this discourse, is a matter of obeying the divine commandments; it is these which express the divine desire. Following God's will is not therefore a matter of individual conscience, but of following received law. Abraham passed on (ימסור) to Isaac and Jacob. In the same way the commandments of God are now in the possession of the covenant community, which will pass them on to its 'children.' Hence the opening address, 'children,' which expresses exactly the relationship within the community between its members and new entrants, or would-be converts, as the discourse may have originally had in mind.

In what do these divine commandments consist? Schiffmann observes that at Qumran מצוה can refer to sectarian halachah, although it pre-eminently denotes divine commandments, including those which may have been derived by exegesis.[47] This conclusion does not seem particularly helpful here, but it is precisely the range of meaning of the word מצוה in CD which explains its use here. On the one hand, the commandments of God rejected by the pre-exilic generations have no sectarian value; they are not privileged knowledge. On the other hand, the audience is about to realise that the state of affairs is different in the new covenant. In III,13f. we read that when God established this covenant with the remnant, he revealed to them the 'hidden things' (נסתרות) in which Israel had gone astray, as the result of which the remnant dug a well, established a halachah. One of the most obvious features of this halachah to the newcomer is the calendar, and it is this which is particular mentioned at this point—holy sabbaths and glorious feast-days. Talmon has suggested[48] that the מצות referred to in connection with the pre-exilic period here also denote calendrical matters, and he comments on the significance of beginning the catalogue of rebellion with the Watchers who, according to I Enoch 6-

8, revealed the secrets of the lunar calendar to men. In fact, I Enoch does not explicitly ascribe this to the Watchers, but rather 'all unrighteousness on earth and . . . the eternal secrets which were in heaven' which may include calendrical and astronomical knowledge, but does not make a point of it. In support of Talmon, however, one may cite Jubilees 6. This records the initiation of the Noachic covenant and the celebration of the covenant renewal at the Feast of Weeks (or Oaths). Especial stress is laid on the injunction against eating blood; 'blood' occurs 12 times in vv. 7-14 (translation from Charles):

> The man who eats the blood of beast . . . he and his seed shall
> be rooted out of the land . . . command the children of Israel
> to eat no blood, so that their names and their seed may be
> before the Lord our God continually . . . And this whole
> festival [Weeks] was celebrated in heaven from the day of
> creation till the days of Noah . . . and Noah and his sons
> observed it . . . till the day of Noah's death . . . and from the
> days of Noah's death his sons did away with it until the days of
> Abraham, and they ate blood. But Abraham observed it, and
> Isaac and Jacob and his children observed it up to thy days
> [Moses'], and in thy days the children of Israel forgot it.
>     . . . The years will come upon them when they will disturb
> (the order) . . . and they will confound all the days, the holy
> with the unclean . . . for they will go wrong as to the months
> and sabbaths and feasts and jubilees . . . and they will eat all
> kinds of blood with all kinds of flesh.

In Jub. 6, the liturgical/calendrical context is Weeks and the celebration of the covenant; the issues raised are the eating of blood and the observance of the solar calendar. The general similarities to our passage are quite remarkably close. In particular may be noted the recurrence of 'children,' 'names' in conjunction with 'seed' in Jub 6,13; CD IV,5, and the mention of removal from the land as final punishment in Jub 6,13; CD III,10. A minor difference occurs in that the children of Jacob are not in CD regarded as following the will of God even until Moses' time; a major difference is that CD does not stress as an issue the eating of blood. The explanation may be that this did not constitute an issue in dispute between the community of CD and its hearers as it possibly did in the case of Jubilees. Nevertheless, the sin of eating blood is mentioned in CD II,6. The CD passage is also uninterested in the great figures of Israel's past, except for the patriarchs: Noah is included only implicitly and Moses not at all; the author wishes to concentrate all positive revelation on the exilic covenant of his community.

The differences between the two passages are, indeed, rather minor compared with the similarities. The likelihood that both stem from a common tradition is extremely strong. The possibility of direct dependence of CD on Jubilees—or at least a direct connection— in this instance cannot be overlooked.[49]

The value of the Exile in this review of history is, as in the previous two discourses, not typological but historical. As an event it marks the birth of the new age of the community. For this reason, Stegemann is totally misguided in attempting to make 'those who held fast to the commandments of God' in III,12 members of communities in the second century BCE. As I remarked previously, this kind of interpretation is really eisegesis, based on a presumption as to the historical context of the document. On the other hand, Jaubert, Rabinowitz and Murphy-O'Connor are correct in recognising those referred to as the exilic generation, or some of them. Cothenet shares Stegemann's historical identification, but at least he sees the difficulty of applying it here; he remarks therefore that the text refers to the exilic survivors with whom the Qumran community identified itself. Such a suggestion is no improvement on Stegemann's; nevertheless, there is nothing at all in the text to hint at a typological meaning; the text obviously *does* refer to an exilic generation and equally does *not* refer to another, more recent generation. No defence of the plain meaning of the text is needed; the phrase 'who were left over of them' is completely unambiguous. The language is that of remnant, of survival, and it is survival of the Exile and remnant of the pre-exilic Israel of which the text plainly speaks.[50]

The sequence destruction—remnant—covenant has been discovered now in all three discourses, and in each case the same historical period is embraced. Here we are given further details of the high point of that sequence, the renewed covenant itself. It comprises four elements; 1. the revelation; 2. the human response; 3. the divine forgiveness; and 4. the making of the 'sure house.' While these are presented in our text as if three separate and successive events, it is possible that we should see at least the first three as aspects of a single event, the forging of the covenant. Let us consider these four elements in turn:

1.  *The revelation.* The נסתרות concerning which Israel had gone
astray are now revealed to the remnant of Israel. Two verbs are used of
this divine revelation, גלה and פתח. Denis objects that the phrase has
been inserted, possibly under the influence of Ezek. 44,2 and
Lev. 23.[51] Opposing this suggestion, Murphy-O'Connor contrasts the
fourfold use of 'his' here with the fourfold use of 'their' in III,10. This
may appear a slender basis for dissent but a more telling argument
against Denis is that the issue of the solar calendar is implicit in the
whole of the preceding historical review; the Jubilees 6 passage quoted
earlier refers to the calendar as something in which Israel 'went
astray,' echoing the vocabulary here. There is, nevertheless, a
difficulty in deciding precisely what is governed by each of the two
verbs גלה and פתח. Rabin and Dupont-Sommer end a sentence at
'astray,' leaving גלה to govern נסתרות, which is very neat, since נגלות and
נסתרות are contrasting technical terms[52]; the remainder is then
governed by פתח. This solution is eased if the phrase 'which a man
should do and live by' is removed as a gloss, with Lohse and Murphy-
O'Connor. Rabin, who retains the phrase, is obliged to insert 'these'
before 'opened' to recapitulate the object of the verb. But *is* the phrase
a gloss? Rabin notes it as a citation of Lev. 18,5, while Lohse and
Murphy-O'Connor suggest it is inspired by the contrasting threat in
line 17 'and those who despise it shall not live.'

In fact, the phrase in lines 15-16 is a quotation from Ezek. 20, where
it occurs three times, in vv. 11, 13 and 21. In each instance, the 'them'
refers to 'statutes and judgments' (חוקים ומשפטים)—but *also to*
'sabbaths'. In Ezek. 20,21, whose context is the lawgiving at Sinai and
the wilderness wandering of the Israelites, occurs the divine statement
'I said I would pour out my fury upon them to accomplish my anger
against them in the wilderness,' coupled with a threat to disperse Israel
among the nations. However, God did not carry out this threat, but
rather 'gave them also statutes that were not good and judgments
whereby they should not live.' Vv. 33ff. draw a parallel between the
wilderness and the Babylonian exile:[53] 'I will bring you into the
wilderness of the people, and there I shall plead with you face to face, as
I pleaded with your fathers in the wilderness of the land of Egypt . . . and
I will bring you into the bond of the covenant.' And when the people
have been restored to their land ' . . . there shall you remember your
ways and all your doings in which you have been defiled, and you shall
loathe yourselves in your own sight for all the evils which you have
committed. And you shall know that I am Yahweh, that I have dealt

with you for my name's sake, not according to your wicked ways' (vv. 42-44).

The Ezekiel passage provides a connection between the phrase 'which a man should do and live by,' sabbaths, covenant in exile, and recognition of sins. The Holiness Code, Lev. 17-26, which also includes the quotation and promises the ending of exile and restoration for Israel on condition of repentance, has been shown to lie behind the specific injunctions of CD VI,11ff.(see below); it refers to the covenant with the patriarchs and gives as the reason for the exile of Israel from the land the need for the land to enjoy the sabbaths of which it has long been deprived. The Holiness Code provides a connection between the exile of Israel and the desolation of the land, and also affords a pretext for the notion that the Exile *is of a predetermined length*, thus enabling calculations of that period to be undertaken. The relevance of this last point to our present passage will shortly emerge.

In view of the close ideological connections of our passage, Lev. 17-26 and Ezekiel, the quotation 'which a man should do and live by' should be retained as original, and we should instead regard as a gloss 'and those who despise it shall not live' which occurs shortly afterwards (see below). Accordingly, פתח לפניהם does not have a formal object, although what precedes constitutes in sense its object. God opened, they dug. There is just possibly a play of images behind the conjunction; 'open' can be used in connection with the divine provision of water.[54] The point of the statement is, I think, that the revelation is of divine origin, but the halachah is a concrete human response to it, which the community of the covenant enshrines. The will of God is realised in the community. At another level, the audience may appreciate that while they have so far received revelations from the community (see the rubrics of the three discourses), the community itself is taught by God. There is no mention here of a human instrument of this teaching, such as we have undoubtedly in VI,1ff. and, of course, in I,11.

2. *The human response.* The revelation of his will by God is not sufficient; a human response of obedience is required, and this necessitates the formation of a code of legal ordinances, a halachah.[55] Study of the law is also required. There is little doubt among the commentators[56] that the well is the law, as stated in CD VI,4, but not simply revealed law; it is halachah, constructed by exegesis. That the

Qumran halachah was derived exegetically has been argued by
Schiffmann, who of course depends a great deal for his conclusions on
the evidence of CD. Indeed, two excellent examples of exegetically
derived halachoth are furnished in CD IV,20-21 and V,7b-10. But in
these cases, the basis of exegesis is Mosaic torah. What form was taken
by the divine revelation and its resultant law mentioned here is not
easy to decide. What is the relationship between the נסתרות, the Mosaic
law, and the halachah? Murphy-O'Connor suggests—although he is
careful to do no more than raise the possibility[57]—that 'there were not
two distinct events, but that deeper insight into the meaning of the law
was considered revelation.' The possibility is certainly by no means
remote; the Pharisaic oral law was deemed to be revelation insofar as it
was ascribed to the Sinai lawgiving to Moses, yet the exegetical origin
of much of this oral was beyond question. Moreover, the נסתרות which
God revealed are here described as having been those 'in which all
Israel had gone astray.' According to Jubilees 6, whose points of
contact with the present passage have been noted, the solar calendar,
the prime object of revelation, was revealed to Moses, and said to have
been revealed previously to Noah. It was therefore once known and
followed, but had to be revealed again. The point is that within the
theological perspective in which CD and Jubilees are both to be seen
there is no contradiction between a previous and a subsequent
revelation of the same law. Whether or not the solar calendar
originated as a theological doctrine in the Babylonian exile,[58] both CD
and Jubilees regard it as being once upon a time known and
subsequently forgotten or lost. What is therefore revealed might well
be, therefore, not a new scripture, but a fuller understanding (בינה) of
the will of God as expressed in Mosaic law. There is in any case
nothing in CD itself which we could identify as the content of a divine
revelation apart from and yet underlying the halachah. That the
Priestly Code, or the Holiness Code may be what is meant seems
rather far-fetched, and yet this possibility is one which merits
investigation, since it has been shown that the Holiness Code
underlies CD halachah (see the comments to VI,1ff. in the following
chapter), and since it has been plausibly maintained by Jaubert that
the calendar of CD is also reflected in the Priestly literature of the
Pentateuch. But these lines of inquiry will need to be pursued
elsewhere.

However, on the assumption that the divine revelation of law and
the sectarian halachah are not distinguishable, an explanation of the

conjunction of נסתר and נגלה is possible. The point made here is perhaps not about different bodies of doctrine, but a single body of doctrine hidden (נסתר) from Israel but revealed (נגלה) to the community. What is being communicated is the theological claim that the נסתרות are now in the possession of a privileged group, and not of all Israel; only this group can fulfil the law and the 'requirements of God's desire.' Where does this leave the rest of Israel outside the community, who claim that *they* are the covenant people in possession of the law? It has now been explained in all three discourses that these people are no longer the covenant people, the true Israel. In the material which follows this third discourse, it will be demonstrated that the obedience to the law of those outside the community can only be a charade; the fact that they do not have the law is demonstrated by examples, and their predicament is explained as one of ensnarement by Belial, whom God has allowed to deceive them into thinking that what they do is righteousness. Once again, the deeper one reads into the individual components of the *Admonition*, the more clearly emerges the coherent argument of the whole.

3.  *The divine forgiveness.* The divine forgiveness is even more difficult to interpret than the previous two items: are those who 'defiled themselves' and those who were pardoned the same group? Who said 'it is ours'? and to what were they referring? Dupont-Sommer, Rabin, Lohse and Stegemann, among others, consider that two different groups are concerned here. Murphy-O'Connor sees the inherent unlikelihood of this, but resorts to the conclusion that 17b-18a is an interpolation, intended to explain 17a. (It is remarkable how many 'explanatory' interpolations seem to have the opposite effect.) No one seems to think that those defiling themselves *are* the saved remnant. As to what is meant by 'this' in 'this is ours,' Stegemann believes it is the well, while Cothenet and Murphy-O'Connor apply it to the land, as in Ezek. 11,15 from where the phrase is apparently taken. There the land is claimed by those who were *not* exiled to Babylon. Murphy-O'Connor then comments that II,18b 'begins with an awareness of pardon without any explicit avowal of sin' and reminds us of the prophetic belief that pardon was the first effect of the covenant, referring to Jer. 31,31f., Ezek. 16,62f. and 36,25f..[59] More relevant texts are those which express—and no doubt inspired—the ideology of CD regarding the land, the Exile and the covenant. One such text is Ezek. 20,43f.:

There shall you remember your ways and all your doings in
which you have been defiled, and you shall loathe yourselves
in your own sight for all the evils which you have committed.

Another is Lev. 26,40f.:

But if they confess their iniquity and the
iniquity of their fathers in their treachery which they
committed against me and also in walking contrary to me, so
that I walked contrary to them and brought them into the
land of their enemies; if then their uncircumcised heart is
humbled and they make amends for their iniquity; then I will
remember my covenant with Jacob . . . with Isaac and . . . with
Abraham, and I will remember the land.

On the evidence of these texts, pardon is not unconditional, but
depends upon acknowledgement and confession of sins. It should also
not be forgotten that in I,8 we have the 'root' considering its trespass
and consequently being given a revelation (וידע, I,11; cf. וידעם, II,12)
by God. In both the first and third discourse, then, the *Heilsgeschichte*
of the community includes an acknowledgement of sin.

But what sin? The biblical texts I have cited suggest that the sins for
which repentance is required are those which drove Israel from the
land in the pre-exilic period. Now, הם התגוללו can equally well refer to
the 'diggers of the well' or the 'despisers,' and it is possible to
understand והם as emphatically denoting another group. On the other
hand, a nominal clause with a perfect tense may be translated as a
pluperfect: 'for they *had been* defiling themselves . . . ' In this case, it
applies to the remnant who now, as a result of the revelation of God's
will, became aware of their past sins, aware that they were disobedient.
Acknowlegement of this brought divine pardon. This must, in my
view, be the correct interpretation here. In the first place, it coheres
with I,8ff. (and incidentally confirms that the 'root' and the remnant in
that passage were originally identical), and in the second place it
provides the basis of the argument to which this discourse builds; the
same perception of sin is being *given* (through the discourse) to enable
'those who come after' to recognise both their sin and God's just *rîb*,
and thus to be admitted into the covenant. In any case, I can see no
purpose in the text referring to a *different* group here; the only group
other than the community of whom criticism is appropriate is the pre-
exilic Israel, and no further strictures upon them seem warranted at

this particular point. Nor, if והם. . . לנו is a gloss, can I see its point. I can, on the other hand, see the point of ומואסיהם לא יחיה as a gloss, namely to pick up the preceding phrase אשר האדם יעשה וחיה בהם and to indicate that those who depart from the halachah of the group (מואסיהם) will not live. This gloss could well reflect a concern with defection from the covenant community of which there is evidence in the supplementary material at the end of the *Admonition* (see ch. V below). This suggestion would also account for the anomaly of a plural subject with a singular verb. If the phrase originated as a marginal gloss in the form מואסם (='*he* who despises them,' corresponding to the בהם of line 16) לא יחיה, it might have been brought into the text at this point, causing the singular מואסם to be altered to מואסיהם because it now appeared to be the antecedent of והם which followed. On this hypothesis, however, the scribe will have forgotten to change the verb into the plural. Surprisingly the commentators make little or no comment on the grammatical difficulty of this phrase, and suggest no explanation for it.

The description of the remnant as defiled with the 'impiety of man' and 'ways of impurity' does not necessarily contradict the earlier statement that they 'held fast to the covenant.' For this statement by itself does not imply that the remnant obeyed the divine will completely, since such obedience became possible only after the divine 'revelation' and the new halachah. It means that they were unknowingly in breach of the divine will. It is true that פשע אנוש and דרכי נדה would seem on the evidence of CD and the Qumran scrolls to be terms more likely to apply to non-members: דרכי נדה does not recur in CD but is found at 1QS IV,10; התגללו בדרכי זנות occurs at CD VII,5 (XIX,17); התגללים בדרכי רשע at 1QS IV,19; and התגולל ברוח נדה at 1QS IV,21; אנוש + פשע occurs also at 1QH XI,10; and נדה with אנוש at 1QS XI,15. Such parallels seem to constitute evidence in favour of this phrase being a gloss, probably a Qumran gloss. But against this the phrase שבי פשע appears twice elsewhere in CD, at II,5 and XX,17. We also have immediately following in line 18 כפר בעד ענם וישא לפשעם, which undoubtedly refers to the offences of the remnant. On balance, therefore, I view 17b-18a as original and as applying to the remnant. They are specifically said to have claimed—in the words of Ezekiel— 'this (land) is ours.' But their departure from the land was precisely what taught them the folly of this claim, and the *raison d'être* of the community is their waiting for God, upon the fulfilment of his dispute with Israel, to grant the land to be reoccupied by the members of the covenant.

4.   *The making of the 'sure house'.* The phrase 'sure house' is almost certainly a quotation from I Sam. 2,35; 25,28 or I Kings 11,38. The first of these biblical passages presents the 'sure house' as a priestly dynasty promised to Zadok, the second a royal dynasty promised to David and the third a dynasty to Jereboam. If its use in our passage is a deliberate allusion to one of them, then by widespread scholarly agreement it is the first. Thee following material strongly supports this conclusion. The biblical text undoubtedly referred to Samuel, but its use here may mean that it was understood by the author to apply to Zadok. This attribution explains the following Ezekiel midrash, which I suspect was originally an independent source, attached to the preceding section which ends with הנה at the beginning of line 20. The intervening material, from המחזיקים to להם, is puzzling. My guess is that it is probably redactional and designed to form a bridge to the midrash. But its character is determined more by what precedes than what follows. The words אדם, חיי, מחזיקים and חקים are all found (חיי as חיה and יחיה) in the preceding lines, and the whole phrase could be read as an esoteric explanation of the phrase יעשה אדם ויחיה בהם—they who 'hold fast to it' (בהם יעשה) are for eternal life (ויחיה) and the glory of Adam is for them (אדם).

This observation is perhaps a little fanciful, and it is possible to understand המחזיקים ... להם in a more straightforward manner; but neither way of reading the phrase assists us with הוא כאשר חקים אל להם. This phrase is a unique introduction to a midrash in CD—indeed, also in the Qumran corpus—and I do not believe that we have the text in its original form, or that חקים can mean 'swore', as Rabin translates. 'Confirmed' and 'established' are better, though the use of קים ביד with reference to a scriptural citation is unparalleled. I cannot but suspect the double occurrence of הקים אל within eight lines (and nowhere else in CD) as more than coincidental; my suspicion is that some of the text may be missing and that the present clumsy formula is the result of a scribal adjustment to that loss. But since the train of thought here has remained apparently undisturbed, the problem need not detain us.

The phrase 'sure house' leads very smoothly into the Ezek. 44,15 midrash. 'House' in the OT can be taken to designate the Temple or a dynasty, as commentators have generally acknowledged; in fact it would seem in this instance to be applied to a priestly dynasty, but a dynasty also which will enjoy the exclusive privilege of serving God in the Temple. The biblical text refers back to the fidelity of the Zadokite priests in times before the Exile; but the interpretation of the text applies all the terms to the community, which, as we have seen, was established as a covenant community only after the Exile. The word 'strayed' (תעה), however, which provides a verbal link with the preceding passage (line 14), is also used in CD to describe the situation of the Jewish people outside the community in the post-exilic period (see above on II,13) and in this sense will presently be attributed to the activity of Belial (see below).

How much of the meaning of the biblical text is being brought into play in this midrash is an important question. Perhaps the 'standing before God to offer fat and blood' is now to be understood by the audience as a claim by the community to be exercising a quasi-sacrificial function, possibly even regards itself as the true Temple? This conclusion would be, I think, both rash and premature; rash because this element in the text is not interpreted in the midrash, whose interest lies in the identity of the priests, the levites and the sons of Zadok and because there is not even a hint in the midrash of any sacrificial function ascribed to any of the three groups; and premature because the attitude of the community towards the Temple can and must be evaluated in the light of more explicit statements which occur later.

It is nevertheless curious that the point of the midrash, the identification of three groups, is brought out of the text only by the addition of the copula twice; for the biblical text reads 'the levitical priests, the sons of Zadok.' There is no evidence of a textual variant on which our midrash might be based. What, then, is the importance of the three separate categories? There are two major lines of scholarly interpretation: one, represented by Stegemann, Murphy-O'Connor and Cothenet, takes them to be three different terms for the same entity, namely the entire community; the other maintains that they refer to different sections of the community. Scholars inclining to this latter view usually think of a hierarchical structure within the community, comprising priests, levites and laymen.[60] Schwarz, however, concludes that the terms apply to different stages in the past, present and future of the community,[61] a view which has support from the argument of the text itself. The activity of the priests is placed definitely in the past, while the sons of Zadok arise 'at the end of days.'

The participle of the verb עמד is used because those who 'stand' (the verb in CD refers to historical coming into existence[62]) are of the present generation. (That the time for decision is short, and hence the end of the Exile and devastation of the land at hand, is made clear presently.) These two groups, then, are mutually exclusive. But they are by no means discontinuous, for as I commented earlier it is precisely the *continuity* between past and present is being stressed in this discourse. This concern motivates the inclusion of the ensuing genealogical list, after which the author declares that the covenant which God established for the first ones whom he preserved is also offered to those who follow. The argument reaches its climax in an appeal to the audience to accept that offer and make the decision to join the 'house of Judah' (= the 'sure house'). As II,2-13 has already told us, the 'men of name' occur in every generation.

Schwarz errs, then, in presenting her three stages of the community as being of substantively different character. The correct interpretation, in my view, is that of Dupont-Sommer, who sees in the 'priests' the founders of the community, in the 'levites' those who joined later, and in the 'sons of Zadok' the eschatological members. Maier is of substantially the same opinion. It is quite in keeping with the rhetoric of the *Admonition*, and especially of the present discourse, that the term conveying the greatest prestige should be reserved for those to whom the document is addressed.

It is the description of the first group, however, which has created the greatest problem of interpretation. Much attention has been paid to the phrase שבי ישראל, and three possible translations have emerged. The first two identify the verb as שוב and translate the noun as respectively 'penitents' and 'returnees.' The third identifies the verb as שבה and translates 'captives.'[63] The translation 'penitents' does not explain the phrase 'who went out of the land of Judah,' which therefore has to be taken as an independent item of information. The majority of scholars have preferred this view once they believed that CD spoke for the Qumran community and that this community was not involved in any emigration from Judah. Separation of the two phrases also allows the exit from the land of Judah to be taken symbolically, denoting a spiritual retreat from Judaism or from Jerusalem into either the wilderness (Stegemann) or to Qumran (most other interpreters). This exegesis is as sound as its premises; on purely linguistic grounds it is undoubtedly the weakest of the three alternatives, for while a translation 'penitents of Israel' is grammatically possible, wherever

שוב is used in biblical or post-biblical Hebrew with the meaning 'repent,' the noun which follows it as direct object denotes whatever is repented of. Whether שוב used absolutely and without any supporting indication from the context can mean 'repent' is questionable.[64]

The other two translations both permit the phrase 'who went out from the land of Judah' to explain שבי ישראל, by referring to a literal exit into captivity. שבי occurs frequently in Chron.-Ezra-Neh. to describe the exiled community. The term שבי ישראל does not itself occur, the nearest to it being השבים מן השבי in Neh. 8,17. The group designated by this phrase had, of course, literally 'gone out of the land of Judah,' and those at least who returned with Ezra appear to have possessed a strong Zadokite ideology. It is this group whose ideology comes to expression in the words of Ezekiel on which the present passage is based. Are these observations of relevance to CD?

Once we set aside the assumption that the community of CD is the Qumran community, once we recognise that the community is claiming to have been founded in the Exile, and once we appreciate the influence of biblical language on the *Admonition*, it becomes virtually impossible *not* to take the phrase שבי ישראל as possessing an exilic association. The only question then left, as Murphy-O'Connor has seen, is whether we read שְׁבִי ('captivity') or שָׁבֵי ('returnees'). He prefers the latter, because it implies absence, and hence exile, anyway; and because the return of this community to Palestine is presupposed by the *Sitz im Leben* of the Missionary Document, which he regards as addressed to Palestinian Jews, not to mention the presence of the community of Qumran, among whom this document was preserved.

The connection between the returning Zadokites from the exile of Chron.-Ezra-Neh. and our community—also appealing to Zadok and also nurtured in exile—deserves very close study, since there are also strong ideological parallels, of which the theology of the Holiness Code is one of the most obvious examples. I do not believe that these links can plausibly be construed as an attempt on the part of the CD community to identify its own predicament typologically with that of the returning exiles of the 5th century BCE. But even if this possibility were entertained, it would require us to postulate an exile, real or symbolic, from which the CD community itself had *returned*. Now, the Qumran community is frequently understood as having depicted its presence in Qumran in terms of an (voluntary) exile (cf. 1QS VIII,13f.); but if this understanding is correct, the predicament of that community is the *exact opposite* of that of the 5th century returnees

—going into exile instead of returning from it—and the Qumran community could therefore compare itself with them only with great difficulty. In any case, it has already emerged that CD's ideology of exile is that it has persisted for centuries, which is at variance with the supposed exilic symbolism of the Qumran community. However, it would seem to be equally at variance with the ideology of the earlier returnees; those rebuilt the Jewish state in Palestine, while our community does not believe that the return has yet taken place. Yet this variance may be of less substance than at first appears, as Ezra 9 suggests. Clearly a detailed comparison of CD with documents of the immediate post-exilic period is urgently needed.

I prefer, against Murphy-O'Connor, to translate שבי ישראל by 'captivity' because the ideology of the community is that it has not, at least theologically, 'returned,' but is still in the exilic 'period of wrath.' Indeed, I am not persuaded that the *Admonition* originated in a Palestinian context, although it was in Palestine that it achieved its present form. A satisfactory translation of שבי ישראל is probably out of reach, for I suspect there may be a polemical edge to the term, not devoid of the biblical resonance of Chron.-Ezra-Neh. A translation connoting both captivity and exile would be, in my view, superior both linguistically and ideologically. But at any rate, the burden of proof lies with those who would maintain that a symbolic exile is referred to here. Arguments so far adduced in favour of this interpretation virtually all have to be dismissed as based on external and *a priori* considerations, rather than exegetical ones, which are the most compelling. We shall have to return briefly to this issue when we later encounter reference to 'Damascus' as the place of exile (VI,1ff.).

To return now to the question of the three groups of the Ezekiel midrash: Iwry has argued that היוצאים מארץ יהודה means 'originating from Judah,' 'of Judean ancestry.'[65] If he is correct, שבי ישראל could apply to all members of the community whether or not they had themselves physically left the land of Judah. But as I have explained, I do not regard שבי ישראל as applied in this passage to the whole of the community, but to those who founded it, so that I prefer to translate more literally 'who went out of the land of Judah.' Iwry's translation makes the interpretation of the 'levites' more difficult. On the view that all three terms designate the totality of the commmunity, 'those who joined them' can only be a pure play on words (הלוים/הנלוים). But since the author has taken trouble to emend the biblical text so as provide three groups, I prefer to take the phrase literally, as I take the statements about the other groups. The original members of the covenant were, in the words of III,13, 'left over' from those destroyed at the time of the Exile, and were later 'joined' by others. Being of the שבי ישראל, and thus having once left the land of Judah, is not prerequisite for membership of the covenant, for the people of this covenant do not form an exclusive society; the *Admonition* is itself addressed to would-be members who come from outside. The 'levites' represent those who in the past entered not as of birthright, but as an act of *choice*. Were such people necessarily Jewish? The existence of proselytes within the community is apparently intimated by the listing in CD XIV,4 of four groups; priests, levites, Israelites and גרים, i.e. non-Israelites, but members of the covenant community nevertheless.[66] A precarious conclusion? It is the most natural translation of the term, and sanctioned by Ezekiel 47,22f.

Finally, then, who are the 'sons of Zadok'? They represent, I think, those who presently constitute the community, who join it at the 'end of days.' It also includes, potentially, those who are being addressed. According to II,2-13, men are 'called by name' in each generation. Those who *choose* (cf. II,14) to enter the community are themselves *chosen* (בחירי ישראל). These will bear the name 'sons of Zadok' by virtue of belonging to the 'sure house' which God established. In the remaining lines of this discourse, the author will reassure those who enter the covenant now that they will enjoy the same benefits as those with whom God first made that covenant.

The phrase קריאי השם deliberately anticipates הנה פרוש שמותיהם. The names of the 'priests,' 'levites' (and 'sons of Zadok'?) are contained in a list which has been omitted from our text. פרוש שמות must be translated as 'list of names'[67]; both the phrases containing שם, קריאי השם and פרוש שמותיהם, also occur in II,2-13, whose close connections with this discourse have already become clear, and will presently become clearer still.

The list itself apparently contained the following elements; פרוש שמות, פירוש מעשיהם and שני התגרר, מספר צרות, קץ מעמד, תולדות. What kind of a list could this have been, and what could have been its purpose? Clearly, one cannot accurately describe it as a mere genealogy. We may begin unravelling its meaning by recognising its *predestinarian* character. Now, we have observed conceptual and verbal parallels between the preceding material and II,2-13. These parallels continue: CD II,9ff. reads וידע את שני מעמד ומספר ופרוש קציהם לכול הוי עלמים ... 'and He knows the years of their existence (=their lifespan?) and the number and list of their periods for all beings in eternity' (the translation is neither felicitous nor certain, but the vocabulary is the issue here). This phrase contains elements from all of the items (פרוש, שמות, קץ מעמד, מספר שנים) except מעשיהם and תולדות. The former occurs in the preceding line (II,8), although there it refers to God's foreknowledge of the deeds of the wicked. תולדות is a *hapax legomenon* in CD, but that this word can bear a predestinarian nuance in the Qumran community is proved by its use in 1QS II,13.19 (twice) and IV,15—all in the so-called 'Discourse on the Two Spirits,' where it means not a literal but a 'spiritual' ancestry (if one may express it thus crudely). Yet it is difficult to see how exactly a תולדה in this predestinarian sense could be represented in a list; we perhaps ought to translate שמותיהם לתולדותם as 'their names according to their *generations*,' that is, arranged not by line of descent, i.e. 'vertically,' but generation by generation, i.e. 'horizontally.' I do not therefore agree with Murphy-O'Connor's view that the missing genealogy constituted the pedigree of the community and hence their status as Jews and their right to address their fellows. For while Murphy-O'Connor believes the group to have attempted to make converts in Palestine (by means of this document), I believe it must have done so also in exile (hence the נלוים of the preceding midrash); the group is constituted not by *descent* but by *membership of a covenant*. Predestination and heredity are alternatives, and תולדה is used, I believe, with at least predestinarian nuances; the names are there not by virtue of descent but by virtue of election.

Also worthy of discussion is the significance of the term צרותיהם. What are these 'sufferings,' and what is their meaning in a list of names? As with תולדה, we receive no assistance from the rest of CD. However, once again, the word occurs in the 1QS 'Discourse,' at III,23: וכול נגיעיהם ומועדי צרותם . . . 'and all the blows that smite them and the times of their suffering (are due to the dominion of his hatred [sc. the angel of darkness]).' Our present passage is no more dualistic than II,2-13, but the suffering of the righteous (which in 1QS is attributed to the angel of darkness) may be a motif which antedates the dualistic context of the 1QS 'Discourse.' Perhaps suffering is presented here as proof of election, inasmuch as suffering is part of the profile of the righteous. But perhaps more plausible is the suggestion that suffering constitutes an act of atoning for the land by the exiled remnant. This notion, or a closely related one, is present in 1QS VIII, where 'suffering the sorrows of affliction' is one of the duties prescribed for the Qumran 'council,' who are also said to 'atone for (כפר בעד) the land.'

Two other terms may be considered briefly. The first of them is התגורר. Apart from the occurrence, already mentioned, of גר (apparently meaning 'proselyte') in CD XIV,5, we also find in VI,5 שבי ישראל היוצאים מארץ יהודה ויגורו בארץ דמשק. In the light of this phrase, שני התגורר here may be taken to refer to the length of time spent in exile outside 'the land of Judah,' amongst aliens and in the 'land of Damascus.'[68]

Finally, we come to פירוש מעשיהם. We have seen that מעשיהם is used in the predestinarian discourse, II,2-13, and it occurs also in 1QS III,14; IV,16.20. It is frequent throughout the *Admonition*. The phrase 'dealings of God' (מעשי אל) occurs in I,1, while in I,10 the deeds (מעשיהם) of the 'root' prompt God to send them a 'teacher of righteousness.' This word is therefore not always used in a predestinarian sense. However, it is *sometimes* so used, as is פרוש, and the two words used together, in the context of other predestinarian vocabulary, surely convey such a sense, to be understood in the light of II,7-8: ידע את מעשיהם, and II,9: וידע... פרוש קציהם.

There are several further problems arising from this missing list which cannot be easily solved. In what form can 'sufferings' or 'works' be included in a *list*? The most plausible suggestion I can offer is that four phrases are being used here in synonymous parallelism:

A     period of their lifespan     number of their afflictions     B

$A^1$     years of their residence     list of their deeds     $B^1$

If the text is to be taken this way, the phrases are not to be read both independently and literally. 'Number of their sufferings' and 'list of their deeds' do not thus imply a further enumeration, but a kind of closer definition. If these terms were, on the other hand, to be understood literally, they would seem to be much better suited to a *heavenly* book, in which an account of all the deeds and sufferings could be kept of all those predestined (cp. Dan. 12,1). But this suggestion founders on the implication of the introductory הנה, as well as of the material which follows the lacuna. Moreover, there is clear evidence of the keeping of lists of names in the CD community. According to CD XIV,3ff., at every 'meeting of all camps' the names of all present, priests, levites, Israelites and גרים, were to be written down. We should recognise that this keeping of names (attested also in the Qumran community, cf. 1QS V,23) is more than a mere 'register of

If the text is taken in this way, we do not read all of the phrases literally and independently. 'Number of their sufferings' and 'list of attendance' but constitutes a ritual of some great significance, and not without predestinarian overtones. But a treatment of this topic is best undertaken in the context of a discussion of the phenomenon within Jewish sectarian literature generally.

The full significance of the missing list does not become evident until we consider the material which follows. There can be no doubt that the same document continues beyond the lacuna. The proof of this is that God's forgiving 'those who came after them' is explicable only on the basis of the originally preceding list of names; the phrase כפר אל בעדם in IV,10 resumes כפר בעד עונם in III,18, while השנים האלה in IV,9 and 12 must have as antecedent the שני התגוררם of 4c-5a.

The continuity of the material at this point is nevertheless obscured not only by the absence of the list but by a corruption of the text immediately after the lacuna. Two restorations, broadly, have been proposed, and two interpretations of the restored text offered. The first proposed restoration, אנשי הקודש הראשונים (alternatively אנשי תמים הקודש ...), endorsed by Rabin, Dupont-Sommer and Cothenet, corresponds to a phrase in XX,2, and Cothenet also alludes to similar phrases in 1QS VIII,20.23. The second restoration is הקדושים הראשונים, preferred by Charles, Rabinowitz and Murphy-O'Connor).[69] The former restoration assumes a lacuna and haplography, the latter haplography only. In fact, the two possibilities differ in implication in only one respect. The latter must refer to members of the community, while the former could refer to either members or non-members. Technically, the latter is preferable, because it accounts for the corruption rather better; and it ought to be accepted, whether correct or not, simply because it does not preempt the question of the identity of the ראשונים. We have to base our understanding of this word not on the balance of intrinsic probability of one restoration over another but on the meaning implied by the context. Now, the phrase ברית ראשונים in I,4, III,10 and VI,2, according to both Denis and Murphy-O'Connor, refers to the Mosaic covenant and the ראשונים are therefore the pre-exilic generations. Certainly באי הברית הראשונים means the pre-exilic generations in III,10, the most important of the three occurrences. In the other two, the ראשונים may be the patriarchs.[70] Moreover, the negative atttitude towards the באי הברית הראשונים in III,10 is contrasted by a positive attitude here towards הקדושים הראשונים. It was because of this discrepancy that Denis assigned IV,6bff. to a source different from that of I,1-IV,6a.[71] But this procedure quite ignored the signs of continuity within the material which have already been mentioned. Murphy-O'Connor, who assigns both III,10 and IV,6f. to the same document, nevertheless suggests that there were among the pre-exilic generations some men who exercised the discernment to which the phrase 'justified the righteous and condemned the wicked' (Deut. 25,1) refers. The statement in III,12f. that God made his covenant with those who were left over from the pre-exilic generation, who held fast to his commandments, is quite compatible with this view.

An alternative view takes account of the fact that הראשונים here is an adjective, the noun being הקדושים. This observation is enough by itself to counter any argument based on the use of ראשונים as a noun elsewhere, even if such usage were unambiguous. Hence those referred to in line 6 may be the founders of the community. It remains possible on this view to understand the ראשונים of line 10 as the pre-exilic generations, but it is difficult to believe that the same word is used twice within a short space to denote different groups. The use of ברית הראשונים is by no means decisive, since the covenant which is being discussed in the context of this phrase is the covenant of the community. It can be argued on grounds of plot and of vocabulary that in both lines 6 and 10 ראשונים designates the *first members of the exilic covenant*. First, it is quite clear that the point which is being made in the text is not that there is a continuity between the first (i.e. pre-exilic) covenant and the covenant of III,13. This continuity has been established earlier. It is rather that there is continuity between the covenant relationship of the first members and that of those who follow. Second, the same phrase הקים ברית is used in both IV,9 and III,13, (whether הקים in III,13 means 'established' or 'confirmed'), and therefore probably refers to the same covenant. Third, the ראשונים of line 6 are those whom God forgave (כפר אל בעדם); in III,18 God forgave (כפר בעד) the members of that same covenant. Fourth, the phrase 'who came after them,' הבאים אחריהם, refers more naturally to successive members of the *same* covenant than to a *new* covenant group, and might even be seen as as explicit contrast to אשר נותרו מהם, a quite differently expressed relationship. If הבאים means 'who entered *the covenant*,' as it well may, this argument is confirmed. Fifth, כפרוש and התוסרו are both used in CD of community law, which is not represented as being either known or accepted by the pre-exilic generations.

The ראשונים are therefore, here, at any rate, the founder members of the community covenant and the phrase which we have decided to

restore הקרושים הראשונים in line 6 refers in my opinion back to the
missing list. If that list consisted, as it is said to have done, of all the
members of the community by generation, the 'first ones' on the list
will be the first generation who entered the covenant (those who were
'left over,' the remnant of the pre-exilic covenant), and whose sins
were pardoned by God. 'Those who came after them' are their
successors. On entering the covenant, they too had their sins pardoned
in return for accepting the 'exact' (פרוש) interpretation of the law.
Implicitly, the audience is being made an offer: you too can join this
covenant; your name can be added to the list of those whom God has
'chosen' from of old; your sins will be pardoned, if you will accept
proper observance of the law.

The argument sustains a masterful balance between the theme of
choice and predestination, the rubric expressing the former (as does
the review of pre-exilic history, a history of stubborn pursuit of human
will in preference to God's), the vocabulary towards the end sug-
gesting the latter. But this balance could not be achieved, nor the effect
accomplished, had not the predestinarian discourse of II,2-14 immediately
preceded. In fact, it can be argued (although this kind of argument is
incapable of proof) that this third discourse brings together all the
themes of the first two discourses: the original choosing of the remnant
from the ruins of the old covenant and the desertion by God of the
remainder of Israel. The climax of this third discourse is a direct
challenge: the covenant is not closed; the pardon of God is still
available, the choice between one's own desires and God's will is *not* a
matter of past history. That choice is not foreclosed. Choose. Now.

So the discourse ends with the warning that the time for decision is
short. Adherence to the פרוש התורה, the outward sign of the true
covenant, will be required 'until the completion of the period of these
years' (עד שלים הקץ השנים האלה). A similar phrase recurs in line 10
(ובשלים הקץ למספר השנים האלה אין עוד . . .). What is this קץ and what
is the 'number of these years'? The word אלה must refer back to a
designated or implied period. In the preceding description of the
(missing) list of members we found the phrases מספר צרותיהם, קץ מעמדם
and שני התגוררם. Full weight must be attached to the first word of each
of these phrases, which reveal that the list itself did not function simply
as a catalogue of names, but in some way as a *calendar*, the calendar of
an epoch. The significance of the words 'period,' 'number,' 'years,'
does not lie in the biographical information they may have contained
about individual members. It is not the periods, numbers and years of

individuals which carry any significance; the list *as a whole is a record of 'the period,'* and, moreover, *a period of a defined length.* For we are told in line 10 that it will be completed, that its completion is according to the numbers indicated by the list of names, and, inferentially, that the epoch is nearly complete.

This interpretation is not speculative, but arises from a detailed attention to the text itself. Moreover, support is given by a reference in CD XVI,2 to a 'list of the periods of Israel's blindness' (פרוש קציהם לעורון ישראל) which it is claimed can be learned in the 'Book of the Divisions of Times into their Jubilees and Weeks'—recognised by most scholars as the book of Jubilees. Appeal to a list of pre-exilic(?) epochs makes the calculation of post-exilic epochs fairly certain and a list of post-exilic epochs very plausible.

To move from a reconstruction of ideology to a reconstruction of history is tempting, but fraught with difficulties. I have outlined the ideology of the community as a belief that the desolation of the land and the anger of God continue as present realities, and that *this* period, inaugurated at the beginning of what we call the 'Exile,' is the 'period of wrath.' The length of such a period is implicitly calculable. That such calculations were made in late post-exilic Judaism is well-known; the book of Daniel computes 490 years on the basis of Jeremiah and fragments from the Qumran texts, especially 11QMelch, suggest an identical period.[72] I have now argued that its calculation is involved in the list which this discourse once contained. The biblical origins of the calculations of this community are also identifiable. A major influence on CD is the Holiness Code, Lev. 17-26; from it is derived the ideology of the desolation of the land, the importance of sabbaths, and the jubilee reckoning. In Lev. 26 we also find the hint of a calculation of the time of punishment: in vv. 18, 21, 24 and 27 God threatens to punish Israel sevenfold. It is possible that this provided a clue to a determined period of exile, in principle calculable. One would suggest a sevenfold multiplication of the number of sabbaths needed by the land.

It is perhaps futile to attempt to deduce the result of the calculation for this community, but we know that 490 (70 x 7) in Daniel and 490 or 500 (10 x 49/50) in 11QMelch were computed. A calculation of a period is found also in CD I, based on 390 years from Ezekiel, a secondary calculation, but one nevertheless which may reflect an adjustment from a later period. If, for instance, a calculated period such as 490 years were to elapse by a significant timespan, one might expect either a new figure to be set, or a new computation by means of which the original figure might be stretched so as to include the present time. It is possible to account for the interpolated figure of 390 years in CD I in such a way. Since 390 is not based on jubilee cycles, I think it unlikely that the CD community originally computed it, but it might well be the result of an adjustment by means of which an event of calendrical importance (i.e. the arrival of the 'teacher of righteousness' might be dated on the basis of a biblical text, while the 'jubilee' figure of 490 remained to be completed in the not too distant future.)

This speculation remains, nonetheless, without any verification at present, although it is an important aspect of the ideology of the community which requires further investigation. Likewise, the historical implications of such calendrical computation belong, at present at any rate, to the realm of conjecture. A crucial difficulty in Murphy-O'Connor's reconstruction of the origins of the Essenes is that he cannot find a plausible reason for the return of exiles from Babylon in the period required by the conventional Maccabean dating he adopts for the emergence of the community in Palestine. This dating is firmly established for him as a result of his preference for reading literally and accepting the chronological data of CD I (one of which he has to halve[73]). There is, of course, a real dilemma here whatever date is adopted. For it seems probable that the CD community, or part of it, *did* return to Palestine at some time, as a result of which the Qumran community itself subsequently came into existence. What motivated this return? Is it that the return of Murphy-O'Connor's Essenes had something to do with calculations of the end of the 'period of wrath,' the final occupation of the land by those for whom it was truly destined? There is no evidence in CD to suggest that the end of this period would be a signalled by political events (as in the case of Daniel, where the 'jubilee' calculation is a rationalising reflection upon political events), but by some kind of genealogical calculation alone. It is far from probable that a group of exiles with the ideology expressed in CD would return to Palestine for other than ideological reasons, and Murphy-O'Connor's reason does not fall into this category. But while there may be scope for further investigation along these lines, once the evidence of the chronological data in CD I has been removed, there is no internal basis for computing the date at which the community of CD returned to Palestine, or the period intervening between this return and the formation of the Qumran community. The historical circumstances of such a return are difficult if not impossible to deduce from CD itself, and the issue is complicated if, as Murphy-O'Connor has argued very soundly, not all of the community came to Palestine, but many remained literally in exile.[74] This historical question has *not* yet been answered, and it would be rash to attempt an answer on the basis of the very limited observations offered in the present study.

If we cannot determine the calculation of the period, and can only conjecture its relevance, if any, to the history of the community, we may deduce that for the redactor of the *Admonition* its end was imminent. When this period is completed, we are now told, there will be 'no more uniting with the house of Judah.'[75] Both intrinsically and from the context we should understand the 'house of Judah' to be the community, for the whole of this document is about joining the commmunity. Indeed, the community has been presented as originating with Judaean exiles, so that conceivably the term בית יהודה evokes not only the בית נאמן of III,19 but also the היוצאים מארץ יהודה of IV,3. We shall also see that where 'Judah' is used elsewhere in CD of a nation rather than of a country, it is the community which is implicitly identified.[76] If, as Murphy-O'Connor argues, behind this document originally stood a group of recently repatriated exiles, we might perhaps see some deliberate irony in their invitation to Judaean residents to join the 'house of Judah.' Referring to Palestinian Judaism as 'Ephraim' later in the *Admonition* may be an alternative tactic to the same effect. The biblical origin of the phrase להשתפח לבית יהודה must not be lost either; Isaiah 14,1b reads 'The Lord will have compassion on Jacob and will again choose Israel, and will set them in their own land, and aliens will join them (ונלוה הגר עליהם) and will cleave (ונספחו: n.b. CD has ש for ס) to the house of Jacob.' It is not difficult to see the relevance of this text not only to this particular passage (and the preceding midrash on Ezekiel), but to the *Admonition* as a whole.

The imminent removal of the opportunity to join the community is finally rammed home by the use of two further biblical texts, quoted without comment. The first is Hab. 2,1. Its function here is misunderstood by all those commentators who seize on the interpretation of the verse in the Qumran *pesher*, which reads 'God told Habakkuk to write down the things which will come to pass in the last generation, but he did not make known to him the consummation of time (גמר הקץ: 1QpHab VII,2).' It is not necessarily significant that the same text is used twice in eschatological contexts, for the words are intrinsically amenable to such exegesis. גמר הקץ is indeed close to שלים הקץ, but the interpretation of the biblical text in CD and 1QpHab is quite different. In 1QpHab the standing on the watchtower is in order to receive a vision, as in the biblical text itself. Here it is matter of being left to one's own resources. The image is not that of a place from which one looks out, perhaps for the coming of judgment, but of a flimsy building. The watchtower was erected from stones cleared from one's vineyard, and stood out in the countryside, outside city walls, vulnerable to attack. It is an image here to be contrasted with the 'sure house' of the community.

Building imagery is continued in the next biblical citation, Mic. 7,11. Some commentators have found in the 'wall' a symbol of separation, namely between the community and those outside it. In this they have been perhaps influenced by the use of the phrase 'builders of the wall' elsewhere, and especially in IV,19. The wall, in their view, is that built around the community, whether by the community itself or by outsiders.[77] This interpretation finds no support in the context, except in a misreading the preceding biblical quotation. The biblical text refers to the extension of the limits of the future Israel, and is best understood in this way as transferred to the community, which is confirmed by the presence of the word חוק, understood as an allusion to the law by which the 'house' of the community is established. Although this precise significance of חוק does not become apparent until VI,7f., the theme of 'law,' which commences with the material immediately following, is neatly introduced. And with these final urgings to consider carefully the choice with which it confronts the reader, the historical part of the argument of the *Admonition* reaches its close.

## III   LAWS: IV,12b–VII,10a

*Summary:* This section of CD contains more numerous and varied sources than the previous section, with evidence of redactional links. IV,12b–V,16 is linked by redactional phrases to the surrounding material, and is itself composite, containing a midrash and an interpretation of this midrash which was itself probably once independent and has been secondarily expanded at some stage. V,17–VI,11a is an originally independent composition of the same genre as the discourses of the first section of the *Admonition*. It is separated from them because its purpose in CD is not to disclose the true state of affairs between God and Israel, but to explain the origin of the community halachah. VI,11b–VII,4a presents some of the laws of the community and is followed by a promise to those who observe them and a warning to those who do not, VII,4b–6a.9–10a. This original, brief warning has been expanded by two sets of material, which form the subject matter of the following two chapters.

At first sight there seems the most natural transition between 12a and 12b accomplished by the phrase ובכל השנים האלה. The material which follows Murphy-O'Connor describes[1] as a critique of practices considered to be orthodoxy by the contemporaries of the community. Such a critique forms, in his opinion, a natural sequel to a statement of the necessity for choice (IV,12a) in showing that the choice called for is complicated by the activity of Belial.

It is with some reluctance that I dissent from this analysis, for from the rhetorical point of view his account is a plausible one. However, it forms part of a larger analysis which posits a single document from II,14–VI,1 and requires a termination in the middle of an historical summary whose literary unity seems to me beyond question. Once the impossibility of ending the document at VI,11 is acknowledged, a complete re-appraisal of its scope becomes necessary. I agree with Murphy-O'Connor that a source-critical approach is required, and the generally cogent source-criticism of this material by Stegemann, ignored by Murphy-O'Connor, provides a sound basis for a more adequate account of the redaction of this material. It is unfortunate that here, as throughout his analysis of CD, Stegemann did not use source-criticism constructively, but only as a means of dividing the material into sections which he could treat independently.[2]

IV,12a-VI,10a is made up of quite disparate material which comprises a midrash, an application of the midrash to specific practices, a review of the by now familiar *Heilsgeschichte* of the community, and a list of community laws. It is evident that these components do not fit together perfectly, and where they join redactional work can usually be identified. The Isaiah midrash in IV,12b-19a is dependent on IV,19bff. for its inclusion here, but did not originally belong with it. If IV,12bff belongs to the same original document as II,14-IV,12a, that document must have been a composite one, and once we accept this much, there is no point in the *Admonition* at which one could cogently argue that such a composite document must have terminated. Yet there are no indications that the material from II,14-IV,12a is not a literary unit. It is best regarded, I suggest, as a constituent source. Whether as such it was combined into a larger document *before* its incorporation into the *Admonition* is impossible to say; but it seems futile to assume an intermediate stage of redaction for which there is no evidence. IV,12b furnishes a plausible conclusion to the material beginning at II,14, which at this point has fulfilled the requirements of its opening rubric. It also marks a transition from the subject of history to that of law.

But these considerations must be set in perspective. It is a central argument of this book that the plot and structure of the *Admonition* are the product of a single redactor (or author). The extent of his skill is such that it is precarious to distinguish constituent sources on the basis of their individual 'plot' or 'purpose.' It is not only impossible but unnecessary to decide in every case between the definitive level of redaction, which created the original 'Damascus Document' and any previous redaction which may have created literarily complex sources.

The redactional seams in the material are quite discernible. If the foregoing arguments are sound, it would be reasonable to regard the initial phrase of IV,12ff., ובכל . . . ישראל, as composed by the redactor in order to furnish a link with the preceding discourse. There is clear evidence of another redactional link in the proximity of two similar formulae, כי אם למילפנים in V,16 and כי מלפנים in V,17. An examination of the context reveals the unlikelihood that both phrases belong to source-material. Furthermore, the sequence of the two blocks of material on either side of V,16-17, namely the preceding critique of law outside the community and the following description of the origin of community law, can be satisfactorily explained only in the light of the plot of the *Admonition*; hence the presence of a redactional suture between them is hardly unexpected.

How, then, is the sequence of the material to be explained? The account of the community in V,17-VI,11a is in form and content very similar to the first and third discourses of the historical section of CD, and is surely an independent source. Its function, separated from them and embedded in diverse and non-historiographical material, becomes clear only when *law* is identified as the uniting theme of this part of the *Admonition*. It then emerges that this further account of community origins fulfils quite aptly the argument being constructed by the redactor. This argument can be illustrated as follows: the preceding passage presents some examples of halachah outside the community and exposes it as an outcome of the activity of Belial. This naturally anticipates an introduction of the true halachah which, by contrast, must be seen to be an outcome of the activity of God. V,17-VI,11 describes the origin of the law of the community in exactly this light. Once the basic point has been established, the next stage is to present the main lines of this halachah. On this analysis, the material between IV,12b and VII,4a exhibits both a rhetorical progression from criticism of outsiders' behaviour to revelation of insiders' behaviour and also a parallelism in the presentation of the two alternatives, namely; (i) Belial's work + concrete examples and (ii) God's work + concrete examples.

The cohesion between the various sources in this section lies not so much (as in the historical section) in their intrinsic similarity of content and ideology as in the argument to which they contribute, and which can only be considered as the product of a very able redactor. It is true that the redactor has not been able to disguise his activity, and we are accordingly obliged to consider in more detail than in the previous section the character of the sources and the extent of the redactor's work. At the same time, the presence and arrangement of the source-material can be clarified and explained only in the light of the redactor's intentions. In this regard, previous interpretation of this part of CD in particular has been inadequate.

*IV,12b-V,16: Critique of Judaism outside the community.*

Stegemann,[3] who also does not attribute IV,12bff. to the same source as the preceding material, makes the ingenious suggestion that there is an original connection between the occurrences of 'Belial' in IV,13 and V,18. It is certainly striking that Belial does not figure elsewhere in the *Admonition*, but this is hardly conclusive. The mention of Belial in IV,13 is necessitated by the following midrash, which speaks of the 'nets of Belial.' Yet Belial does not figure in the interpretation of the midrash, and his appearance in V,18 casts him in a quite different time, place and rôle. His rôle in IV,13 has, indeed, been widely misunderstood, for it is usually held that the text describes the unleashing of Belial in a 'pre-eschatological' epoch so as to lead Israel astray. But I have argued that the 'years' of IV,9f. refer to the whole period of the existence of the community, from the time of God's 'turning his face from Israel.' If IV,12.13a is redactional, as I have suggested, it is possible that the redactor did not use the phrase בכל השנים האלה in the same way as IV,5.9.10. But such a conclusion would have to be argued for, and strong objections can be brought against it. There is nothing in the present passage to suggest that the activity of Belial is confined to a recent, brief period. Nor is it necessary to assume that the halachic practices criticised are of recent origin. On the contrary, the view that Belial is let loose during the whole period in which God has turned his face from the land is required by the thrust of the argument being developed, by the meaning of קץ חרון in I,5, and by the statement of II,7ff., in which God is represented as causing (or allowing) Israel to stray ever since hiding his face from the land. In other words, the activity of Belial extends over the whole history of the CD community.

Within the perspective of the *Admonition*, then, such an interpretation is virtually inescapable, while the view that Belial's loosing is confined to a 'pre-eschatological' period is difficult to make sense of. What, on this view, could be the *significance* of the letting loose of Belial? Unlike writings (such as Daniel or Revelation) which present a period of intense persecution or wickedness preceding the eschatological salvation, the *Admonition* does not hint at persecution, nor (as we have seen, and will see again in this chapter) does it condemn the present time as of exceptional wickedness. The fact is that the usual interpretation of this passage is influenced by *a priori* assumptions about the historical context of CD and of the Qumran community (the 'Hellenistic crisis') and not by sound exegetical considerations.

Correspondingly, to regard halachic disagreements as the occasion for the formation of the CD community is to disregard what the text actually says and what everything preceding it implies. The visitation of Belial is *not the cause but the outcome of God's anger with Israel*. The reader has been told that at the time of Nebuchadnezzar God abandoned Israel and made a covenant only with a remnant, which is the community. The community's knowledge is contrasted with the ignorance of those outside, and those whom God has chosen are contrasted with those whom He has allowed to stray. The covenant was inaugurated by a revelation of the divine will, which prompted the development of halachah. Therefore, the breach between the community and Judaism outside it goes back—according to the ideology of the community—to the Exile; it is to that time that the halachic differences are to be traced , and it is from that time that God allows those he has rejected to go astray. The activity of Belial throughout this time is to be understood by the reader as an amplification of the predestinarian account in II,2-13.

The major point which the *Admonition* seeks to establish in this passage is, I think, a demonstration of the claim earlier made that God had abandoned Israel and deals now only with the community. This explains why the halachah of non-community Judaism is not criticised on the grounds of being different from that of the community, for this would be a circular argument. The criticism of non-community halachah is justified on the basis of Mosaic law, public, not esoteric; in the language of III,13-14 נגלות, not נסתרות. What is at issue is admittedly an *interpretation* of the Mosaic law, and the interpretation offered represents no doubt part of the community's peculiar halachah. But the argument is, I think, not: 'we have the law, so our interpretation of the Mosaic law must be right'—which would, again, be circular and devoid of cogency. Rather, the argument is: you can see that their (your?) interpretation is contrary to (revealed) scripture, whereas ours is not. Who, then, is the true Israel? Who has been led astray? Where is Belial at work? This passage is a demonstration that those outside the community are misled, and consequently that their halachah is demonstrably wrong; it is thought to be right by those who follow it only because they themselves are misled by Belial. The aim of this demonstration, as Murphy-O'Connor has already perceived in respect of his Missionary Document, is to prise the audience away from their allegiance to the law as they know it and have been taught it, and to introduce them, gently, to the more stringent law of the community.

Having asserted his thesis in IV,12b–13a, the redactor uses, to open his demonstration, a midrash on Is. 24,17 which identifies the three elements in the text as three nets of Belial: whoredom, wealth and defiling the sanctuary. He apparently had also to hand a list of criticisms about the practices of contemporary Judaism. The two components are most readily understood as independent sources because they do not correspond exactly with each other; only two of the 'nets' of the midrash can be fitted to the specific criticisms. But the redactor has overcome this discrepancy by means of the phrases הם ניתפשים בשתים בזנות in IV,20, and וגם ממעים הם in V,6. Both phrases borrow vocabulary from the midrash, ניתפשים, זנות and טמא מקרש. The first phrase reconciles midrash and exposition by establishing that only two of the nets are in question, the second condemns as defilement of the sanctuary an activity which really has nothing to do with the sanctuary at all. Together—and only together—these phrases make the connection of the accusations with the midrash plausible. The second phrase in particular is important in betraying the fact that the 'accusations' source used by the redactor originally dealt with sexual irregularities only.

What may be said about the origin of the sources in this section? It is not the midrash itself, interpreting the Isaiah text as referring to Belial's nets, which is attributed to 'Levi son of Jacob,' but only a statement about these nets. Therefore, even if that statement could be assigned to some lost work or a lost part of a known work containing words of Levi, we cannot determine the origin of the midrash itself. The term 'Israel' (the accused) is probably to be understood as the whole nation, and the identity of the 'nets' does not necessarily betray any sectarian basis. There is indeed a rather close parallel to these 'nets' in Ps. Sol. 8,9ff, which mentions illicit sexual union, plundering of the sanctuary, and pollution of the sanctuary, and in Jub. 7,20 where three criticisms of Israel are given as fornication, uncleanness and iniquity. While in the former of these parallels the accusations are arguably directed against Jewish leaders in particular, they may have a more general target in the latter. From neither can we infer anything specific about the offences or the target, and equally, the accusations in our midrash could be applied at almost any time in Israel's history by one group to another. It is probable that such a three-fold accusation is conventional. I would regard it as extremely probable that the 'three nets of Belial' was an allusion recognised by the audience, and hence the use of the midrash is an appeal to an 'objective,' authoritative source, over and above the biblical text itself. For this reason, as well as because it provided an opportunity for supporting the opening assertion from a biblical text, the midrash was sufficiently valuable to the redactor to justify his adjustment of the specific criticisms to its three categories.

It is only these specific criticisms which may help us to identify the ideology of the group making them, and their target. The target in question is not altogether clear because it is referred to as the 'builders of the wall.' To identify them simply as 'Israel' counters the objection that while Israel as a whole is said to be ensnared in all three nets, and any individual Israelite will be ensnared by one or other, the 'builders of the wall' are ensnared in specifically two. And since the 'builders of the wall' are associated with specific accusations, it appears that a well-defined group within Israel is being isolated. The qualifying phrase אשר הלכו אחרי צו הצו הוא מטיף אשר אמר הטף יטיפון confirms this impression. Indeed, if the entire passage is original, the group in question can be accurately identified. Jeremias[4] represents a large number of commentators who have concluded that those designated are the followers of the 'Man of the Lie' who is not only a protagonist in the *pesharim* but also appears in CD I,14f.: איש הלצון אשר הטיף לישראל מימי כזב.

But this deduction, which seems at first sight reasonable, conflicts with the argument being pursued in the *Admonition*, in which it is Israel as a whole which has been contrasted with the community. To attack a specific group at this point makes no sense. At the very least, such a group would have to be representative of Jewish practice, for an argument from abuse would undermine the opening assertion. One could not establish that Belial is leading Israel astray by pointing to the excesses of a group which the rest of Jewish society would oppose. The fact that such excesses were the exception would prove the contrary—that Belial was not leading *Israel* astray. And to furnish an instance of halachic practice in which the community and Jewish society in general were in agreement would totally undermine the entire thesis of the *Admonition*! It is unlikely, therefore, that the redactor intends to attack a specific group, unless perhaps those who claimed to be the religious leaders of the Jewish community, and stand as its representatives.

However, logical as these arguments may seem, they require to be justified exegetically. The phrase 'builders of the wall' must be regarded as original, because it is the antecedent of אשר הלכו אחרי צו and of הם ניתפשים.[6] It may, however, either belong to the 'accusations' source or constitute a redactional phrase. The biblical context of the term בנה חיץ, Ezekiel 13,10, might provide us with the answer to this question. The passage deals with a wall, which the people have built, and which false prophets daub with plaster. The prophet predicts that God will bring the wall down in his anger. Elsewhere in the *Admonition* this image is developed rather fully (VIII,12ff.; see below). Here, however, neither the rôle of the false prophets nor the anger of God is the issue, only the fact that the wall was built *by the people*, and that it fell. The sudden appearance of the title 'builders of the wall' seems to me best accounted for as inserted by the redactor as part of his linkage between the midrash and the accusations, and prompted not only by its aptness (when its biblical context is recognised) but because it recovers the motif of the wall introduced in IV,12a, where the image of each man standing upon his own flimsy structure is succeeded by that of the extended wall round the community. The allusion to Ezekiel 13 rounds off the imagery, and not only by providing the 'wall' which those outside the community build for themselves, but by providing the clue to the imagery as a whole, for in Ezek. 13,4 the prophets are accused of not having built a גדר על בית ישראל. In the biblical passage, therefore, גדר and חיץ are directly contrasted, and this contrast is taken up in our passage and strengthened by the quotation of Micah 7,11, whose גדר is taken to refer to the community itself. The redactor is prompted by the Micah quotation to turn to the Ezekiel passage in order to amplify the significance of the גדר. In sum, 'builders of the wall' is a rhetorical as well as a redactional element in our text.[7]

It follows from the preceding argument that the 'builders of the wall' are Israel—that is, those of the nation outside the community. The qualifying phrase אשר הלכו אחרי צו, quoted from Hosea 5,11, does not necessarily define them more closely. If it is original, the phrase provides an apposite reference to a doomed Israel following after a false commandment (צו), reinforcing the comparison between Israel's halachah and the community's which drives the entire argument of this section of the *Admonition*. In fact, the biblical context of this quotation is employed elsewhere in CD; the 'princes of Judah' of Hosea 5,10 are identified as targets of criticism in VIII,3ff., while 'Ephraim,' to whom 5,11 applies, is identified with Israel outside the community in VII,9bff.

Although presupposed by the secondary phrase which follows it (הצו הוא מטיף . . . יטופון) it is possible that this quotation is nevertheless a gloss. Grammatically it fits into its context only as a parenthesis and both Stegemann and Murphy-O'Connor regard it as secondary for this reason and also because it apparently introduces an individual figure, the מטיף. Stegemann observes that the word צו in Hosea 5,11 does not indicate an individual figure nor does the present quotation of that phrase. Here he takes issue with Jeremias, who had identified the 'Spouter' with the 'Man of the Lie' of the Qumran *pesharim* and the 'builders of the wall' with his community, which had, in Jeremias' view, broken away from the Qumran community. Stegemann makes the obvious point that the general accusation voiced in IV,12bff. is of deception by Belial and not desertion from the community, and that the specific faults are presented not as breaches of community law by those who are familiar with it, but failure to follow the proper meaning of the revealed Mosaic law. Accordingly, while agreeing with Jeremias' identification of the 'spouter' and his community, Stegemann regards the reference as secondary. This conclusion is well-founded and also supports our own conclusion that the *Admonition* has been glossed by the Qumran community.[8]

The outcome of all of the preceding discussion is as follows: the 'builders of the wall' are the whole of Israel outside the community. Murphy-O'Connor is entirely correct, therefore, when he recognises that what is attacked is not the heterodoxy (or heteropraxis) of a rival sectarian group, but safe orthodoxy. An attempt has been made at a subsequent stage, however, to direct the thrust of this passage against a specific group, an attempt which may be plausibly ascribed to the Qumran community.

We may now turn our attention to the specific accusations, which we classify as follows:

| | | |
|---|---|---|
| 1. | IV,20bf. | they marry two women in their lifetime |
| 2. | V,6bff. | they pollute the sanctuary in that |
| | (a) | they fail to observe laws about menstruation, and |
| | (b) | they marry their nieces |
| 3. | V,11b | they have made their holy spirits unclean |

How can these be correlated with the categories of the midrash: whoredom, wealth and fornication? Any attempt at a complete correlation is futile, because there is no mention whatsoever of riches.[9]

Some degree of harmonisation is to be expected, however, in view of the use of the midrash.

If we abstract the last of these accusation as being generic, we are left with three items. But how many original accusations are there? Scholars may be divided broadly into two camps, depending on whether they see two or three nets. Some believe that the *number* of accusations is intended to equal the number of nets of Belial, even if the *identification* of the three nets does not correspond. Of these three accusation, then, one relates to sanctuary defilement and two to sexual relations. According to this interpretation, the words הם ניתפשים בשתים בזנות mean 'they are caught in whoredom *in two respects*,' and hence are intended to explain that the net of riches mentioned in the midrash is replaced by a second net, as it were, of whoredom.[10] A difficulty with this view is that the two kinds of whoredom are not, as one would expect, listed first, followed by that of sanctuary defilement, but occur as the first and third accusations. To meet this objection, it has been further suggested that V,6b-7a, the second accusation, is out of place and should be placed after the accusation which it presently precedes.

A second group of scholars find only two accusations, and translate IV,20b as ' . . . are caught in two [sc. nets]: in whoredom by . . . .'[11] While the meaning 'in two respects' is by comparison rather forced, the preceding statement 'he who escapes one is caught in the other, and he who escapes the other is caught in (yet) another' (IV,18-19a) does suggest that the word שתים refers to the nets. This interpretation is not without its own difficulties: it makes good sense of the first two accusations, which correspond to two of the nets of the midrash, but it does not account for the third accusation, marrying one's niece. Some scholars[12] suggest that this third accusation is a second example of the (second) net of sanctuary defilement. But the only way in which this interpretation can be made even remotely plausible is by applying it to priests, a recourse adopted by Jeremias and Murphy-O'Connor. Yet there is nothing in this passage to suggest that this accusation *alone* is confined to a section of the Judaean population, Equally, there are no grounds for applying *all* of the accusations to priests. In any case, if priests are the targets of all the criticisms, then they all equally entail defilement of the sanctuary.

The easiest way to dispose of this problematic third accusation is to dismiss it, with Stegemann, as a secondary expansion. However, there are no supporting grounds for this view which must be regarded as a desperate resort.

A way of approaching this problem which in my opinion is the most fruitful has been overlooked because of the presumption that defilement of the Temple is one of the key issues of the *Damascus Document*. As we shall argue in due course, it is not. But even aside from this issue, it will surely be conceded that our document seems to have found a rather feeble example of sanctuary defilement. Sexual intercourse during a period forbidden by law would indeed render a man unclean, and the presence of such a man in the sanctuary would consequently pollute it. It may be that here we are faced with a conventional accusation, for Psalms of Solomon 8, 13 reads 'they trod the altar of the Lord (coming straight) from all manner of uncleanness; and with menstrual blood they defiled the sacrifices as (though these were) common flesh.' The words quoted, incidentally, apply to all Israelites, not priests alone. But whether the accusation is conventional, or represents a serious issue of disagreement between the community and those outside it, this example calls into question the suggestion that Temple defilement is a crucial element in the ideology of the *Damascus Document.* Is this example the best that the community could instance in pursuit of its contention that Belial had netted Israel in Temple defilement?

The accusation of defiling the sanctuary may be felt to attract suspicion in that unlike the other two specific accusations, its first part does not cite a biblical text as its basis. Now the employment of a biblical proof-text in these accusations is more than a formal device. It underlines the claim that these accusations are not based on esoteric sectarian principles but on *the law as revealed to and acknowledged by those both inside and outside the community.* The accusations expand the point made in the midrash that the nets appear as righteousness: that is, they are accepted outside the community as being not in breach of the law, but consonant with it. Now, if the law regarding the period of uncleanness of a menstruant were in dispute between the community and outsiders—as is the case with the other two accusations—it is surely required that the community will argue from scripture that its own interpretation is correct. How else can it prove that the observance of the law, the 'righteousness', of the outsiders is a 'net of Belial'? Here we find no such scriptural appeal.

Despite this last point, however, my conclusion is that the accusation of defiling the sanctuary is present here simply because it *was* present in the list of accusations used by the redactor as a main source. The actual charges we find deal two with forbidden marriages and one with female ritual uncleanness, and I therefore suggest that the source from which the accusations are drawn, or that part of it which was used, *was exclusively concerned with sexual offences*. On balance, this consideration outweighs the omission of a scriptural citation in the case of the second accusation. I do not therefore believe that this brief second accusation is a gloss, for without it the accusations would not be consistent with the midrash. It was retained because it corresponded with one of the nets of the midrash. Had the redactor himself invented or inserted this accusation simply in order to provide a closer correspondence with the 'nets' of the midrash, he would surely have found a better example, or found one with a biblical proof-text to match the others and to suit his purpose. The most plausible explanation must be that he found this accusation in his source material, and found good reason to retain it. Obviously, the issue of Temple defilement does not indicate any formal breach with the sanctuary either on the part of those responsible for the source-material (midrash and accusations) *nor for the redactor and his community*. (Did the writers of the Psalms of Solomon abandon the Temple?)

Before leaving this passage, it is worth noting that there are nonetheless traces of secondary expansion within it. Several scholars accept or imply that the first accusation has been enlarged, probably from V,1b-6a. As to the meaning of 'two wives in their lifetime,' I see no reason to depart from the literal meaning of the text and follow Murphy-O'Connor in concluding that the community disapproved of any second wife, possibly on the grounds that marriage was intended for procreation only. It may be relevant that Josephus ascribes precisely this motive—and a test of fertility—to the Essenes (War II, 8.13).

We may now consider the final accusation, of 'defiling their holy spirits' (V,11bff.). It is regarded by Stegemann as secondary in view of its undoubtedly different character, but this is not entirely convincing. The paragraph could represent a coda to a series of specific accusations. Its point certainly is not to specify some breach of Mosaic law, but to present the culmination of preceding criticisms. What it amounts to, at any rate, is that these people are dangerous, and should not be associated with. This is a perfectly plausible conclusion to a list of accusations whose point was to encourage dissociation from the rest of Israel. The climax of the description is the claim, expressed by means of two biblical quotations, that Israel is ignorant, which is perfectly in keeping with the tenor of the argument that their practices are wayward through the deception of Belial, and the insistence several times earlier in the *Admonition* on the perception enjoyed by the community.

Nevertheless, this passage does not quite accord with the point which IV,12bff made in introducing the material, namely that Israel is ensnared by Belial. This final criticism expresses a certain bitterness, not at all stifled by being couched almost entirely in biblical language. The phrase in V,11bf. 'with a blasphemous tongue they have opened their mouths against the ordinances of God's covenant, saying that they are not established' (ובלשון גדופים פתחו פה על חוקי ברית אל לאמר לא נכונו), deserves especial attention. According to Stegemann, the covenant in question is the Mosaic one, and accordingly the 'builders of the wall' are accused of conscious violation of the Mosaic law. If this interpretation is correct, the accusation seems to go beyond that of the previous ones, and indeed of the thesis that these violations are the work of Belial. It makes of the 'builders' protagonists and deliberate violators rather than blind victims of divine desertion and diabolical deception. Murphy-O'Connor, on the other hand, takes the covenant in question to be that of the community, and infers that the 'builders of the wall' had rejected the halachah of the community: 'the accusation levelled here is no longer one of erroneous interpretation of the Law but of rejection of revealed truth.'[13] In favour of this suggestion is that deliberate opposition to the community law does not conflict with ignorant departure from the Mosaic law. We may also consider the implication of חוקי ברית אל in its present context. The account of the origins of the community law which follows in 17ff. furnishes an elaborate, even cumbersome word-play on מחוקקות/מחוקק/חוק. This feature enhances the probability that the חוקי ברית אל refers to the community's law. It is also more probable that the word ברית would be reserved for the community's covenant, since in its view no other covenant remained valid, and certainly not for those outside the community.

Murphy-O'Connor has further suggested that this community attempted to proselytise and to advertise its claims to be the true covenant and the true possessor of the law, and was opposed and rejected by the religious authorities. Such a state of affairs is a very plausible context for these criticisms, although they need not address formal opposition by religious authorities but dislike, and perhaps ridicule on the part of outsiders, all of whom are, on our argument, 'builders of the wall.' But conclusions about the historical context of this document are premature.

An apparently new element is introduced into the argument with the phrase 'he who associates with them . . . ' Both Stegemann and Murphy-O'Connor agree that the word הקרוב (this reading is found in a Cave 6 fragment) introduces a formal warning. (The restoration of כהר ביתו to כהרבותו, 'the more he does it' is agreed by Rabin, Lohse, Maier, Stegemann and Murphy-O'Connor.) Accordingly, association with the 'builders of the wall' brings guilt, and the more the association, the more the guilt. This incidentally increases the difficulty of regarding the 'builders of the wall' as apostates of the community, with whom association would hardly attract *degrees* of guilt. The addition of כי אם נלחץ, 'unless he is forced,' is a further problem, which Jeremias tries to dispose of by taking as a gloss. Even as a gloss, however, the phrase attracts the same question. Stegemann follows Jeremias here, because he also believes, with the majority of scholars, that the warning is addressed to insiders. On this view, the text warns insiders not to be close to the 'builders of the wall' because this will attract punishment. But such a statement is surely too obvious to require expression. The phrase makes better sense not as a warning against a possible *future* act, but a warning about a *present* state of affairs. All those associated with the 'builders of the wall' will not escape punishment, and the closer they are to these men, the greater their guilt; that is to say, *the greater one's piety according to the external standards, the greater one's guilt according to the community's.* The qualification 'unless he is forced' *may* be a gloss, although on a proper understanding of the text this supposition is not required. Murphy-O'Connor retains it, remarking that the pressures to conform to the standards of the religious authorities may have been strong; to renounce them would certainly attract the possibility of ostracism, even persecution.[14] The degree of association between members of the community and the outside world is not very clear from the *Laws* of CD, but it may be significant that the first of the injunctions presented in the *Admonition* (VI,11ff.) is to 'keep apart from the children of the Pit.' If our phrase in V,15 is also to be read as anticipating the withdrawal from society which joining the community would entail, it may be understood as a warning that once a newcomer has joined the community, further association with present friends and neighbours will court danger; not merely because these are ensnared by Belial, but because they have shown opposition to the true covenant of the community.

There are significant comparisons and contrasts to be drawn between V,11b-15 and VIII,3bff, where an attack on the 'princes of Judah' suggests that the religious/political authorities outside the community are exercising a competing claim for the loyalty of newly-arrived members. Here, possible entrants are being weaned away from old allegiances; in VIII,3bff. they are being warned against backsliding. In both passages, there are explicit and implicit comparisons with the halachah of the community sketched in VI,11ff. (for details, see below on VIII,3bff.)

### The origin of community halachah: V,17-VI,11a

The next source to be used by the redactor opens in an historio-graphical vein, and is introduced, in my view, at V,17 by the phrase הם גוי אבד עצות. This view may seem at first sight an arbitrary one, but certain observations and deductions support it. 15b-16 anticipate the opening statements of the next passage in several respects; first, the phrase in 15b 'for in ancient times' (כי למילפנים, omitting אם as an error) anticipates the identical phrase in 17b, a circumstance best explained if the former is a part of a redactional link; second, the phrase ויחר אפו בעלילותיהם (words all culled from elsewhere in CD) anticipates the desolating of the land in V,20; third, the biblical quotations following, Is. 27,11 and Deut. 32,28, express almost exactly the same sentiment (the first has בינות, the second בינה), and are juxtaposed asyndectically.[15] It is probable that the first of them is also part of a redactional link.

15b-16 thus brings us from the train of thought of the preceding passage—Israel's seduction by Belial away from the Mosaic law—to that of the next passage, which commences with historical examples of Israel's capacity to be misled.[16] This passage therefore begins with the phrase הם גוי אבד עצות, which is a plausible opening: the nation of Israel is without counsel and understanding. This expresses in a converse way the characterisation of the community in I,1-IV,12a as possessing בינה, understanding. In this case the lack of understanding is contrasted with the precepts which the community has inherited from its founder.

The success of this redactional material in effecting a smooth transition (though not without trace) is measured by the fact that Murphy-O'Connor makes no source-division here, but sees only a natural progression in the argument of his 'Missionary Document.' In his view, V,15b-VI,1 reinforces the warning of the preceding lines by reminding the would-be convert that historically God has not allowed the guilty to escape. He also observes several parallels between II,14ff. and V,15b: the 'understanding' of line 17 echoes the introduction to his document at II,14, the 'kindling of God's anger' occurs also at II,21 and III,8 and the 'devastation of the land' occurs in III,10. Hence the document ends with a punishment on those who are 'typologically identified with them,' i.e. the men who have 'opened their mouth against the precepts of the covenant of God.' 'An historical event of the past is seen as a paradigm for God's action in the future.'[17] We have encountered the theory of a typological interpretation of the Exile in CD before, in the case of I,1ff. Here, as there, the theory fails because the point at issue is clearly *not* the punishment of the wicked but the history of the faithful, and the desolation of the land is very firmly an historical event which represents the end of the old Israel and the beginning of the new dispensation, the covenant with the community. There is in V,17ff. no threat of punishment, implicit or explicit. The foolishness of Israel, from the consequences of which it was once delivered, was definitively punished at the time of the Exile, a punishment which persists to the present time.

Because he does not interpret the ideology of CD in this way, and, more specifically, does not realise that VI,17ff. is a community *Heilsgeschichte* which may be closely compared with I,1ff. and II,14ff., Murphy-O'Connor not only divides the source-material wrongly, but is at a loss both to explain the material in lines 18-19 and also to identify the event referred to in line 21 as the 'desolation of the land.' Of the identity of this event, he writes 'it is a matter of some debate,' but he inclines to an incident at the end of the pre-exilic period.[18]

Stegemann's analysis is also different from that suggested here, for he takes V,15-16a as marking the conclusion of a source, and the following material, consisting largely of scriptural phrases, as redactional. A new source begins for him with 17b, כי מלפנים. As we have seen, he is attracted to the double mention of Belial here and IV,14, and believes the two passages to have run consecutively in the original form of the material. IV,10-13 deal with the author's own time (the *Endzeit*), while V,17-19 is a reference to an earlier incident, and V,20-VI,11 a second 'period of desolation' attending the formation of the community in the early second century BCE.[19] But Stegemann rightly rejects Jeremias' assertion that the phrase 'removers of the bound' is a designation for the community of the Man of the Lie,[20] for the phrase is not, he argues, used exclusively in CD of this group. Similarly, we may remark, יִנְבְּאוּ שֶׁקֶר in VI,1 is close, in content if not in wording, to phrases such as מַטִּיף כָּזָב, but it can hardly be denied that 'false prophecy' is strongly attested in the OT as one reason for the divine punishment of the Exile, the event to which the text must surely refer.

But both Stegemann and Murphy-O'Connor completely misread V,20ff., Murphy-O'Connor because he wrongly divides the sources[21] and Stegemann because he brings to his exegesis an *a priori* conclusion about what the history of the CD community is and when it began.

The correct interpretation of the passage is as follows: the opening criticism of lack of understanding (V,17) is illustrated by one historical reference only, that of Moses and Aaron and their opponents. The example is perfectly chosen; Moses and Aaron, as founders of the covenant and its law, represent divinely-inspired leadership. Against them were false leaders who led Israel astray. The straying persisted, rebellion against the laws of Moses (and the prophets) was continued by 'removers of the bound' and the land was devastated. By contrast, those who entered the covenant which God (re-)established afterwards with the remnant adhered to the precepts which *their* lawgiver established, while the rest of Israel strays in ignorance. On this reading of the passage, its contribution to the argument of the *Admonition* is readily appreciated. It moves from the sorry relationship of Israel, past and present, to its law and towards the relationship of the covenant community to its law.

Even a superficial comparison of V,20-VI,11, I,1ff. and II,14ff. will show that the historical schema is, in all major respects, identical in each of them; moreover, they all display substantial verbal agreement. The straying of Israel, the desolation of the land, the restoration or re-creation of the covenant with 'Israel and Aaron,' the 'well' and the salvation which this new covenant community enjoys in the present and future comprise a sequence whose reference is unambiguous. It is the same story of the origin of the community which we have met before, and we have already been able to conclude that it begins with the destruction of the land by Nebuchadnezzar. The following comparison with II,14ff. displays the basic identity of the *Heilsgeschichte* in each case. (I,1ff. may also be compared.[22])

| | | | |
|---|---|---|---|
| 1. | rebellion against God | II,17b-III,9a | V,17b-19 |
| | (failure to occupy the land | III,7 | V,17b-18 ?) |

2.  straying leading to desolation of
    the land                                  III,9b-12a          V,20-VI,2a
3.  covenant with the remnant of the
    destruction                               III,12b-13a         VI,2a-3a
4.  divine revelation                         III,13b-16a         VI,3a
5.  halachah of the remnant (well)            III,16b-17a         VI,3b-4a
6.  biblical quotation/midrash
    applied to constituents of the
    remnant community                         III,21-IV,4a        VI,3b-9
7.  the eternal nature of the new
    community.                                III,19-20           VI,10-11a

These parallels, which display significant verbal resemblance also,
demonstrate both the unity of V,17-VI,11 and its historical referent.
Ambiguity is present only in respect of the wording of V,20f.:
ובקץ חרבן הארץ עמדו ... ותישם הארץ כי דברו .... But it is clear on reflection that the desolation of the land (תישם) followed and was caused by
the activity of the 'removers of the bound.' The phrase ובקץ חרבן הארץ
must include what is indicated by תישם הארץ, and therefore is not to be
read as conveying strict chronological sequence, but introducing the
period of which the following verbs describe the events. In accordance
with its usage elsewhere in CD, קץ denotes an extended period of time,
an epoch, and I should regard it as comprising not only the Babylonian
invasion, destruction and exile, but the whole period up to the present,
during which the land is, in the eyes of the covenant community,
desolate.

Once the events referred to in this passage have been correctly
identified, we are in a position to amplify our knowledge of the
community's origins, at least as the community presents them. Those
who dug the well are the שבי ישראל who 'went out of the land of Judah
and dwelt (גרו) in the land of Damascus.' The first two items in this
phrase we have met before; now we learn that those who left the land
and went into exile call their place of exile 'Damascus.' The phrase
'covenant in the land of Damascus' does not occur in the original
*Admonition*, but 'new covenant in the land of Damascus' occurs in
VIII,21 = XIX,33f.; XX,10-12 (where we shall argue that the word
'new' is a Qumranic gloss), and the currency of the phrase without the
word 'new' may be taken for granted (see on XX,10-12 below). There is
no point in arguing at length that Damascus is used as a symbol of
Babylon (or the Assyro-Babylonian captivity), since this inter-

pretation is demanded by the context, and it is for scholars of a different persuasion to establish their case. The view which Rabinowitz, Jaubert, Schwarz and Murphy-O'Connor all advanced (despite divergences in other respects) is given further support in the present study by our analysis of the argument of the *Admonition*, as a whole. On the basis of this argument, however, one may only conclude that the community *claimed* to have originated at the time of the Exile. It will have to be argued that this theological perspective is also a true historical one. Equally, however, the recognition of this perspective undermines the conventional view that the community originated in the Maccabean period, and it requires to be shown that the exilic perspective of this document cannot be historically accurate before the possibility may be dismissed.

We can also learn more from this passage about the origin of the community's halachah, for its derivation is now traced to an individual, called דורש התורה, 'the Interpreter of the Law.' This figure reappears in VII,18 where he is placed in Damascus, and although it appears that the passage may be secondary, the datum nonetheless offers a measure of confirmation. By contrast, the title in the Qumran scrolls is applied either to an eschatological figure (4QFl I,11-12)) or to an office within the Qumran community.[23]

If the title designates an historical individual, whom the community remembered as its lawgiver, the second Moses, as it were, it is unlikely that we can identify him. Candidates such as Ezra or Nehemiah[24] are not only quite speculative but also rather improbable. Comparison of this passage with I,11 has convinced most scholars that the title 'Teacher of Righteousness' there may refer to the same figure as the title 'Interpreter of the Law' here. (In the account given at III,21ff. no individual figure is present.) This in turn has been seen to confirm the equation Qumran=Damascus by a majority of recent commentators. But in addition to the difficulties involved with respect to the identity of Damascus, there is one passage highly embarrassing to the identification of the two figures, namely the reference to 'he who teaches righteousness at the end of days' in VI,11. It has even been (seriously) suggested that the historical 'Teacher of Righteousness' would be reincarnated or resurrected.[25] A more sober explanation is that the 'one who teaches righteousness' is not the historical 'Teacher' but another figure.

There is, of course, a similarity between the place of the 'Interpreter of the Law' in V,7 and the 'Teacher of Righteousness' in I,1ff. But in fact that place is not *identical*, as an examination of the two passages will readily reveal; the arrival of the 'Teacher' is placed well after the formation of the 'root' and even further from the survival of the remnant, while the 'Interpreter' is placed at the very origins of the remnant community. The 'Interpreter of the Law' in CD is a past figure; the 'one who teaches righteousness' of VI,11 is a future figure. What prevents the most obvious conclusion that the present passage looks back to a figure of the past but *predates the arrival of a figure upon whom the title was bestowed?* Only the presumption that the covenant of CD is the covenant of the Qumran community, established by one known as the 'teacher of righteousness.' If that presumption is abandoned, this *crux interpretum* is not only no longer a problem; it also provides an answer to the claims of the historical 'Teacher' and gives an insight into the relationship between those who accepted him as the awaited figure, and those who apparently did not.

A difference between the Num. 21,18 midrash here and the Ezek. 44,15 midrash of III,21ff. is that here two groups are distinguished instead of three. Commenting upon the earlier text, I argued that its three groups were to be distinguished temporally. Here, the distinction is not dissimilar, and indeed, more explicit: we are shown those who *dug* the well on the one hand, and those who *have come to dig it* on the other. It is conceivable that such a distinction here is a purely formal one, deriving from the biblical text, but nothing stands in the way of a literal reading, viz. to accept the distinction as a real one between those Judaean exiles with whom the covenant was established, and those more recent converts who have joined the community. Such a reading entails the openness of the community to new converts and supports our suggestion that the argument of the *Admonition* is addressed to outsiders, inviting them to participate in the rewards which the covenant brings as well as the responsibilities which it demands.

Accordingly, the קץ הרשיע, during which the laws of the community will be observed is not a 'pre-eschatological' period, as is often thought, but the 'years' of IV,9.10.12, the period of Belial's activity, the period of God's wrath in I,5, the period of the desolation of the land in V,20; that is, the period from the initiation of God's *rîb* in the sixth century BCE until the present; or, more precisely in this case, the period from the inauguration of the covenant community until the arrival of 'one who will teach righteousness.' According to prevailing assumptions of the 2nd century BCE origin of the community, its distinctive laws would need to be of recent origin, formulated for a brief period of observance.

This seems to me to be intrinsically implausible, supposing a good deal of recent legislative activity, contradicting the statements of CD about the longevity of its covenant and covenant laws. But there is certainly no room for doubt that the 'period of wickedness' is a concept intimately bound up with the community's halachah. קץ occurs in VI,4, XV,7 and XII,23, in each case in conjunction with the observance of certain regulations or laws. In XII,23 it emerges that this era will come to an end with the arrival of the Messiah, and this raises the suspicion that the phrase 'teacher of righteousness', or 'one teaching righteousness' in our passage designates no other than a (priestly?) 'Messiah.'[26]

*Main points of the community's halachah: VI,11b-VII,9*
The general outline of this passage is clear: laws, followed by promises and warnings. Murphy-O'Connor assigns all of this to a single document, which he calls the 'Memorandum.' He finds within it two interpolations at VII,6b-8 and VII,13c-VIII,1a. Stegemann identifies a *Gemeinderegel* from VI,11-VII,4, followed by a blessing formula; and he finds VII,6b-9a to be interpolated between this and the curse formula which originally extended only as far as VII,13b. Denis sees here a 'petit code' of 12 precepts in VI,11-VII,4, concluding with an epilogue in VII,4-13.

I agree with Murphy-O'Connor's contention in favour of the unity of this passage, and also with his choice of the term 'Memorandum.' But I disagree in one important respect with his view of this document's function. It was not, in my view, written to *remind* community members of what they had once learnt, but to introduce for the first time the basic tenets of the halachah which were to be remembered, and which would be present somewhat more fully (but hardly in their completeness) in the *Laws* which follow the *Admonition*. The contents of VI,11ff. are not in fact 'laws'—at least, they are not 'casuistic' even if they could be regarded as 'apodictic.' They can only be understood as statements of general practice or principle, and I shall designate this particular list as 'injunctions,' to distinguish them from the *Laws* proper in CD IXff. My assessment of the contribution to the plot of CD of these injunctions and the following promises and warnings has already been made clear. What must occupy our attention chiefly in the following analysis is their character. If, as I suggest, they are a selection of the community's legislation designed to give would-be entrants an idea of the community's halachah, they will show us the most important respects in which the community felt it differed *from the practices of its environment*.

The injunctions tell us a good deal about the ideology and the attitudes of the community. The most controversial and difficult item to interpret is the first, 11b-14. Murphy-O'Connor reserves discussion of this paragraph for separate treatment, since he regards it as comprising an introduction to the following injunctions rather than the first of the series. Against Murphy-O'Connor, I shall argue that while the phrase וכל אשר הובאו בברית is an introductory phrase, the remainder of this paragraph should in fact be read as the first injunction. But because of the extended discussion required of this paragraph, I shall follow Murphy-O'Connor in reserving it for discussion until the remainder of the injunctions have been dealt with.

Here is a summary of the injunctions as I analyse them:

1.] לבלתי ...
לעשות כפרוש התורה לקץ הרשע [
(on this first injunction, see below)
2. להבדל
להנזר
(ולגזול ... ירצחו is secondary)
4. ולהבדיל ולהודיע
5. ולשמור כפרושה
כמצאת באי הברית החדשה...
6. להרים כפירושיהם
7. לאהוב
(introductory)
7. ולהחזיק
9. ולדרוש
(general)
10. ולא ימעל איש
11. להזיר כמשפט
12. להוכיח כמצוה ולא לנטור
13. להבדל כמשפטם ולא ישקץ איש כאשר הבדיל אל

This list can be divided into two sets, 1-6 and 7-12. The first concerns relations with outsiders, the second relations with insiders. Given the presence of introductory and general injunctions, this could yield a 5+5 decalogue or a 6+6 dodecalogue. (In either case the biblical precedents draw attention to the purpose of these injunctions as I have understood them.) In the first set, three of the injunctions are defined by פרוש and one by מצאת; in the second set, two are defined by משפט and one by מצוה. The group is enclosed within references to the principle of 'division': at the beginning, to separate from outsiders and at the end, to separate (holy from profane) within the community, 'as God has separated them.'

1.   The introduction defines the totality of the obligations: to do 'according to the law as detailed.' פרוש in a legal sense is used only in CD.[27] It occurs three times in the present section (lines 14.18. 20). In XIII,6 the מבקר instructs the priest in the פרוש התורה; in XIV,17f פרוש מושב and פרוש המשפטים are both linked with the 'period of wickedness' according to a probable restoration of the text. Schiffmann's view is that פרוש at Qumran (by which, for this legal usage, he means CD) 'is another term for the law derived from scripture by interpretation.'[28] This conclusion is based on the parallelism between פרוש and מצאת in lines 18-20 in our present section (no. 5), מצאת having been previously defined as sectarian halachah. In Neh. 8,8 we read ויקראו בספר בתורת האלהים מפורש ושמו שכל ויבינו במקרא 'and they read from the book, from the law of God clearly(?) and they gave the sense, so that the people understood the reading.' מפורש is translated by the RSV 'clearly' but in the margin 'with interpretation,' these two readings reflecting the major alternatives offered by biblical scholarship. Another possible rendering[29] is 'in translation.' The idea may be present already in this Nehemiah text that the meaning of the law can be brought out fully only by explication (פרש) conducted by those qualified, as a result of which perception (בינה) is gained. The same idea is perhaps also present in Dan. 12,3 if such a rôle is entrusted there to the משכילים (note שכל in Neh 8,8).

The use of פרוש in the legal sense, and of בינה, in CD is consistent with this concept: 'understanding' is predominantly the outcome of an *exegetical* process. It is not the result of individual inspiration, but of inspired *teaching* transmitted within the community. This is of course especially true within the domain of halachah, but it can be applied wherever בינה is used in CD. Indeed, the purpose of the *Admonition* as a whole is to impart בינה, in the course of which the frequent allusion to, as much as quotation of, scripture serves first and foremost to give the impression that scripture and the esoteric knowledge of the community are in unison. (Only in the case of II,2-14 is direct dependence on the testimony of scripture questionable. Even here, however, there is an abundance of scriptural verbiage which invites the audience to consider that they are hearing an exposition of scripture.)

We have just seen (on VI,10 above) that observance of the חוקות (פרוש התורה=) was prescribed for the 'period of wickedness,' which would end with the arrival of 'one who would teach righteousness.' The significance of this period for the life of the community may now be understood, given what we have previously learnt of the ideology of the community. The goal of this scrupulous observance is not the holiness of the community; rather, this is only the means. The goal is the ending of God's *rîb* with Israel and his granting once again of the land, after its period of desolation, to those fit to occupy it. The observance of the precepts has an eschatological dimension, in the sense that its context is a restricted period of time whose fulfilment is awaited. This is why in CD the פרוש התורה is always mentioned together with the period during which it has to be applied. The two ideas, the law and the period, are inseparable. Exact obedience to the law of the community of the covenant during God's *rîb* is understood by the community as atoning (if this is an acceptable translation of כפר) for the long history of Israel's iniquity before the Exile. Also, since iniquity polluted the land, its repossession must be won by righteousness. Such a view could be, and undoubtedly was, developed from Lev. 17-26 in particular. We have already noted the influence of the Holiness Code on CD, and will presently draw attention to its considerable influence on these injunctions in particular.[30]

2. From the point of view of the audience addressed by the *Admonition*, the fundamental implication of the observance of the law כפרוש is separation from those outside the community, who are outside God's saving plan for Israel, and designated here בני השחת, 'children of the Pit,' or 'children of corruption.' I prefer the former translation because these outsiders are defined not positively as wilfully disobedient so much as negatively as those abandoned by God and destined for destruction. Moreover, XIV,2 states that 'the covenant of God is established for them that they may be saved from all the מוקשי שחת: here the translation 'Pit or 'perdition' must be preferred to 'corruption.' However, in the sense that these men behave not according to the law, their *way* is corrupt; CD XV,6 reads 'and this is the ruling (משפט) during the whole period of wickedness concerning everyone who turns from his corrupt way (השב מדרכו הנשחתה) ... they shall apply to him the oath of the covenant ... '; and XIII,14 forbids

any of the באי ברית from giving to or receiving from the בני שחת 'except for cash' (כי אם לכסף).

3. Refraining from 'unclean wealth of wickedness' is defined with reference to offering vows, 'devoting' (חרם) and the wealth of the sanctuary. What is meant can again be elucidated with the help of the *Laws*. XVI,13 reads 'let no one vow (ידור) to the altar anything obtained unlawfully (אנום)'; XVI,14bf. stipulates '[let no] one declare holy (יקדש) the food of his mo[uth to G]od, for that is what is meant by "they trap each other with חרם".' הון by itself seems a neutral term in CD (at XX,7; IX,22, X,18 and XIII,11 it is used of the property of a community member, in XII,7 of the property of Gentiles, and in XI,15 it also has a neutral sense) and only when coupled with רשעה does it acquire a pejorative sense (see e.g. VIII,5). The 'wealth of the sanctuary' is here too used in a neutral sense, referring to Temple property. Any abuse of Temple property may be meant, but in conjunction with vowing and devoting what may be at issue is the kind of abuse by which pledging something to the Temple acquitted one from repaying a debt, an abuse also criticised in the New Testament.[31] Vowing, devoting and the existence of Temple property are therefore not criticised *in themselves*, but for their *abuse*—unless the *Laws* and these injunctions contradict each other. Property illegally acquired ('wealth of wickedness') may not, then, be used in dealings with the Temple, for this would defile it, and it is for this reason called '*unclean wealth.*'

The presence of biblical quotations after this injunction is unique, and the passage obtrusive in that it cannot be made to fit into the text without the provision of some such phrase as 'and not' (so e.g. Rabin). Murphy-O'Connor takes the quotations, therefore, as a gloss intended to explain why the property of the Temple is 'unclean wealth of wickedness,'[32] since as we have noted he interprets all of these injunctions within the perspective of VI,11b-14a, which in his view express rejection of the Temple cult. In fact this gloss—it probably is secondary—is more plausibly an attempt to explain what is meant by the preceding clause, commenting that the abuse of vowing or devoting to the Temple amounts to depriving the underprivileged of their rights. In other words. the glossator understood the injunction is precisely the way we suggested it shoud be understood.

4. The conjunction of להבדיל and להודיע (cf. XII,19f) betrays a quotation from Ezek. 22,26: 'her priests have done violence to my law and have profaned my holy things; they have made no distinction

between the holy and the common, neither have they taught the difference between the unclean and the clean.'(Lev. 10,10 is similar, with ירה instead of ידע.) In the Ezekiel passage the responsibility for distinguishing and teaching distinctions lies with the priests. It is therefore significant that in CD this responsibility is laid upon the members of the community. In CD III,21ff. we encountered another passage from Ezekiel concerning priests, levites and sons of Zadok and also applied to the community. We may therefore suggest that this community regarded itself, rather than the Temple priesthood, as the proper guardian of cultic matters, and no doubt considered the priesthood to be in error. This much is in any case implied in the community's already expressed rejection of Israel as being led astray, and it cannot be maintained that any specific rejection of the Temple, motivated by any specific abuses on the part of its priesthood, is indicated. 'Rejection of the Temple' is in any case far too imprecise a phrase to be used to any benefit. In a certain sense, of course, the community has 'rejected the Temple' just as it has the rest of the post-exilic Jewish nation. Nevertheless, it is an inescapable fact that the laws in CD imply continued use of the Temple by the community.

5.   The importance of the sabbath for the community is evidenced in the *Laws*, and implicit in the solar calendar which embraces a system of sabbath years and jubilees; biblical scholarship has recognised observance of the sabbath as pre-eminently a concern of the Jews in Exile. Its importance in CD is hardly surprising. The reference to the festivals, and especially to the תענית raises some difficulty. For in contrast with the considerable volume of Sabbath legislation in CD X,14–XI,23 there is no festival legislation as such and no mention at all of the Day of Atonement. Why are they specified here, and, moreover, qualified by the unique phrase כמצאת באי הברית החדשה בארץ דמשק whose meaning, if an integral part of the text, can hardly differ in implication from פרוש? Why, in any case, does the text not read simply ולשמור את יום השבת ואת המועדות ואת יום התענית כפרושה, if the festivals are to be included?

There seems to me a strong probability that ואת המועדות . . . . דמשק is a gloss. It will be argued below that the phrase 'new covenant in the land of Damascus' occurs elswhere in CD in a section of the *Admonition* which has been secondarily appended to the original document, where it is clear that a new or revised version of the original covenant is meant (see ch. V, on XX,12). Since the 'community of the new covenant' may well have abandoned the Temple cult (see XX,23), it would follow that a different manner of celebrating the major festivals—as opposed to merely a different date of celebration—would be required (cf. 1QpHab XI,6-8), and this state of affairs is a plausible explanation for the expansion of the text of the original *Admonition* at this point.[33]

6.   הרים in Num. 15,17-21 is a technical term for the dough-offering and in Num 18,19ff for the giving of the tithe. It certainly implies some contact with the Temple cult.

7.   This introduces specific injunctions, which deal with internal relations and provides the general heading of 'loving one's brother,' i.e. one's fellow-member.

8.   According to CD XIV,13-15 two(?) days' wages in each month are set aside to 'strengthen the hand of the poor and needy' as here. In accordance with injunctions 2 and 7, the beneficiaries are to be understood as community members.

9.   Is this a specific injunction or another general heading? Injunctions 10, 11 and 12 could be taken as falling under this rubric, but to do so would entail a rather negative interpretation of 'seeking the welfare.' Although injunction 12 seems to be a positive example of concern for a fellow-member's welfare, we shall argue that its motivation is otherwise. The issue is of little consequence, but I regard this as a separate injunction.

10.   Lev. 18,6, איש איש אל כל שאר בשרו לא תקריבו, forbids an act of גלות ערוה, in this case meaning incest. An identical meaning is taken here by Lévi and Cothenet. But Murphy-O'Connor objects that this is too weak for the verb מעל, and it may be added that incest seems to be covered by the subsequent injunction. In CD IX,16f. occurs the phrase כל דבר אשר ימעל איש בתורה, and in I,3 מעל is used of Israel's deeds in forsaking God. In XV,13, where the same verb may plausibly be restored, it also seems to have a fairly wide meaning, as it has also in XX,4. In sum, מעל can apparently be used in CD for any offence within the community. Accordingly, this injunction is best taken as applying to any offence in respect of *family obligations* (e.g. *ge'ullah*), over which the community elsewhere expresses concern (see XIV,15f.).

11.   The text apparently reads 'to refrain from whores.' This meaning is unlikely because such a prohibition would be self-evident, and because it is at the very least unlikely that whores existed within the community. Since זנות is also found in VIII,5 where ms. B reads זנות, we ought to translate 'whoredom' or 'lust' and interpret it, as in IV,20ff., of a second marriage and perhaps also of any marriage within

forbidden degrees. It therefore includes all incestuous relationships.
12.   This injunction is also spelt out at IX,2-8, where the bearing of a grudge (תמור) and reproving are brought together. It is for this reason that I take the two verbs as comprising a single injunction. IX,2ff is unusual in presenting its law together with a scriptural quotation (from Lev. 19,18 and 17), and makes it clear that reproof is *obligatory*, not an act of charity, and that it is *formal*: it must take place before witnesses prior to any official complaint being brought against the offender. If a member sins, and another fails to reprove him, the latter bears the sin of the former on his account. It is probable that מצוה is used in our present text rather than the more usual משפט because of IX,7-8; 'because he did not carry out the commandment (מצוה) of God who said to him: Thou shalt surely reprove thy neighbour and not bear sin because of him.' In other words, a מצוה—in this case at least—appears to designate a specific and explicit commandment of God in scripture, משפט and פרוש the community's interpretation of such commandments.
13.   Commentators agree that this injunction refers to dietary laws. הבדיל is not 'taught them to distinguish' as Rabin translates. It means either 'as God has divided (clean from unclean) for them (the community); or, possibly, 'as God has set them (i.e. members of the community) apart,' following the train of thought in Lev. 20,25f., with the ל in להם expressing the direct object). The dietary laws receive a fuller exposition in XII,11f.

A number of important conclusions and additional observations can now be offered:
   (i) Some of the items in the second part of the list are either general or may overlap. The reason for this may be the desire to reach an appropriate number of basic injunctions (a decalogue or dodecalogue) without undue complication or qualification.
   (ii) The injunctions are extensively paralleled in the *Laws*, and are probably directly derived from a larger body of community legislation much of which is included in IX-XVI (The case of no. 12, where we explained the use of מצוה from the quotation of a biblical text in the *Laws*, points to this.)
   (iii) Most of the injunctions are also paralleled elsewhere in the *Admonition* by criticisms of outsiders, which suggests that they have been selected as being especially significant to *outsiders*, for whom

different standards would hitherto have applied, rather than to existing members of a community whether or not disaffected. This point will be illustrated further: a table of comparisons between criticisms of outsiders' practices and community injunctions is given below on VIII,2bff.

(iv) Murphy-O'Connor has demonstrated in detail the close connections between these injunctions and the Holiness Code (Lev 17-26), concluding that the latter stands if not directly, then at no great distance behind this list. He enumerates the following points of identity:

| Injunction | 3 | Lev. 20,25 (but cf. 10,10) |
|---|---|---|
| | 4 | 23,3.4f.27f. |
| | 5 | 22,2 |
| | 6 | 19,18 |
| | 7 | 19,9f.34 |
| | 8 | 19,18 |
| | 9 | 25,25 |
| | 10 | 18,6f. (but of illicit marriages) |
| | 11 | 19,17f. (cited in IX,2-8) |
| | 12 | 20,25 |

These detailed and verbal parallels vividly illustrate the influence of the Holiness Code upon the ideology of the *Admonition* to which we have already drawn attention. The purity which the Holiness Code enjoins is intrinsically bound up with the present defilement of the land and with its future re-possession; it is a code written by exiles who believed that the disaster which had occurred resulted from Israel's previous pollution of the land it had been given, and which had now been purged of its inhabitants to 'enjoy its sabbaths.' It is therefore in a very accurate sense a law for the 'period of wrath,' and consequently a very proper basis for laws to be in force 'during the period of wickedness.' Especially worth quoting for the light it sheds on the ideology of CD is 26,32ff. Comment is unnecessary; the numerous points of direct contact can hardly be overlooked:

> And I will devastate the land . . . and I will scatter you among the nations, and I will unsheathe the sword after you; and your land shall be a desolation, and your cities shall be a waste. Then the land shall enjoy (RSV mg: pay for) its

sabbaths as long as it lies desolate, while you are in your
enemies' land; then the land shall rest, and enjoy its sabbaths.
As long as it lies desolate it shall have rest, the rest which it
had not in your sabbaths when you dwelt upon it . . . and you
shall perish among the nations and the land of your enemies
shall eat you up. And those of you that are left shall pine away
in your enemies' lands because of their iniquity; and also
because of the iniquity of their fathers . . . But if they confess
their iniquity and the iniquity of their fathers in their
treachery which they committed against me, and also in
walking contrary to me, so that I walked contrary to them and
brought them into the land of their enemies . . . and they
make amends for their iniquity, then I will remember my
covenant with Jacob . . . Isaac . . . and Abraham, and I will
remember the land . . . I will for their sakes remember the
covenant of the first ones.

We are now at the point where we can consider the introductory
paragraph to these injunctions, 11b-14.[34] Murphy-O'Connor states
that they must all be read 'in the light of the introductory lines' and
concludes that 'the group addressed by the Memorandum is defined
negatively by opposition to the Temple and positively by adherence to
a special interpretation of the law.'[35] He observes that the phrase 'to
act according to the exact interpretation of the law' appears elsewhere
in the documents from Qumran only at CD IV,8, in a source 'which in
addition contains a severe critique of the Temple.' We have discussed
this source and reached a different conclusion regarding its attitude to
the Temple. Murphy-O'Connor seems here to be straining for
evidence to support his interpretation, perhaps aware that the
injunctions themselves appear to imply continued participation in the
Temple cult.

The *Laws* are even clearer than the injunctions in spelling out the
community's continued use of the Temple, as the following extracts
testify:

XI,17f.    Let no man offer on the altar on the Sabbath except the
           burnt-offering of the Sabbath; for thus it is written: 'apart
           from your Sabbath-offerings' (Lev. 23,38 = Holiness
           Code).

XI,18f.   Let no man send to the altar a burnt-offering or a grain-offering of frankincense or wood by the hand of any man affected with any of the types of uncleanness, thus enabling him to convey uncleanness to the altar, for it is written: "The sacrifice of the wicked is an abomination but the prayer of the righteous is like an offering of delight' (Prov. 15,8).

XII,1f.   Let no man lie with a woman in the city of the sanctuary so as to convey uncleanness to the sanctuary with their impurity.

IXI,13    Let no man vow to the altar anything unlawfully acquired.

IX,14     . . . apart from the ram of the sin-offering, he [the priest] shall have everything.

Murphy-O'Connor dismisses the laws in CD relating to the Temple cult as theoretical formulations, while he regards its laws regulating behaviour towards Gentiles as proof of the non-Palestinian provenance of the community.[36] Yet he offers no argument for this discrimination. Stegemann, on the other hand, rightly recognises that the community (communities) to which these laws refer did participate in the Temple cult.[37] The extent of this participation emerges as follows:

(i) Offerings could be made on the altar, specifically the Sabbath *tamid*. This law *is* strictly theoretical unless members of the community were Temple priests (which is unlikely, but not inconceivable); it states a law which *ought* to be in effect at present. Even so, by permitting the *tamid* on days other than the Sabbath this law condones the Temple cult. Almost certainly, it implies that the practice in the Temple was to offer the Tamid on the Sabbath also.

(ii) Burnt-offerings and meal-offerings could be sent to the altar, but not by the agency of a man ritually unclean. Of paramount importance is the proof-text used, which compares the sacrifice of the wicked with the prayer of the righteous. It furnishes an ideal text for any community wishing to claim that the Temple cult could be dispensed with by those who lived righteously. But the text is not used that way at all. It is, *on the contrary*, used to specify the need for absolute purity in all matters concerned with sacrifice.

(iii) Rabin comments on the third item that this law probably applied to pilgrims who would, frequenting the Temple at a festival period, be in any case in a state of purity. At all events, it can hardly apply to residents of the city. Whether or not they are visiting as pilgrims, the law reminds community members of the sanctity of the Temple. Note, incidentally, that in the *Laws* the word 'altar' is used. This prevents us from concluding that the community maintains only the sanctity of the city or of the Temple. It is the altar, the place of sacrifice which is the issue; the altar is for the community still a valid place of offering and can be polluted by unclean sacrifices, including those of community members themselves.

(iv) Vows are permitted also; these frequently entail sacrifice and in addition are an area of *voluntary participation* in the Temple cult and hence enlarge the extent to which community members were permitted (expected) to avail themselves of it.

In the light of this impressive evidence of participation in the Temple cult, how are we to construe 11b-14? Schechter and Charles render, in effect, 'none who have entered the covenant shall enter the sanctuary... unless they take care to do...' This disregards the usual meaning of לבלתי, and translates as if the text read ולא יבואו. Lévi proposed taking לבלתי in its regular sense, translating, in effect, 'all who have entered the covenant not to enter the sanctuary.' But this requires translating אם לא as 'because not' rather than 'unless,' which it regularly means. Lagrange agrees with Lévi over לבלתי but takes אם לא as introducing an oath. Dupont-Sommer follows Schechter and Charles, while Rabin suspects there may be a lacuna between לבלתי and בוא, and translates 'brought into a covenant not to.. [but have not fulfilled their words, have come] into....'

Murphy-O'Connor has reviewed the options[38] and presented his own conclusion. This is to accept (with Lévi) that ברית לבלתי must mean 'an agreement not to,' and to take ויחיו as interrogative. He makes the point that according to Mal. 1,10, which is quoted here, the 'closers of the door' are behaving righteously, in opposing wrongful sacrifices, and there are no examples in CD where the basic sense of a biblical text is reversed. His translation of the passage is:

> 'All those who were persuaded to enter into an agreement not to enter the sanctuary to kindle his altar in vain, shall they be closers of the door, as God said; "Who among you will close its door that they may not enter to kindle my altar in vain?" unless they shall be careful to act...?'

This does not seem to be any great improvement on the alternatives. It is still a clumsy translation, it equates the doing of the 'exact law' with non-entry of the Temple, which, if it is not assumed *a priori*, is a highly controversial conclusion to draw from a conjectural translation, and it assumes that the 'covenant' here is not the covenant of the community, as elsewhere throughout CD, but some kind of otherwise unmentioned 'agreement.'

In fact, none of the proposals, including Murphy-O'Connor's, is convincing. The unintelligibility of the text may be due to some idiomatic peculiarity, or to some corruption or deliberate scribal interference, in which case we shall get nowhere by arguing about which phrases or words in the paragraph do *not* mean exactly what they appear to, or indeed by confining our attention to linguistic considerations alone. No translation arrived at in this manner should be accepted if it contradicts unambiguous statements elsewhere in CD. Accordingly, the paragraph may mean that those who have entered the covenant must observe the law exactly as specified for the 'period of wickedness,' but it can hardly mean that they reject the Temple, at least not totally.

A clue to the riddle of this paragraph lies in one of its features which has not hitherto been observed, namely the manner of reference to the biblical text. We have a *paraphrase* of the text followed by a *quotation* of it. The paraphrase and the quotation are insufficiently different to account for the presence of both. Such a double method of reference to the biblical text is unparalleled in CD and puzzling. Even if the entire paragraph were to make perfect sense, one would be justified in suspecting that the text is not entirely in order; more precisely, that it has been expanded. But to confirm the suspicion an explanation of the present state of the text is required. There seems no such explanation if the expansion is understood to comprise the words אשר אמר . . . חנם, which, as noted, simply repeat the preceding text. But if the expansion is taken to include ויהיו מסגירי, it can be seen to amplify an original biblical quotation or allusion consisting of only three words, להאיר מזבחו חנם; the interpolator recognised the source of the allusion, expanded it, then drew attention to his erudition by adding the formula אשר אמר, which is therefore to be seen as referring primarily to the phrase מסגירי הדלת rather than to the whole of the preceding allusion. There is a similar, if not identical, phenomenon to be observed in the difference between the A and B texts of VIII,2bff.,[39] which may assure us that we are not postulating a hypothetical process of expansion. Moreover, the

additional words may have been theologically motivated if they
originated from within the Qumran community which adopted a
harsher attitude towards the Temple (see below on XX,22bff.).

On technical grounds, therefore, and quite apart from any considerations of the overall sense of the paragraph, ויהיו ... חנם can be
isolated as a probable interpolation, leaving us with the original
לבלתי בוא אל המקדש להאיר מזבחו אם לא, 'not to enter unless'—which
makes perfect sense. The only remaining problem is the opening
phrase וכל אשר הובאו בברית. There are two reasons why ברית might be
taken to denote a special 'agreement' (as Murphy-O'Connor desires)
rather than the community's covenant. The first is the juxtaposition of
ברית and לבלתי. Yet, tempting as this juxtaposition is, to take the two
words to mean 'an agreement not to' leaves the sentence without a
vital main verb. The second reason is the use of the *hophal* of בוא rather
than the usual *qal*. However, if it is correct, as some scholars believe,[40]
that באי ברית means 'members of the community,' the *qal* participle
connoting a state and not an act, the use of the *hophal* may be intended
to refer to the act of entry itself, and accordingly to those who have just
entered. The stress is then on the process of transition itself; those who
undergo this process are warned that their previous unconditional
association with the Temple cannot continue without the qualifications imposed by the community covenant. These qualifications are
provided in the first few injunctions which follow.

Since, therefore, we need to posit no special 'agreement' beyond the
community covenant in CD, the only remaining problem is the lack of
the main verb. But if we regard this paragraph *as the first injunction*,
the lack is explained, for the injunctions which follow are introduced
by the preposition ל+ infinitive, and do not have a main verb either.
ללבלתי+ infinitive is the negative form of this construction. The
infinitives which introduce each injunction are not, on this view,
grammatically dependent upon לעשות כפרוש התורה in line 14, for this is
itself in a subordinate clause introduced by כי אם 'unless.' Rather, they
all (including לבלתי בוא) introduce *conditions of the covenant*, and the
phrase כל הובאו בברית defines those to whom the conditions apply.

My restored original text and its translation is therefore as follows:

וכל אשר הובאו בברית
לבלתי בוא אל המקדש להאיר מזבחו חנם ...
אם לא ישמרו לעשות כפרוש התורה לקץ הרשע
ולהבדיל . . .

and all who have been admitted into the covenant:
(are not) to enter the sanctuary 'to light His altar in vain' ...
unless they are observant in doing according to the law as detailed for
the 'period of wickedness':
to separate ...

It is certainly significant that the first of the injunctions is about the
use of the Temple, and the allusion to Mal. 1,10 does imply a criticism
of it, or perhaps a criticism of its priests and the laws by which they
administer it. There may also appear to be a discrepancy between the
ideology which we detected behind the covenant of the community
and its attitude towards the Temple. It may even be asked how in any
case the community could participate in a cult which apparently
observed a different calendar.[41] The question cannot be answered
neatly. One can only reply that the evidence of CD clearly implies such
participation. And indeed, upon reflection, the implied objection is
seen to carry little weight. The book of Jubilees implies the use of a
solar calendar but expresses no rejection of the Temple. Likewise the
critical statements of Jesus regarding the Temple and its priests did not
imply abandoning its use. Although the Temple was built by, and for,
and administered by, those who did not belong to the true Israel, this
fact did not in the eyes of the community prevent its use by those who
were the true Israel. The sanctuary might be frequently polluted by
others, but that was no reason why a member of the covenant should
pollute it; by failing to offer his sacrifices according to the law he was
failing to be completely holy himself; whether the Temple was being
constantly defiled by others was irrelevant. It must also be borne in
mind that the community need not have reached the point where it
could envisage any kind of Judaism without a Temple. Could perfect
obedience to the law be exercised without cultic activity? There are
texts from the Qumran community itself which may be taken to imply
such a doctrine, but that represents an advance on the attitude in CD,
and perhaps a definitive one. It might be suggested that a community
which had lived in exile would have little practical dealings with the
Temple, and so could avoid any conflict of principles. That may indeed
furnish part of the explanation; but being distanced from the Temple
would not in itself make any difference to the ideology, and in any case
CD exhibits evidence of having been used, if not composed, in
Palestine.

In conclusion, therefore, we cannot deduce from this passage precisely what was the ideological stance of the community towards the Temple, nor the exact extent of their participation in it. I would suggest that the Temple issue was not very important within the community, for virtually nothing is said of it in CD apart from this passage. The real importance of the Temple issue was probably that it represented an alternative allegiance; it was regarded by its authorities and by the majority of Jews, to be a symbol of God's presence, and perhaps therefore a guarantee of a continuing divine commitment to Israel. The community's belief, on the other hand, is that this Israel is not the true Israel, that God has abandoned it for good and entered into a covenant with a remnant, who more than once describe themselves in priestly terms. These terms do not amount to a claim to be an 'alternative Temple,' but rather to the fact that the community must fulfil the highest definition of holiness, namely priestly holiness.

Nevertheless, the claims of the commmunity constituted a direct challenge to the status of the Temple, which must now become no more than a means of fulfilling the cultic obligations of the law. No doubt, this restricted use of the Temple was to pertain only for the 'period of wickedness,' after which the community expected that it would possess the Temple fully, or perhaps would receive another from God. Either view can be supported with reference to the Qumran scrolls or, more pertinently, the book of Jubilees. In brief, the attitude of the community of CD to the Temple was cool, but neither indifferent nor hostile.[42]

The injunctions are followed in VII,4b-6a by a promise to the faithful, המתהלכים באלה על פי כל יסורו ברית אל נאמנות להם. There are some problems here; should יסורו be read יסורי (e.g. Dupont-Sommer) or perhaps יסורי with ברית supplied after it (Rabin)? More importantly, how is the phrase to be construed? Rabin has 'All they that walk in these ... the covenant of God shall stand fast with them'; Dupont-Sommer offers 'For all who walk in these (precepts) in holy perfection, obeying all His instructions, the Covenant of God is assurance that ... ' (similarly, Charles); Lévi, Maier and Cothenet read, in effect, 'All those who walk ... are assured.' The text is almost certainly corrupt, for a grammatically suitable subject for נאמנות (found in both A and B texts as well as at XIV,2) is absent. The passage is not important enough for our purposes to demand a decision or provoke a new suggestion. We need only comment that אלה and יסורים can hardly denote the same entity, and since אלה can refer only to the

preceding injunctions, it is the significance of יסורים which poses the
question. The verb יסר occurs twice in CD: IV,8 reads 'the פרוש התורה
in which the first ones were instructed (התוסרו)'; and in XX,31 there is
blessing on 'those who have been instructed (התיסרו) in the former
ordinances (משפטים) in which the men of the community (יחיד[43]) are
judged.' The noun יסור occurs once only elsewhere: VII,8 reads
כמשפט היסורים (the B text has יסורים). From all of these passages, if they
are consistent, we learn that the יסורים were the laws by which the
community was ruled (שפט), which were traced back to the founders of
the community (ראשונים), and which constitute the proper meaning
(פרוש) of the law. In this case, then, the יסורים are the whole body of
laws, while אלה are the injunctions, that is, the summary, the main
principles, which have just been given. These express the essence of
the פרוש התורה by means of a mixture of the general and specific; the
possibility that they may represent the rules by which new entrants
into the community are required to abide until they become full
members, while theoretically attractive, cannot be accepted in view of
the formulation כל המתהלכים באלה . . . על פי כל יסורו. The יסורים are
implied by such formulae as כמשפט and כפרושה within the injunctions.

Finally, a word about the promise itself. The A and B texts both
contain a promise to the faithful that they will be made to live for a
thousand generations. We have commented already on the ideology of
the community in respect of its own mission. We can also say
something of the rewards which it offered to individual members.
Already in III,20f. those faithful to the covenant were offered eternal
life and the 'glory of Adam,' a promise in line with the statement here.
A question which must perhaps remain open is whether the community
offered this hope unconditionally to all members throughout its
history, or whether the restoration to the 'glory of Adam'—by which
chiefly immortality seems to be meant—is entailed in the restoration
which is expected at the 'end of days' when the 'period of wickedness'
ends. I raise the question not because it can be answered but because it
brings into play the contrast (which can of course be overstressed)
between on the one hand an *historical* and *corporate* hope, in which a
community becomes the seed of a new Israel whose promises will at a
definite future time be fulfilled, and on the other hand an *existential*
and *personal* hope, in which the community offers salvation to each of
its members. The fact that there is abundant evidence from the
Qumran texts of both kinds of belief suggests that either they were not
necessarily incompatible or that this community was divided on the

question. The CD community's list(s) of names could be taken as evidence of a belief in the individual salvation of all members, if understood as a kind of 'book of life' (Dan 12,1); but, as I have argued,[44] such a list could have other purposes.

The following paragraph (6a-9a) is widely regarded as an interpolation because its conditional style contrasts with the apodictic style of the preceding material (Cothenet), because it has no context (Maier) and because it is out of place in following the promise (Stegemann). Murphy-O'Connor thinks it may have been a 'floating' fragment inserted because of the verbal connections in פי אל, התהלך, היסורים and כמשפט. I believe a better reason can be adduced for its presence, which does not entail recognising it as an interpolation at all. The burden of this fragment is that a child whose parent is a member of the community—a state of affairs which can occur in the 'camps'— shall also be subject to the laws of the community. The original text of CD was addressed to new entrants; having brought them to the point of choice by argumentation, it offered them the principles of its halachah. Obeying these brought divine rewards. But not all members entered the covenant by conversion. Some were in the community by birth. What is their status? This text tells us the children of community members are subject not only to the Mosaic law (על פי התורה) but also to the regulations of the community, כמשפט האסורים. In the light of this interpretation, the paragraph is certainly not out of place in its present context, and the introduction of a reference to camps is not odd if only in such settlements would children be born. Nor its its placement after the promise problematic. Had it been placed, say, immediately before כל המתהלכים in 4b it would have fitted no better. The paragraph was not necessarily composed by the redactor, although this should not be ruled out.

## IV   WARNINGS: VII,9-VIII,19

*Summary:* A brief statement in VII,9-10a, directed at those who are contemplating entering the community, but will decide not to, comprises the original formal warning which corresponds to the preceding promise in VII,4b-6a. This has been expanded by two following passages, which are addressed to those who have already entered the community, and assure them that those outside the community, numerous and powerful as they may seem, are nevertheless destined to perish, together with all those who follow them. Escape from the visitation of God lies only with the community itself. Despite wide superficial differences between the two passages, VII,10-VIII,2 and VIII,2-19, they exhibit strong thematic similarities, and the second of them was quite probably composed precisely for its present setting. These two passages, almost certainly to be regarded as supplementary to the original *Admonition*, reflect antagonism towards authorities outside the community whose opposition to it remains a threat to its newly acquired members especially. Some opposition from these authorities is the most likely reason for the addition of the material.

In accordance with the covenant-formulary structure of the *Admonition*, a warning follows the giving of the laws and the subsequent promise. But the warning is itself a complex unit. All the material from VII,9 to the end of the *Admonition* may be assigned to it from the purely formal point of view, but clearly the extent of such material is exceptional and quite out of balance with the rather brief promise. There is little doubt that an originally briefer warning has been considerably expanded.

There is a very brief notice in VII,9-10a, which in my opinion perfectly balances the preceding promise and probably constitutes such an original warning. It is addressed to *would-be converts*, and is followed by material in which *members of the community* are encouraged in their commitment, and warned against apostasy. Here we find descriptions of, and threats against, external authorities or groups, whose punishment is contrasted with that of the community members.

In VIII,20ff. the *Admonition* continues with threats against *erstwhile members of the community who have already deserted*. This material envisages a rather different situation from that implied in the rest of the *Admonition*. Not only has apostasy already taken place, in specific circumstances and with apparently severe repercussions, but *the community which speaks in this passage is not the original community* of the *Admonition*, but a group claiming a new covenant, employing some new terminology, and beholden to a new leader-figure, called the 'teacher.' Such a group can only be seen as an offshoot of the community represented in the rest of the *Admonition*, and ought to be identified with the Qumran community. This material cannot be regarded as an integral part of the original *Admonition*, although it has been shaped to form the conclusion to a Qumranic recension of the document. Therefore, although this material is formally to be included under 'Warnings,' I shall consider it separately in the following chapter.

Our task is now to investigate the source-material and the redactional history of VII,9-VIII,19. Our provisional identification of the phrase וכל המואסים . . . עליהם as the original warning is supported by an examination of the following material, VII,10-VIII,2a. At VIII,1b-2a is a formula which partly recapitulates VII,9b-10a, and concludes an illustration of the fate awaiting those outside the community. VII,10a-VIII,2a may accordingly be seen as a self-contained unit consisting of a series of midrashim. In my opinion, this material is to be understood less as a warning to outsiders than as an encouragement to those entering the community to hold fast to the small and powerless remnant to which they are now electing to belong, and which alone is spared the divine anger. This unit is almost certainly later than the original *Admonition*, and the partial recapitulation in VIII,1b-2a betrays redactional activity by which the new warning has been brought into the formal warning of the *Admonition*.

VIII,2b-19 is to be seen as another self-contained unit. It is closed in VIII,18b-19 by another formula which again recapitulates the warning formulae of VII,9 and VIII,1b-2, although here the warning is directed unambiguously at those within the community who have abandoned the 'commandments of God.' This unit also contrasts the wickedness of those outside the community with those inside, and at first glance seems to be composed from more than one source. Yet it exhibits such basic thematic links with VII,9-VIII,2, and is so heavily dependent on the rest of the *Admonition* for its vocabulary that one may doubt whether it ever existed as an independent source.

Both VII,10-VIII,2a and VIII,2b-19 focus on the coming fulfilment of the divine *rîb* and the behaviour of outsiders to an extent not hitherto met in the *Admonition*. The tone of contrast between the community and those outside is considerably sharper than previously, and the emphasis on the coming divine salvation/punishment quite probably reflects an increasing engagement with, and rejection by, those outside the community as well as an awareness of the danger of apostasy. This supplies a further reason for doubting that either of these passages belonged to the original *Admonition*.

Before we comment on the content of all this material, we must confront the major problem posed by the discrepancy between the A and B texts. This will involve us in considering the structure and argument of the material. After the opening formula, the A text has a midrash on Is. 7,17 followed by a midrash on Amos 5,26; 9,11 and Num. 24,17. The B text has instead a midrash on Zech. 13,7 and Ezek. 9,4. Apart from this major difference, there are minor deviations of varying degrees of significance between the A and B texts. Some scholars explain the state of affairs by considering both as faulty copies of the same original (Rabin, Denis), while Carmignac believes that one of the two must be regarded as the original, and argues in favour of the priority of B, thereby imputing a good deal of haplography to the A text. But the most careful and certainly the most persuasive account of the problem derives from the analysis of Murphy-O'Connor.[1] He regards the Amos-Numbers midrash of text A as an interpolation for three reasons:

1. The virtual repetition of the phrase in VII,13 'and all who turned back were given over to the sword' (וכל הנסוגים הוסגרו לחרב) at VIII,1. The two instances stand on either side of the Amos-Numbers midrash.
2. The midrash displays no inseparable links with its present context. Its concluding phrase, 'these escaped in the time of the first visitation, but those who withdrew . . .' (VIII,1) explains the point of the Amos-Numbers midrash and returns the reader to the point at which the midrash had begun; and 'these' refers back to those who escaped in VII,14 and not to the sons of Seth in the midrash. The phrase is therefore a redactional link.
3. The midrash is not entirely in harmony with the context, for it is

concerns the 'sceptre-prince' and not the punishment of the wicked.

Murphy-O'Connor then argues that the Zechariah-Ezekiel midrash of the B text is original. Its absence from the A text can be accounted for by the scribe's eye jumping from the phrase הוסגרו לחרב in VII,13 (part of the original text of the midrash but now missing from the B text) to הסגרו לחרב in XIX,13 (also part of the original text, but consequently now missing in the A text!). Murphy-O'Connor argues that the scribe's visual jump would be unlikely had the interpolated Amos-Numbers midrash been present; he therefore concludes that it was added after the Zechariah-Ezekiel midrash had been accidentally omitted.

Finally, Murphy-O'Connor explains the absence from the B text of the Isaiah midrash. He suggests that the scribe's eye jumped from the phrase 'the prophet Isaiah son of Amoz' (ישעיה בן אמוץ הנביא), before the Isaiah midrash, to 'Zechariah the prophet' (זכריה הנביא), after the midrash.

To set out the results of this argumentation clearly, here are the original contents of VII,9-VIII,2 (excluding the minor differences) as Murphy-O'Connor has reconstructed them:

1.  the introduction, 'all who despise ...'
2.  the Isaiah midrash, VII,10b-13 (preserved only in the A text)
3.  the Zechariah-Ezekiel midrash, XIX,7-12 (preserved only in the B text)
4.  the concluding formula, 'thus is the case ...'

On this analysis, the loss of the Isaiah midrash in ms. B and of the Zechariah-Ezekiel midrash in ms. A are both the result of scribal error. By losing the Zechariah-Ezekiel midrash, the A text lost the theme of salvation, so that a suitable interpolation was required to restore it. There is one difficulty, however, with Murphy-O'Connor's reconstruction of the process, although in most respects it is so persuasive. As I understand it, the explanation supposes that the phrase 'these escaped at the time of the first visitation' (VII,21) is part of the original text, since it is also included in the Zechariah midrash (XIX,10). But it is argued that this phrase, together with the whole midrash, had been lost in the A text *before* the Amos-Numbers midrash was interpolated. How, then, did the interpolator of that midrash come to use the same phrase when adapting his material to the context? The recent modification of Murphy-O'Connor's account by G.J. Brooke[2] overcomes this difficulty. According to Brooke, the omission of the Zechariah-Ezekiel midrash and the insertion of the Amos-Numbers midrash were part of a single process of *replacement* within the A text. The reason he suggests for such a replacement is that the editor of the A text wished to substitute a passage anticipating *two* Messiahs (the Star and the Sceptre) for a passage in the B text referring to only *one* Messiah. Such an alteration, Brooke observes, would bring the text into line with the majority opinion at Qumran.

I concur with Brooke's conclusion regarding the process, but disagree regarding the motive he ascribes to it, as I shall presently show. In order to complete discussion of this question, and because the Amos-Numbers midrash is apparently not part of the original text, I shall consider the contents of the midrash here rather than during discussion of the rest of the material. Because the midrash is secondary, we cannot assign any independent value to its witness regarding the historical traditions of the community. However, since its implications in this regard are consistent with those of the rest of CD, they should be allowed weight. The midrash speaks of the exiling of the books of the law and the prophets to 'Damascus'; the books of the law are the 'tabernacle of the king' who is interpreted as the 'assembly' (קהל). Also mentioned is one called the 'Interpreter of the Law' who comes (or: 'came') to Damascus. It is here that I take issue with Brooke over his understanding of the Numbers quotation. It seems to me rather that the 'Interpreter of the Law' is the Star, and belongs to the history of the community (the קהל), while the Sceptre is an eschatological figure. I also prefer to translate הבא as 'came' because both the 'Interpreter of the Law' and 'Damascus' are elsewhere in the *Admonition* firmly associated with the *origins* of the community which lie already well in the past. The 'Interpreter of the Law' is mentioned also in CD VI,7, while the Sceptre *may* correspond to the 'one who will teach righteousness' which, as I have pointed out earlier, is probably to be understood as a messianic title. The community looked *back* to a founder figure, who was a lawgiver, and *forward* to another figure, to whom 'teaching (or even 'raining') righteousness' could be ascribed as well as 'striking the sons of Seth.' Since both descriptions are derived from biblical texts it is unwise to attempt to read very much into them. In each case the context has played a determining rôle; in VI,11 the context is law while here it is about divine visitation. The (Messianic) title has been chosen accordingly.

Let us develop a hypothesis from this suggestion. We learn from CD

XI,22 (cf. XII,16 and XIV,18) that the קהל of the community took place in a בית השתחות (house of worship) where ritual cleanliness was required. The 'my tent' of the Amos text is uninterpreted, but nonetheless significant because it deviates from the MT (מאהלי for מהלאה); it almost certainly means the Temple, and the midrash therefore teaches that study of the law has been exiled from the Temple to the קהל in 'Damascus' (where, we infer, it takes place in 'houses of worship'). Hence it is being claimed that the law had been transferred from the Temple to the (place of worship of the) community—presumably at the time of exile, when the Temple was destroyed and the community, according to CD, was established.[3] If this inference from the midrash is justified, we are now in a position to explain the community's attitude to the Temple, the Temple authorities, and their estrangement from the law. We have already concluded from our examination of other passages in CD that the community did not believe the law was presently with Israel, nor had been since the divine rejection of Israel. The law was given to, and kept by, the community alone. This belief very plausibly accounts for the place of the Temple in the ideology and in the life of the community as I have expounded it; the Temple remains legitimate *for those, and only those, who have the law*; and, as VI,13f. states, the Temple is not to be entered *except* by those observant of the law 'detailed for the period of wickedness'; otherwise, resort to the Temple amounts to 'vain lighting of the altar.'[4] The full significance of the Temple reference in the first injunction of VI,11bf. is now clear.

With our treatment of the Amos-Numbers midrash concluded, we now turn to the original passage as reconstructed earlier.

*The original warning: VII,9-10a*
The wording of the opening formula of the warning parallels that of the promise in both vocabulary and syntax, both lacking a main verb:

כל המתהלכים באלה      ברית אל נאמנות להם
כל המואסים באלה      בפקד אל להשיב עליהם

This obvious parallelism presents us immediately with a problem; to whom is the warning addressed, those within the community or those outside it? The phrase וכל המואסים (in the A text, VII,9) is not decisive for its verb has no object, leaving it uncertain whether rejection of the community laws, of the community itself, or of God is meant. The B text adds 'the commandments and the ordinances' (במצות ובחקים) to make clear that those threatened are members of the community, so that the warning parallels the promise in VII,4b-6a and is intended to be understood as belonging with the preceding injunctions. The recipients of the warning are those who have just heard the injunctions, and while any divine visitation will obviously embrace non-members of the community, it is specifically those who have heard and then rejected the laws who are addressed here. We may also note that the verb מאס, as well as מצוה and חקים, occur in Lev. 26,14-15, the beginning of the warning which follows the Holiness Code, whose influence on the preceding injunctions we have already noted. While this does not suggest the priority of the B text, it does support the interpretation which that text makes explicit, and, as Murphy-O'Connor argues, shows that the redactor of the B text recognised the biblical basis of the community injunctions.

Accordingly, those warned here are not apostate members of the community, as is frequently suggested, but new members, possibly initiates, who have, earlier in the *Admonition*, been instructed in the history and identity of the community, brought to the point of choice, and given some of the basic principles of the community laws (but not the laws themselves, which follow the *Admonition*), may decide to turn their backs on these laws. They are warned that their fate will be the same as those who never approached the community. By contrast, in VIII,19 those who *have* actually apostasised are said to have rejected *and* deserted (מאס and עזב).

There is a further difference between the A and B where B has the phrase 'to return the reward of the wicked upon them' after 'all who despise the commandments and statutes,' whereas in A it follows the phrase 'when God shall visit the earth.' In the A text the phrase 'to return the reward of the wicked' defines the purpose of the divine visitation[5] but in the B text describes the consequence of rejection of the law. In consequence of this shift, the antecedent of the word עליהם, in the A text the wicked, becomes in the B text the rejecters. This alteration could be understood as a deliberate reflection within the B text of a sharpening of the attitude towards potential apostates which is observable elsewhere in the criticism of the 'princes of Judah' (VIII,2bff.), and is possibly induced by the fear or the fact of defection. Alternatively, one might argue that the phrase להשיב גמול רשעים עליהם was accidentally misplaced in B, leaving . . . וכל המואסים להשיב, 'all who refuse to return,' a nonsensical construction which necessitated the insertion of the phrase במצות ומחקים. But this proposal gives no account of the initial misplacement other than pure error.

### The chosen are always few in number: VII,10-VIII,2

The warning is now developed with the aid of a text from Isaiah which speaks of days coming upon Judah unknown since the separation of Ephraim from Judah. There may be a sign of the secondary addition of this passage[6] in the syntax, which lacks a main verb. The original warning most probably led into the *Laws* which, I think, always followed the *Admonition* as part of the same document (see below in chapter V, on XX,27bff, where it is suggested that traces of such material may remain). The Masoretic text itself is most interesting at this point, for while the context of the verse (Is. 7,17) implies a promise of good times unknown since the days of David and Solomon, the addition of the words 'the king of Asshur' to the end of the verse dramatically changes the promise into a threat: what God will actually bring on Judah is her enemy. At the same time, the departing of Ephraim from Judah now refers—whether or not it did before the gloss—to the destruction and deportation inflicted on the Northern kingdom of Israel. Although the words 'the king of Assyria' are not included in our quotation, they are assuredly part of the text known to the writer, for the biblical verse is cited here as threat and not as promise.

The midrash plays on the meaning and the sound of the verb סור, 'depart': 'Ephraim departed from (סור אפרים מעל) Judah when the two houses of Israel *separated* (בהפרד), Ephraim became ruler over Judah' (שר אפרים מעל יהודה). It continues 'but all those who turned back were given to the sword' (הנסוגים הוסגרו), perhaps playing with the sound of שר/סר). At the same time, it links the departure (סר) with the final handing over (הוסגרו) to the sword as sin and punishment, providing a perfect lesson from history of the perils of turning away. Several scholars, including Jeremias and Murphy-O'Connor, have objected to the translation 'Ephraim became ruler over Judah,'[7] on the grounds that שר מעל is unidiomatic, and that the statement is historically incorrect. Consequently, these scholars favour emending the verb to סר. But סר מעל, if perhaps less odd, is still not idiomatic. Very probably we have a further instance of word-play; מעל means 'act treacherously.' Furthermore, the sort of pedantry which insists that Ephraim did not rule over Judah is misguided. For as a general description of the political relationship between the two states it is far from inaccurate, and for certain periods it could be said that Judah was a puppet of Ephraim. Jeremias and Murphy-O'Connor are perfectly correct, of course, to oppose the view that Ephraim here stands for the community, which has been suggested as the implication of שר אפרים מעל יהודה. The point being made here, however, is that those who 'departed' were, despite their greater numbers and power, ultimately destroyed while the numerically smaller and weaker Judah survived. (We have seen already in the *Admonition* the community's appropriation of the title 'Judah' to itself.[8]) In the light of this argument, the use of שר is perfectly intelligible. Moreover, it is very probably presupposed by the following passage which with delightful irony is a criticism of the 'princes of Judah' —שרי יהודה.

Because of failure to grasp the argument of this passage—an argument which is contained *in nuce* in the Isaianic text itself—it has not been generally realised that the phrase 'and all who withdrew were given to the sword' must refer to 721 BCE, the bringing by God of the 'king of Asshur,' here as well as in the biblical text. Schwarz, for example, thinks of the ravages of Shishak,[9] while Dupont-Sommer and Cothenet refer to the destruction of Jerusalem by Pompey in 63 BCE. We have, of course, to set aside the reference to the flight to the 'land of the north' which belongs to a secondary passage and deals with the theme of exile drawn from the Amos text and not the theme of destruction drawn from the Isaiah text. The original text in fact moves very smoothly from the mention of the 'sword' to the quotation of Zech. 13,7. This describes the punishment inflicted on the 'shepherd' and the 'man who is near to me,' the scattering of the flock and the preservation of the 'poor of the flock,' all of which will occur when the 'Messiah of Israel and Aaron' (the 'sceptre' of the interpolated Amos-Numbers midrash) shall come. It is probable that the phrase . . . והשומרים הצאן in XIX, 9 is a gloss, for it interprets a phrase not in the quoted text, but two chapters earlier, Zech. 11,11. The 'these' who are to be saved are therefore the 'little ones' (הצוערים), and the 'turning of the hand upon' is to be understood in a benign sense (following Dupont-Sommer and Cothenet), not a punitive one (as probably in Zechariah, and as understood by Rabin, Charles and Schwarz[10]). 'Those left' (הנשארים) being 'given to the sword' harks back to the phrase which originally preceded the Zechariah midrash: the sword is one which 'executes the vengeance of the covenant,' another phrase drawn from the Holiness Code, Lev. 26,25, and which, because it is absent from the A text, may be an expansion, probably from the same hand as

במצות ובחקים at XIX,5-6, also drawn from Lev. 26.

Taken together, the Isaiah and Zechariah midrashim present a clear enough argument: apostasy by Ephraim in the past was punished by destruction. The historical 'giving to the sword' refers to 721 BCE. The warning to those who turn from the community is, of course, that their act will incur the same retribution. Both the midrashim represent the faithful community as a small minority (Judah, the poor of the flock), whose salvation is contrasted with the punishment of larger and more powerful groups, designated as 'Ephraim,' and the 'sheep' (i.e. the majority of the flock). The sequel in the biblical text, Zech. 13,8f. makes this point even more clearly:

> In the whole land, says the Lord, two thirds shall be cut off and perish and one third shall be left alive. And I will put this third into the fire, and refine them as one refines silver, and test them as gold is tested. They will call on my name, and I will answer them. I will say, 'They are my people,' and they will say, 'The Lord is my God.'

But the disparity of numbers to which the entire passage alludes implicitly and explicitly throughout is obviously not applicable to those who reject the community compared with those who join it! 'Ephraim' and the 'sheep' are not those who turn away from the community. They represent those to whom apostates might be *attracted*, that is, the society outside the community, the mainstream of Jewish society, the 'establishment.' Their fate has already been hinted at in the opening phrase (according to the A text) 'when God shall visit the earth *to repay the reward of the wicked'*. Those who reject will enjoy no special visitation, but will suffer the fate of all the wicked. In view of what has been stressed earlier in the *Admonition* about the need for choice, rejection cannot be seen from the community's point of view, simply as dissociating oneself from the saved, but as associating oneself with the damned. Would-be apostates are being warned against being attracted towards a numerically greater group, a group which, as symbolised by Ephraim, 'rules' over Judah and which is also characterised as the 'flock' (led by the 'shepherd'). Just as the argument of the *Admonition* up to this point has tried carefully to weaken the loyalty of the would-be initiate to the religion of those outside the community, and to replace it by allegiance to the community, so now it is the size and power of this group which is attacked. They may seem more numerous and more powerful (like Ephraim), but nevertheless, it is they who have gone astray and will accordingly come to nought, and it is Judah, smaller and weaker, which will be preserved.

The warning therefore states: do not be misled by the apparent power and numbers of the society in which you live; it is destined for the sword, and if you ally yourself with it, your fate will be the same. Belong to Judah, not Ephraim; for you know what happened to Ephraim.

What happened to Ephraim is described (XIX,11) as 'the first visitation,' פקדת הראשון. Several emendations of this ungrammatical phrase have been offered: פקרתו הראשון by Rabinowitz, פקרת הראשונים by Rabin and Cothenet, while Murphy-O'Connor thinks that פקרה was the original text, to which a scribe added הראשון, thinking of קץ, not פקרה, and that finally פקרה was changed to פרקת.[11] These different readings amount on the whole to the same thing, although what is referred to by the phrase is not completely clear. There are, it seems to me, two possibilities. The first is that it describes the divine punishment on Ephraim mentioned in the preceding Isaiah midrash. This seems at first sight the most natural interpretation. Those who escaped, historically, are Judah. However, elsewhere in CD the visitation of God *par excellence* is the Babylonian Exile, in the context of which the ראשונים are the pre-exilic generations whose period ended at the devastation of the land.[12] In this case, 'those who escaped' are perhaps the exiles, or possibly more specifically the members of the 'covenant in Damascus,' while it is historically *Judah* which is punished. If the visitation of the Northern kingdom specifically is meant, is there an inconsistency here in the ideology of the *Admonition*, in the representation of the historic divine 'visitation'? I do not think that such stringent limitations ought to be placed on an author or redactor; the argument of the Isaiah midrash here requires a comparison of Judah and Ephraim, and this need not be collated with the description of the divine *rîb* and the origins of the community offered earlier. The Isaiah midrash operates only within the horizon of the division of the kingdoms, the destruction of Ephraim, and the survival of Judah; the destruction and Babylonian exile lie outside. Typologically, since the community alone is Judah, the equation of historical Judah with Ephraim is perfectly permissible.

There is a further consideration to be added. The Ezekiel citation (9,4) used in connection with the 'first visitation,' while it has a

Judaean setting, refers to the 'guilt of the house of Israel and Judah'; in the book of Ezekiel generally the distinction between Israel and Judah is deliberately obscured, and the exile of both nations presented as one. Murphy-O'Connor has suggested that the author of this passage regards the destruction of Ephraim and that of Judah as typologically one.[13] The word קץ is in any case used in CD of a period of time and not a moment, and thus the קץ פקדת הראשון (however we restore the phrase) may well be intended to refer to that period which included the destruction of both kingdoms. I am unable to decide confidently between the two alternatives: on the one hand, I can see no compelling reason to suppose a change in the historical reference from the fall of Ephraim to the fall of the pre-exilic world generally, and if Murphy-O'Connor's suggestion that the text originally read simply פקדה were correct, I should regard this alternative as marginally preferable. On the other hand, the application of the Ezekiel text appears, the more one examines it, to hint at the foundation of the community, showing us that the intrinsic connection between the (Judaean) Exile and foundation of the community is still secure even in this secondary stratum of the *Admonition*.

The citation of Ezekiel is dramatic, and follows the plot of the whole section by stressing not only the inevitable divine punishment on the wicked, but the preservation of the few. It describes the widespread slaughter of all except those upon whom is the mark, beginning at the defiled sanctuary, and it concludes:

> Then he said to me, 'The guilt of the house of Israel and Judah
> is exceedingly great; the land is full of blood, and the city full
> of injustice; for they say, "The Lord has forsaken the land,
> and the Lord does not see." As for me, my eye will not spare,
> nor will I have pity, but I will requite their deeds upon their
> heads.'

There are two further elements in the Ezekiel passage which explain its use. First, it emphasises again the numerical ratio between the many who will be destroyed and the few who will be saved. Also, it reminds those who are to be saved that they are predestined; the 'sighing and groaning' are of no special significance, but the 'mark' might prompt the careful reader to recall that in II,2-14 God was said to have raised men 'called by name' in every generation (see also on IV,3ff.). Those saved are *chosen* (and their choice amounts to deliverance from divine visitation).

VIII,1b-2, while reminiscent of VII,9-10a, is different in one important respect. It refers to the באי ברית who do not 'hold fast' to 'these'; they will be exterminated by the hand of Belial. First, who are the באי ברית? As we have remarked before, some scholars translate this phrase as 'who are in the covenant' or 'members of the covenant.'[14] This meaning is quite possible here. But I prefer to see this warning addressed to those who are *deciding to enter*; it offers a brief reminder to those who have not rejected, but accepted the community laws, that they are also prone to the divine visitation if they do not hold fast to these laws. In my view, the three warning formulae in this section of the *Admonition* each address different groups. In VII,9-10a it is those who, having sought to enter, finally turn their backs. Here it is those who enter who are warned to remain steadfast. In VIII,18b-19 it is those members of the community who have in fact turned their backs on it and left. There is a distinct variation in the three formulae, despite the similarities, which deserves to be given weight. This interpretation also reinforces the argument for the cohesion of the material at this point, which I am also concerned to demonstrate. A further sign of cohesion is the simple reference to 'these' in VIII,2, clearly referring back to the injunctions of VI,11ff. The B text has, unnecessarily if correctly, identified them as החקים.

## A critique of the authorities: VIII,2b-19

This passage as a whole poses two major problems: the identity of the original target (and hence the origin of the critique), and the function of the critique within CD. The material comprises three elements: a critique of the 'princes of Judah' (3-12a), a statement about 'builders of the wall' (12b-13) and a statement about the community (14-18). Both Stegemann and Murphy-O'Connor agree that the middle section is substantially a gloss; Stegemann regards the first and third elements as independent sources, while Murphy-O'Connor regards the whole passage as a single document.

Both scholars also recognise redactional material at either end of the passage, but disagree about its exact extent. Stegemann takes the phrase 'This is the day,' (הוא היום), as far as the beginning of the biblical quotation, to be a rubric for the remainder of the *Admonition*, setting out as its theme the Day of Judgment. Murphy-O'Connor attaches the phrase to the end of the previous passage, leaving an abrupt transition to the quotation which the B manuscript has softened by the addition of the phrase 'as it is (or: 'he has') said' (כאשר דבר). At the conclusion of our passage, Murphy-O'Connor regards VIII,18c-19 from 'and like this case . . . ' (וכמשפט הזה) as a redactional suture, with a further connection in the B text with the word 'and thus' (וכן). (VIII,20-21 are absent from the B text.) Stegemann regards 18cff. as a independent source.

My own view, for which I shall argue in the course of the analysis, is that VIII,2b-18 was probably composed as a sequel to the preceding warning. This conclusion is undoubtedly controversial, for superficially other conclusions seem more persuasive. The passage is to be treated as a single source, although it concludes with a redactional phrase 'and like this case . . . ,' whose presence was necessitated not by this passage but by the addition of the following material. 12c-13 is certainly a gloss, but the reference to the 'builders of the wall' in 12b is original.

Once again, our analysis has to take account of the differences between the A and B texts, and again it is Murphy-O'Connor whose careful comparison of the two provides us with the most satisfactory conclusion.[15] He has established that in every instance of deviation, the A text is closer to the original, and that B can in each case be derived from A. Furthermore, the differences in text B betray a consistent tendency which implies the work of a single hand. This tendency is twofold: to render existing allusions to OT texts more explicit and accurate, and to smooth the transition into and out of the document. The second of these tasks was achieved by adding short phrases at beginning and end and by redirecting what was originally a criticism of outsiders more explicitly towards apostates within the community, by the addition of such phrases as 'and who follow them' and 'covenant of repentance.' Finally, Murphy-O'Connor suggests, the past orientation of the document, which is preserved in the A text, is shifted in the B text towards the present/future. In short, he concludes that a critique of Jewish leaders was inserted rather abruptly into the *Admonition* and only in the B text was any effort made to establish a smoother connection with the context.

This view occupies a position between that of Jeremias and Stegemann. The former had argued[16] (i) that the phrase 'princes of Judah' applied to members of the community, pointing out that 'princes' and 'Judah' are used elsewhere of members of the community (VI,6; IV,11 respectively); (ii) that the phrase 'removers of the bound' is used elsewhere in CD of the community of the 'Scoffer' (I,16); and

(iii) that several verbs denoting treason are to be found. To these arguments Stegemann[17] responded that: (i) 'princes of Judah' was a biblical quotation, and, whatever the attribution of the two words individually elsewhere, the phrase could not be taken automatically to designate the community of the 'Scoffer'; (ii) the phrase 'removers of the bound' did not uniformly refer to that same community (cf. V,20), and (iii) that although several verbs denoting treason do appear, the accusations themselves are not such as would be directed against erstwhile members of the community, but rather against non-members.

Nevertheless, Stegemann was embarrassed by the phrase 'covenant of repentance' in the B text (XIX,16) and attempted, without much plausibility, to apply it to Jews outside the community, on the basis that any Jew could be said to have entered a covenant, and a covenant of repentance, for that matter. Even before Murphy-O'Connor's suggestion, it was clear that neither Jeremias nor Stegemann had a convincing case; but according to Murphy-O'Connor, it was not that both were wrong, but rather than both were right.

But the view that this passage is to be read as a critique of apostates, yet not originally written as such, leaves us in the dark as to why it was attached to the *Admonition* in the first place. It was an attempt to answer this question which drew my attention to the verbal and thematic connections between this passage and the preceding one. 'Judah,' שׂר ('ruled'/'prince'), and 'vengeance' occur in each, but these similarities are not as significant as the identity of theme: the political/religious establishment is destined for destruction, and is to be avoided; by contrast the members of the community are destined for salvation. The most dramatic connection, however, is between the midrash on Is. 7,17 (VII,10ff.), where the end of the kingdom of Ephraim is brought to mind as an example, and where, in the biblical text, the agent of God's punishment is the 'king of Asshur,' and VIII,11 where the punishment on the 'princes of Judah' is executed by the 'head of the kings of Greece'—the latter-day Assyria.

There are also several verbal connections with other parts of CD. Most obviously, the 'builders of the wall' are mentioned in IV,19. But I shall also presently explore the extent to which the criticisms in this section reflect halachic rules presented elswhere in CD. In fact, the extensive verbal and thematic parallels with other parts of CD make it extremely difficult, as we shall see, to conceive of this passage as having enjoyed an origin outside of the original *Admonition*.

We may now consider the text in detail. Our first problem is: where does the document begin? We have seen that Stegemann and Murphy-O'Connor disagree on this question. The whole phrase 'this is the day when God shall visit' (הוא היום אשר יפקד אל) seems linked to the preceding section rather more closely than to what follows. Murphy-O'Connor assigns it, therefore, to the previous passage, arguing that after the reference to Belial it serves as a reminder that the punishment is God's, and also that, as a concluding phrase, it forms an *inclusio* with 'when God shall visit the earth' in VII,9. But against Murphy-O'Connor it can be suggested that the phrase somewhat distorts the rhetoric of the preceding section, which reaches its climax with the assertion that those who do not 'hold fast' will suffer the same fate as those 'visited' on the former occasion. The addition of a further phrase after this climax weakens its impact, especially since it does not really continue the train of thought. Indeed, nowhere in the passage is there any interest in the *time*, only on the *target*; as a final sentence 'that is the day when God shall visit' seems to strike rather a false note.

One can more plausibly argue that the phrase 'that is the day' refers *forward* to the quotation, to the *time* when the 'wrath' shall be 'poured over them,' and even beyond to the final words of the passage: 'his anger is aroused' (חרה אפו). My own preference therefore is to regard VIII,2b-3a as composed specifically to introduce the following passage and link it to the preceding material. A major objection to this view, as Murphy-O'Connor recognises, is that the A text does not offer a smooth connection, reading אשר יפקד אל היו שרי יהודה אשר תשפוך. Unless one follows Murphy-O'Connor in attaching the first three words אשר יפקד אל to the preceding passage, the text is impossible to translate as it stands. Yet the bald juxtaposition which this procedure leaves between the two larger units which respectively end and begin at this point (according to the A text) is contradicted by the verbal and thematic links which bind them together, and which would lead one to expect some kind of redactional seam between them. I propose an alternative solution of the problem: one of the characteristics of the A text in this passage, as against the B text, is that it does not render biblical quotations exactly. In this case, the use of an incomplete quotation results in a grammatically and idiomatically awkward construction. The text perhaps originally read אשר יפקד אל את שרי יהודה... with the quotation itself formally commencing only with את. אשר תשפוך עליהם העברה was perhaps accidentally omitted, and שרי יהודה was then construed as part of the quotation. To make some sense of the text, היו was added from the biblical quotation. The B text, responding to the awkwardness of the A text, has tidied up by adding the phrase כאשר דבר. This solution is, of course, entirely hypothetical, and the question would not have detained us had not an important issue been at stake: whether or not the criticism of the 'princes of Judah' is from an originally independent document secondarily adapted (and not very well in the A text) to its present context. I differ from both Stegemann and Murphy-O'Connor in holding that it is not. The account just given of the opening phrase is not, of course, offered as an argument in favour of this conclusion, but only as an explanation which is consistent with it. The arguments which lead me to that conclusion, and which I have already summarised, will follow presently.

There is less room for disagreement regarding the conclusion of the passage. VIII,18b-19 is formally parallel to VIII,1-2, even using the phrase וכמשפט הזה. If the passage were originally independent, this phrase would have to be assigned to the redactor responsible for its inclusion in the *Admonition*. But this can only lead us to ask why less trouble seems to have been taken over the opening of the passage. Would this redactor have provided a suitable conclusion to a passage he has just interpolated without providing a suitable link with the preceding material? Hence the account just offered of the A text of VIII,2b-3a. On my own view of the origin of VIII,2b-19, that it was composed as a supplement to the *Admonition*, the concluding sentence is an integral part.

Our next problem is to identify those designated as the 'princes of Judah.' Here close attention to the use of biblical quotation and allusion is called for. Since the phrase 'like those who remove the boundary,' כמשיגי גבול, although in the biblical text quoted, is an addition in the B text, the appearance of the phrase elsewhere in the *Admonition* does not necessarily help us—at least, not in any straightforward manner. Indeed, even if it could be argued, as Jeremias does, that the phrase 'movers of the boundary' in CD is a designation of a specific group,[18] the (presumably) deliberate omission of the words from the A (and therefore probably the original) text of our document might imply that this specific group is *not* intended to be identified here!

We can be more optimistic, however, about the next biblical allusion. Murphy-O'Connor has identified כי יחלו למרפא וירק מום as an allusion to Hos. 5,13: והוא .... וירא אפרים את חליו ויהודה את מזורו

לא יכול לרפא. Verbally, the correspondence is faint, if unmistakeable, but the probability of an allusion is reinforced by not only proximity of this text to the preceding quotation (three verses earlier), but also by thematic connections between the context of the Hosea passage and CD VII,10-VIII,2. Hos. 5,11-14 read as follows:

> Ephraim is oppressed, crushed in judgment, because he was determined to go after צו. Therefore I am like a moth to Ephraim, and dry rot to the house of Judah. When Ephraim saw his sickness and Judah his wound, then Ephraim went to Assyria, and sent to the great king. But he is not able to cure you or heal your wound. For I will be like a lion to Ephraim, and like a young lion to the house of Judah. I, even I, will rend and go away. I will carry off, and none shall rescue.

The quotation in our text of v. 10, followed by a probable allusion to v. 13, surely points to the whole biblical passage just quoted. And the biblical passage reveals a fundamental and dramatic connection between our CD passage and the one preceding. In the biblical passage just quoted, we have Ephraim, Judah, and the going of Ephraim to the king of Assyria, the situation presupposed by Is. 7,17, the text which is interpreted in VII,10-13. In that interpretation, it was stated that Ephraim became ruler (שׂר) over Judah; in VIII,3 we find the שׂרי יהודה. Ephraim also 'departed' from Judah (סר) and in VIII,4-5 occurs the phrase לא סרו מדרך בוגדים. One is then prompted to ask whether the threat of vengeance by the 'kings of Greece' is a deliberate allusion to Is. 7,17's threatening Ephraim with the coming of the king of Asshur. It is not going too far, I believe, to suggest that the criticism of the 'princes of Judah' in VIII,19 for following the ways of the 'kings of the nations' is built up from the attitude of Ephraim towards Assyria, because that attitude is spelled out in Hos. 5,11-14 itself.

However, the following of Gentile ways is not the predominant criticism of this passage, and its inclusion is no doubt largely due to its correspondence with the previous passage. We should therefore be wary of taking this particular criticism as especially valuable in identifying the 'princes of Judah.'

Jeremias has pointed out that many of the criticisms offered here of the 'princes of Judah' use the vocabulary of treachery: נזר, בגד, סור, מרד and פרע.[19] But some of these verbs are used negatively, to criticise for *not* 'departing from the way of the people' or *not* 'forsaking the way of traitors.' The verbs of treason do not straightforwardly convey an accusation of treachery, and cannot be taken as evidence, *pace* Jeremias, that 'princes of Judah' were traitors vis-à-vis the community.

In fact, the burden of the criticism of the 'princes of Judah' is that these 'princes' *do not behave like the members of the community*; on the contrary, they behave in precisely the ways to which the behaviour of the community is contrasted earlier in the *Admonition*. The correlation between the accusations in this passage and other parts of CD[20] is most eloquent. In particular, four other passages in CD may be compared, namely:

IV,13-19a     a midrash on Isaiah conveying three broad crimes of which 'Israel' is guilty. It has earlier been argued that this is applied to outsiders generally and not to another sectarian group.

IV,19bff.     an application of the midrash of IV,13ff., where the three broad crimes are developed in terms of specific practices. it applies to outsiders referred to as 'builders of the wall' and criticised for departing from the law of Moses (which the community implicitly follows).

VI,11ff.     a list of injunctions, a selection of important items from the community law.

IX-XVI     a code (probably not complete) of community laws.

| | | IV,13-19a | IV,19bff | VI,11ff | VIII,3ff | IX-XVI |
|---|---|---|---|---|---|---|

(X indicates similar or identical terminology)

| | | IV,13-19a | IV,19bff | VI,11ff | VIII,3ff | IX-XVI |
|---|---|---|---|---|---|---|
| 1 | lust | X | X | X | X | (1) |
| 2 | wealth | X | | X | X | (2) |
| 3 | defiling the sanctuary | X | ? | (3) | | cf. XI,20 and XX,23 |
| 4 | separating from wicked | | | X | ? | cf. XIII,14 |
| 5 | separating clean/unclean | | X(4) | X | | X |
| 6 | keeping the Sabbath | | | X | | X |

| | | | | |
|---|---|---|---|---|
| 7 offering according to the rules | | X | | X |
| 8 loving brother | | X | ? | cf. XX,18 |
| 9 helping poor | | X | | X |
| 10 incest | X | X | X | X |
| 11 reproving brother | | X | | X |
| 12 diet laws | | X | | X |
| 13 defiling "holy spirit" | X | X | | X |

Notes:    (1)    no parallel; cf. however, CD II,16

             (2)    wealth is not condemned as such, only its abuse

             (3)    implicitly in "lighting the altar in vain"

             (4)    see V,7

This table shows thirteen crimes, offences or principles of behaviour. Items nos. 4, 6, 7, 8, 9, 11 and 12 are applied to members of the community. Nos. 6, 7, 9, 11 and 12 are mentioned only in VI,11 and IX-XVI, to which we can add no. 5; it too therefore is applied to the community. Nos. 4 and 8 appear to recur in VIII,3ff. also, but it may well be that different principles are in question in this passage. No. 4, 'separating from the children of the Pit,' ought not necessarily to be equated with 'turning from the way of the people' for the former phrase entails total withdrawal from (regular?) contact with those outside the community, while the latter may be only a matter of not following disapproved patterns of behaviour. No. 8, 'loving one's brother,' although verbally identical in VI,11ff. and our present passage, may denote in the one case specific obligations towards a fellow-member (such as reproving him) and in the other regard for one's fellow Jews. There is certainly a striking similarity between וניתור איש לאחיהו ושנא איש את רעהו in VIII,5 on the one hand and ולא לנטור and לאהוב איש את אחיהו in VI,20 and VII,2 respectively on the other. But the identity of one's fellow will depend on whether one is inside or outside the community, so that the criticism may apply equally in either case. The distinction between אח and רע may be significant in this respect. We may, at any rate, conclude that our present passage does not contain any criticisms which decisively identify the 'princes of Judah' as erstwhile community members.

If we accept that points 4 and 8 are not, or not necessarily, identical in VI,11ff. and our present passage, we are left with seven issues of criticism, nos. 1, 2, 3, 4, 5, 6 and 8, which are applied to outsiders. These are: lust, wealth, defiling the sanctuary, separating clean from unclean (but against outsiders this is directed only possibly in V,7), incest and 'defiling one's holy spirit.'

Three of these occur in IV,13-19a and three in IV,19bff., although in practice incest is identified with lust; defiling the sanctuary is a dubious charge (see above, *ad loc.*). VI,11ff. has all of them. VIII,3ff has lust, wealth and incest and in addition has two items, which were classified as nos. 4 and 8 paralleled in VI,1ff. and IX-XVI. But this classification was tabled simply in order to point to the similarity, and these, as we have already remarked, are not necessarily identical accusations.

In total, then, our present passage contains five points of criticism:

| | |
|---|---|
| lust | (ויתגוללו בדרכי זנות) |
| wealth | (ובהון הרשעה) |
| incest | (ויתעלמו איש בשאר בשרו) |
| separation from people | (לא נזרו מעם) |
| not loving one's brother | (וינגום וניטר איש לאחיו ושנא איש רעהו) |

The first three correspond to nos. 1, 2 and 10; the last two are similar or related to nos. 4 and 8.

There are especially significant verbal contacts between our passage and VI,11ff.:

| | |
|---|---|
| זונות בהון הרשעה | VIII,5 |
| הזונות | VII,1 |
| מהון הרשעה | VI,15 |

(Note the irregular spelling זונות in both cases.)

| | |
|---|---|
| איש בשאר בשרו | VIII,6 |
| איש בשאר בשרו | VII,2 |

| | |
|---|---|
| ולא נזרו מעם | VIII,8 |
| להנזר (מהון) | VI,5 |
| להזיר (מן הזונות) | VII,1 |
| להבדיל מבני שחת (Cf. | VI,14f) |

(These are the only occurrences of the verb נזר in CD.)

The correspondence between these two CD passages has already been observed by Denis and Murphy-O'Connor, both of whom nevertheless stress the difference of tone between the two, in that VIII,2bff. makes no reference to ritual observances peculiar to the community, unlike VI,11ff. But that perfectly valid observation does not diminish or indeed explain the parallels themselves, which are hardly coincidental. We have to adopt one of two conclusions: either the injunctions have in some way developed from the criticism of outsiders, whether this present passage or an earlier document on which it is based; or VIII,2bff. is employing language deliberately reminiscent of the injunctions in order to reinforce the message that to follow the 'princes of Judah' is to reject the community (and specifically its laws). The former alternative is rendered unlikely by the extent of the parallels between the injunctions and the *Laws* of IX–XVI. Therefore, the criticisms used here of the 'princes of Judah' are deliberately reminiscent of the community's own halachah. Literary dependence, however, goes beyond the injunctions. We have also to take into account other terminology borrowed from elsewhere in CD: שרירות לבם (cf. II,17; III,5.11); בוני החיץ (cf. IV,19); לחון ולבצע (cf. X,18; XI,15; XII,7). A significant number of these borrowings have been drawn from II,14–IV,12, in particular the phrase 'and they did each man what was right in his eyes, and chose each man according to the stubbornness of his heart,' which can hardly be other than a deliberate and explicit allusion to the criticism of II,14ff. The 'princes of Judah' are undoubtedly being compared with those pre-exilic generations whose unfaithfulness led to punishment. Underlying the parallel is also the reminder that the choice which II,14ff. initially presented to the would-be entrant is not necessarily a once-for-all decision; there is always the temptation of turning back; the choice has to be made and re-made. The conclusion of this passage makes this point very clearly: one can abandon the community, and such an act is described in the language used in II,14 of the rebellion of pre-exilic Israel (commandments of God; abandon; stubbornness of heart). The author of this passage is therefore acquainted with that document, and his acquaintance with other material in CD makes it probable that he knew an existing *Admonition*, in all probability with the *Laws* attached. It is this evidence, taken in conjunction with the verbal and thematic connections between VII,9ff. and VIII,3f., which supports the conclusion that this passage was composed for its present purpose, and was never an independent document.

The sequel to these criticisms is the threat that these 'princes of Judah' will meet vengeance from the 'kings of Greece.'[21] The 'ways of the wicked' in which the 'princes of Judah' walk are also identified as the ways of the 'kings of the nations,' and, just as with Ephraim, love of things foreign will bring punishment at the hands of foreigners. But this criticism emerges only in the midrash on Deut. 32,33, which develops 'walking in the ways of the wicked.' In any case, love of foreign ways is the kind of criticism which can be directed at almost anyone, by almost anyone, within Jewish society of the post-exilic period. Certainly, it would be foolhardy to base any identification of the 'princes of Judah' (for example, Hellenising high priests) on such a detail. Nevertheless, in this passage the vengeance of God is introduced as a threat, not, as in the earlier part of the *Admonition*, a present fact. Also, it is presented as the work of the 'kings of Greece.' It is true that some scholars regard this vengeance as having already taken place (for example, Dupont-Sommer thinks of the arrival of Pompey in 63 BCE). The opening words אשר יפקד אל of the passage and the words closing the criticisms of the 'princes,' ... וחרה אפו (text B), can refer only to a future punishment, a conclusion confirmed by the use of the participles ושנא ומתעב. In any case, if the 'princes of Judah' had already met their punishment, the purpose of this passage is rather unclear.

However, we do have the words וחרה אפו in the A text, apparently to be read as a past tense, and the fact that past activities *may* be described in the sentence which precedes, VIII,12-13 (XIX,24b-26): 'all this the builders of the wall, and the daubers of plaster did (or: 'do') not understand.' But here we face a complicated problem. Stegemann regards this, together with what follows, as a gloss, since it does not continue the thought of the preceding lines which culminated in the bringing of divine judgment by the 'kings of Greece.' I agree with his conclusion that the sentence is secondary, although I see no lack of coherence with what precedes. The point of the sentence could easily be that those who will suffer the divine vengeance are unaware of its coming. Its incongruity lies rather in its clumsy anticipation of VIII,18, from which it in fact derives its two components 'builders of the wall' and 'arousing of anger.' The reference to the 'builders of the wall' in VIII,12 is quite confusing. Does it refer to the 'princes of Judah' or to some other entity? There is no simple account to be given of the presence of this reference. It is found also in line 18 and in IV,19 where it is followed by the words 'who have followed after צו,' taken from Hos. 5,11. Hos. 5,10 is the biblical source of the 'princes of Judah'! Is the conjunction of Hos. 5,10f. and Ezek. 13,10 ('builders of the wall') in *two* CD passages coincidental, or has one been adapted to the other? Commenting on IV,19 I concurred with Stegemann and Murphy-O'Connor that the phrase 'who have followed after צו' from Hos. 5,11 was introduced secondarily. It might therefore best be seen as a gloss inspired by VIII,12. But VIII,12 is itself apparently a gloss, for although we have here a fuller quotation of Ezek. 13,10 than at IV,19, the connection of the phrase 'builders of the wall' with the context is more difficult to perceive here than in IV,19. A possible explanation of the abrupt introduction of 'builders of the wall' in both texts is that it comprised a well-known allusion within the community, and Schwarz has suggested that both the references go back to a single midrash.[22] Murphy-O'Connor, on the other hand, thinks the two references are independent because in each case they refer to different groups; here rulers, in CD IV Jews in general. His seems too delicate a distinction in this case, and still requires us to accept a coincidence which must be regarded as unlikely. In each passage, surely, the phrase could be taken to apply to those who set the standards of religious life. However, I do agree with Murphy-O'Connor that the term was not originally coined of a particular group, but was used of the Jewish 'establishment.'

Although all of the sentence in VIII,12b-13: XIX,24b-26a is to be regarded as secondary, two stages are to be discerned. The earlier inserted reference to the 'builders of the wall' stated that the anger of God is (was) aroused against them—an awkward anticipation, as I have suggested, of line 18, and also a change of tense from the preceding paragraph, if חרה is to be read as perfect and not participle. Of this earlier insertion the immediate source is probably to be regarded as VIII,18. But there has been a subsequent expansion, taking a slightly different form in each of the two texts. Both Stegemann and Murphy-O'Connor believe that the 'builders of the wall' are not, either in IV,19f. or in the present text, identifiable with a particular group led by an individual. Yet in both passages, as Stegemann has demonstrated, the interpolation of an individual figure, a 'spouter' (identified with the 'Liar'/'Scoffer' in his view) has taken place. Although an investigation of the the origin of such secondary material would be premature at this stage, it can be shown that the connection between the 'builders of the wall' and the 'spouter' is not arbitrary or accidental, but *exegetical*. Mic. 2,11, which is quoted here, provides the source of the 'spouter,' while Mic. 3,5 reads: 'thus says the Lord concerning the prophets, who lead my people astray, who cry 'Peace' when they have something to eat . . .' Compare with this Ezek. 13,8ff.: 'Because you have uttered delusions and seen lies . . . my hand will be against the prophets . . . because they have misled my people, saying 'Peace' . . . when the people build a wall, these prophets daub it with whitewash.' This illustration reminds us that behind the tissue of biblical allusion at the surface of our document lies a further tissue of contextual reference of the kind with which students of the classic rabbinic midrashim—where of course they are explicit—will be quite familiar.

For my own view of the relationship between the references in CD to 'builders of the wall,' see below on VIII,18.

The remainder of in our passage contrasts the 'princes of Judah' with members of the community. Whereas the 'princes of Judah' will be punished by foreign nations, the שבי ישראל will 'dispossess these nations'; whereas the 'princes of Judah' did not detach themselves from the people[23] nor 'depart from the way of traitors,' the שבי ישראל have turned away from the people (contrast VIII,4f. לא סרו מדרך בוגדים and 8 ולא נזרו מעם; is there also a play here on שר/סר, as there was in VII,12f.?). A curiosity of this passage is the phrase כן המשפט 'thus is the case.' Its usage here, apparently as a midrashic formula, is unique in CD. I can only suggest that the author intended a deliberate contrast with VIII,1 or perhaps with VIII,18b; possession of the land is the 'case' (this in in fact Rabin's translation of the word here) with the community, while the wrath of God is the 'case' ('judgment') with the despisers.'

Those here designated by the term שבי ישראל may not be simply all the members of the community. They are described as having 'departed from the way of the people by the love of God for the ראשונים.' Now ראשונים here interprets the 'fathers' of Deut. 9,5//7,8 (the quotation is conflated). Moreover, these ראשונים are set beside הבאים אחריהם, 'those who come after them.' This obviously recalls IV,6ff., where we found that the ראשונים were those who first entered the covenant, and were pardoned by God, with the result that 'those who come after them' will also receive the divine pardon. 'Those who come after' are the converts, and it is they who are quite probably addressed in the present text, who will also receive the 'covenant of the fathers.' There is no reason to suppose that in the material under discussion in this chapter, nearly all of which is secondary to the original *Admonition*, the purpose of that original document has been altered.

Murphy-O'Connor[24] argues that owing to the presence of a qualifying phrase, the connotation of שבי ישראל[25] is different from that in IV,12 and VI,5, and the only translation possible here is 'converts of Israel,' which he applies as a title to Palestinian adherents of the community. But אחריהם must have an antecedent; after whom? Although the text is corrupt in both A and B manuscripts, שבי ישראל can surely be held to apply to the original, or existing community. 'Those who come after them' can hardly be other than the audience of the *Admonition*, and the purpose of this passage is virtually identical to that of IV,6ff. There is a demonstration of the wickedness of outsiders followed by a challenge to join the community and share the inheritance of the ראשונים. Here סרי מדרך העם is used as a deliberate contrast with לא סרו מדרך בוגדים in 4bf. and נזרו מעם in 8. The שרי יהודה are contrasted with the שבי ישראל, and those addressed by the text left to draw their own conclusions. The fact that the community injunctions are implicit in the passage means that those addressed are indeed already among its members. But they need reassurance. They are exhorted here to remember that 'those who come after' will inherit the 'covenant of the fathers' from the שבי ישראל, and not from the 'princes of Judah,' who do not possess it.

Our passage closes neatly by observing that while God loves 'those who come after,' he hates (cf. II,1) those who 'build the wall,' against whom his anger is aroused (cf. I,21; II,21; III,8; V,16). Then the passage concludes with a statement which repeats substantially the original ending of the *Admonition*, but also continues to pick up phrases from all over the *Admonition*—including the 'builders of the wall,' concerning whom it now behoves me to offer the explanation which I promised earlier.

On this subject, I have already supplied what little argumentation is possible. Here is the conclusion baldly presented: the original reference to the 'builders of the wall' is at IV,19 (a reference which has been glossed). It is picked up, as an internal quotation, at VIII,19, which, it has been suggested, belongs to a secondary stratum of the *Admonition*. This reference has subsequently been anticipated in the interpolation of VIII,12-13. Here it was further glossed by Mic. 2,11, by the exegetical process described earlier. This identification brought in also the 'princes of Judah,' and this appears to have prompted the gloss which uses the same Hosea passage at IV,19, as well as the additional gloss identifying צו with the 'Spouter.' This reconstruction supposes a considerable amount of internal exegetical activity of a kind which a close study of the *Admonition* reveals as entirely plausible. I make no apology for the contorted solution; it is in my opinion the simplest consistent solution available, and the truth may indeed be more complicated and even beyond recovery.[26]

Following our conclusion that VII,10-VIII,2a and VIII,2b-18 have been added to an earlier *Admonition*, and that the latter was composed specifically for its present setting, we have now to ask what circumstances may have brought about its composition. Let us begin with VIII,2b-18. We draw attention first to the sharp tone of polemic in this section, directly aimed at contemporary outsiders. Such direct polemic we have not hitherto encountered in the *Admonition*; previous criticism of outsiders has been offered with the specific purpose of persuading would-be converts of the error into which those outside the community have fallen, or rather, been led. The rhetoric here is to the same effect, but is less restrained and emphasises the wilfulness of the 'princes' rather than their blindness, and describes the fate which awaits those outside the community. But it is not difficult to see *how* this polemic works here; it emphasises the distance between these 'princes of Judah' and the men of the community, drawing out the typology used in the previous passage, and assures the men of the community that they have made the right choice. The problem is to understand *why* the criticism appears in this form here.

Murphy-O'Connor has a detailed suggestion as to the origins of the passage, seeing in it a tone of bitter disappointment with a group from whom help might have been expected. He marries the description of the 'princes of Judah' with that of the ruling classes in Ben Sira and identifies them with the 'leaders of Judah' in I Macc 2,15, to whom is opposed the 'covenant of the fathers.' He comments also on the similarity between these criticisms and those directed at the Wicked Priest in 1QpHab. Working from his own view of the origins of the Qumran community, Murphy-O'Connor suggests that at the conclusion of the war with the Syrians and their Jewish protégés in the reign of Antiochus IV, those supporting the Zadokite high priest expected support from the political leaders, the Maccabees. But these betrayed them, and Jonathan assumed the high priestly office; led by the 'Teacher of Righteousness,' the deposed high priest, the Essenes adopted the rallying cry of the Maccabees, 'the covenant of the fathers,' and turned it against those who had coined it. When the Teacher and his followers reached Qumran, a document criticising the

Maccabees was adapted for use against apostates.

The suggestion is supported by some impressive argumentation,[27] but it depends quite substantially on a particular reconstruction of Qumran origins. Moreover, I do not find a tone of 'bitter disappointment' here, as Murphy-O'Connor does, nor any suggestion that the 'princes of Judah' had been expected to give any support to the community. On the contrary, in IV,12bff. we have been led to believe that the community has given up the Jewish establishment for lost. There is certainly nothing in the *Admonition* leading one to infer that the community expected official support. Even more telling is the objection that no criticism of defiling the sanctuary or usurping the high priesthood is made against the 'princes of Judah.' Indeed, there is nothing sufficiently characteristic in the criticisms to permit us to suggest with any confidence what, if any, specific grudges may have led to the composition of this passage. As has been observed, the burden of the criticisms made in our passage is that the 'princes of Judah' do not behave as members of the community do—and there is no implication that they were expected to have done so. However, the addition to an already existing *Admonition* of this direct attack on the behaviour of the 'princes' and the strong contrast between them and the שבי ישראל may imply some exercise of authority on the part of these 'princes of Judah' which had an adverse effect on the stability of the community. If Murphy-O'Connor's suggestion of a Palestinian setting for the passage is taken up, it may be speculated that the community was engaged in preaching its views and gaining adherents in the vicinity of Jerusalem, which incurred the antagonism of the established authorities. Certainly, the most natural application of the term 'princes of Judah' is the literal one, and such an identification itself partly explains the presence of our passage. Overt hostility on the part of the authorities could well threaten the resolve of potential converts and the loyalty of recent entrants, who might consider revoking their commitment. While the earlier parts of the *Admonition* do not necessarily imply that the community had returned to Judah (although earlier references to Judah read well in this context), this passage may very plausibly be understood in the context of a (recently acquired?) Judaean environment. The same may be said of the preceding passage, VII,10-VIII,2, in which Ephraim represents the Judaean establishment whose power and authority are thereby offered as proof of their ultimate fate. V,11b-15a which deals with the 'builders of the wall,' describes them as 'opening their mouth against the ordinances of

God's covenant.' I have earlier suggested the possibility that this passage might be secondary; if this were the case, it could well be assigned to the process which has appended VII,10-VIII,18a to the *Admonition*.

To conclude, then: the expanded *Warnings* encourage (newly-acquired?) members to think of their plight in terms of Judah and Ephraim, and consider the fate of the latter; they then remind them that there can be no compromise with the 'princes of Judah' and that these 'princes' are doomed to punishment. If the stage passed where this predicament was keenly felt, and an internal crisis developed, it is logical that the invective here would be redirected at the new opponents, the new source of threat, at the new alternative claims to authority. We shall presently argue that the final section of the *Admonition* betrays such a split, and introduces us to a new community. In the light of this finding it is possible to endorse Murphy-O'Connor's contention that the B text of VIII,2b-18 has reorientated the original text, as represented in ms. A, towards apostates. For additions such as ברית תשובה in XIX,16 and ובכל החלכים אחריהם in XIX,31f. are plausibly explained in this way. Such a reorientation, if it has taken place, may then be ascribed to the new community which in the next section of the *Admonition* shows itself especially concerned with the problem of defection and the nature of its relationship towards the parent community which produced the original *Admonition*.

## A note on VIII,20

This passage exists only in ms. A. Does it belong with the material preceding or following, or is it a fragment of an independent section? The first of these alternatives is rather unlikely, since VIII,19 is almost certainly the ending of the preceding section. The following section is introduced by a redactional וכן in the B text; in the A text it is left without any explicit conection to what precedes it. While we cannot be sure that the beginning of this next section has not been truncated, it seems self-contained and no plausible connection with VIII,20 can be perceived. The second alternative is therefore also unlikely, and VIII,20 is accordingly to be regarded as an independent statement.

The case of Elisha and Gehazi referred to is almost certainly the biblical episode in II Kings 5,26-7, where the servant had betrayed his master and was afflicted with the disease of Naaman. This is by no means inapplicable to those who abandon the teachings of their master and incur the punishment of those with whom they wrongly have dealings. In fact, the allusion fits extremely well into the theme of the preceding section. The actual words of Elisha in v. 27 are 'therefore the leprosy of Naaman shall cleave to you and to your descendants for ever.' Could the comment possibly be a misplaced gloss on VIII,4 'the defect shall cleave (רבק, as here)'? The Baruch episode is more difficult. Some scholars, e.g. Dupont-Sommer and Maier, propose a reference to a pseudepigraphic work now lost. Rabin and Cothenet allude to Jer. 45,4-5 and Schwarz to Jer. 36,5-7.[28] If we expect another example of a disciple betraying his master and dealing with others (even foreigners?) Jer. 45,5 is the only possibility: 'and do you seek great things for yourself? Seek them not, for behold, I am bringing evil on all flesh.' The words are addressed to Baruch, and possibly generated a haggadah about their origin. It is nonetheless difficult to see Baruch as an unfaithful servant. We cannot in the last resort determine whether this passage is a fragment of larger statement about treacherous servants, or a gloss. There are enough contextual links to prevent us from dismissing it too readily as a mere stray insertion.[29] Nevertheless, the B text has managed without it, and whether we like it or not, so shall we.

# V THE 'NEW COVENANT': XIX,33b-XX,34

*Summary:* The section consists mostly of a series of condemnations of apostates. These presuppose a different community from that of the rest of the *Admonition*, characterised by adherence to a Teacher. The first (XIX,33b-XX,1a) is a general condemnation which 'excommunicates' all those who had once joined the 'covenant in the land of Damascus' and subsequently left. In XX,8b-13 those remaining who apostasise in their hearts are compared with those who have physically left. XX,14-22a is not a condemnation, but a reassurance to the community which has just lost its Teacher. XX,22b-27a concerns the status of a group whose admission to the community is in question, and finally, XX,27b-34 is a reminder of the requirements of the faithful community member and of his reward. XX,1b-8a is a later insertion dealing with rebellion within the community to be dealt with by temporary disciplining. This section has been added to the original *Admonition* later than VII,10-VIII,21, and it is to be attributed to the Qumran community. We must therefore consider the B text of CD (and perhaps also the A text) to represent a *Qumranic recension* of the document.

The material in this section deals with several different topics. We begin our analysis by distinguishing in XIX,33-XX,13a three distinct warnings, marked by the use of similar introductory formulae:

| | | |
|---|---|---|
| XIX,33-XX,1a | וכן | those who entered the covenant and left |
| XX,1b-8a | וכן המשפט | all 'men of perfect holiness' who disobey |
| XX,8b-13a | כמשפט הזה | whoever despises 'the former and the latter' |

Each of the groups incurs a specific threat or condemnation, but *none of them is a threat of eschatological destruction*; they are instead threats of partial or complete *exclusion from the community*. This feature marks an important distinction from the warning of the original *Admonition* in VII,9 and also of the supplementary warnings of VII,10-VIII,19; and hence we should not assume an intrinsic connection between the preceding criticism of the 'princes of Judah' and these paragraphs, despite the introductory formulae which recur in slightly varying form. The formulae found in this section are in fact redactional seams designed to integrate it with the preceding warnings directed at outsiders, and to attach this new material more firmly to the *Admonition*.

Beyond this division into three units, the structure and intention of the material is not so clear. XX,13b-22a presupposes 8b-13a; however, it does not seem to be a warning to apostates but a calculation about their life expectancy. XX,17b is a statement about the members of the community, followed in 22b by a ruling about a group who are (or were part of) the 'house of Peleg.' Finally, from 23b to the end of the *Admonition*, there is another statement about the members of the community.

Stegemann[1] is content to present the material here as a series of independent sources that have been redacted—whether to some particular plan or purpose he does not consider. Murphy-O'Connor, on the other hand, treats the whole of XIX,33-XX,34 as a single document which contains two interpolations at XX,1b-8a and 13b-17a.[2] The material undoubtedly begins by continuing and developing the warnings of the preceding section; it addresses at the outset not *potential* but *actual* apostates; to be precise, those who are deemed never to have been part of the new community. But the arrangement and purpose of the remaining material is not transparent. A fruitful line of approach is to consider the apostasy which the contents imply and to inquire what may have brought it about. At the heart of the apostasy which occupies the opening passages of this section lies the figure of the 'Teacher'; it is obedience to him which constitutes belonging to the community; he is the source of authority. In the opening passage (XX,1) it is stated that only during the lifetime of this Teacher can apostates (or those deemed to be apostates) 'return.' The death of the Teacher therefore brings about a new state of affairs, not only for these 'apostates' but also for his followers, for whom a new system of internal discipline is needed to replace his authority. Most if not all of the material which does not comprise condemnation of apostasy deals with the twin issues of reassurance and community discipline directly provoked by the death of the Teacher.

Apostasy and the death of the Teacher therefore emerge as the two issues which together account for the presence and arrangement of the material in this section of the *Admonition*. Together with other considerations, these two issues lead us to the fundamental conclusion that *the community behind all the material in this section is a different one from that which produced the rest of the Admonition.* In the first place, as has been remarked, the new community has as the basis of its identity and at the centre of its legal structure the figure and authority of a Teacher. This figure does not appear elsewhere in the *Admonition*. True, a 'teacher of righteousness' is mentioned in the opening discourse, but *if this reference is original*[3] it certainly cannot indicate same figure, because there he belongs to the origins of the community which are placed in the Exile. If both references are to the same person, on the other hand, then the earlier one in CD I has to be seen as secondary. I shall develop this point later in the context of the redaction of the *Admonition* as a whole. But we may note for the present that elsewhere in the *Admonition* the original lawgiver of the community is called the 'Interpreter of the Law' whose halachah has been observed for generations (VI,7f.); there is no suggestion that additional requirements, the teachings of a Teacher, or indeed loyalty to an individual figure, are imposed on the community, but only the laws which its founders set up. Beside this is the belief (VI,11) that the laws of the community remain in force until 'one who will teach righteousness' shall arrive 'at the end of days.'

It is consistent to posit that the presence of this Teacher explains the concern with apostasy in our material. Elswhere in the *Admonition* apostasy is mentioned only as a possibility; this may be because the document was designed for new members, but more probably apostasy was simply not a major problem. For the community which produced this supplement, however, the situation is different: the material is concerned hardly at all with Judaism outside, only with those who were, or should have been, among its numbers. What is referred to, of course, is apostasy from the *new* community, namely rejection of its Teacher. In XX,11 such apostates are called 'men of scoffing' and in I,13 an individual 'Scoffer' is identified, through secondary expansion or re-interpretation, as an opponent and contemporary of the Teacher of Righteousness. Both these figures appear in the Qumran *pesharim*, giving further support to the view that the community reflected in this part of the *Admonition* is the one which lived at Qumran.

Further evidence of a new community behind this section of CD is the presence of some new vocabulary. This community uses the term יחד of itself; it employs שוב frequently and in a distinctive way; it refers to the '*new* covenant in the land of Damascus'; and it also seems to employ the word 'righteousness' (צדק) more frequently than elsewhere in the *Admonition*, and in a restrictive, sectarian sense.

On the whole, therefore, Murphy-O'Connor's analysis leads in the right direction; the material here is not arranged haphazardly, but is linked together by similar basic concerns. But what fundamentally holds it together is its provenance, which is not the community of the rest of the *Admonition* but a splinter-group. Hence the following analysis yields conclusions rather different from Murphy-O'Connor's.

*Warning to members of the parent community: XIX,33b-XX,1a*

This first passage condemns 'all the men who have entered the new covenant in the land of Damascus' ושבו ויבגדו ויסורו מבאר החיים. Most commentators, taking the covenant throughout CD to be that of the Qumran community, translate שבו either as equivalent to 'again' (Rabin) or as 'turned back' (Charles, Dupont-Sommer), while Murphy-O'Connor reads 'and returned, but betrayed...' since he believes that the covenant in question is the one forged in the Babylonian exile, the original 'land of Damascus.'[4] In favour of Murphy-O'Connor's view is that שוב without qualification does not connote defection, while to take it as giving the sense of 'again' implies *two* betrayals! Yet the use of שוב in this section makes it almost a motif: XX,10bf. כמשפט רעיהם; אנשי המלחמה אשר שבו [ע]ם; XX,14 איש הכזב [ע]ם אשר שבו עם אנשי הלצון; XX,20 also has שבתם but with a lacuna on either side; XX,23 וישבו עוד אל; XX,32 ולא ישיבו. It can indeed be argued that שוב is used in this section without qualification to connote defection from the community, so that Murphy-O'Connor's objection against such a translation here is invalid. 'Turned back' is not an inaccurate rendering, but does not convey what I suspect is a technical usage for the new community, 'apostasise.'

Two features of this new community, the fact that it calls itself the '*new* covenant in the land of Damascus,' and its adherence to a 'Teacher,' both suggest that it has developed *out of the community responsible for the original Admonition*. Few commentators are prepared to regard the 'new covenant' as anything other than a variant term for the covenant of the rest of the *Admonition*. But the distinction between the two is not a quibble. There is a very sound basis for it in XX,12, where the phrase ברית...אשר קימו באריץ דמשק ('covenant... which they swore in the land of Damascus') is glossed as והוא ברית החדשה, 'and that is the new covenant.' I cannot explain this form of words except on the supposition that the phrase 'covenant in the land of Damascus' was by itself inappropriate or misleading and called for closer definition. If the word 'new' was added as a necessary qualification of the original term, it follows that the new covenant *is not associated with Damascus in the same way as the original 'Damascus covenant'*; there is no need to look for a new 'Damascus' or even the old one, in connection with this new covenant, for the ancient nomenclature is retained in order to stress that this is not a different covenant, while at the same time the word 'new' claims that it must not be equated strictly with the previous one, which has been superseded (or fulfilled) by the Teacher. We should ideally translate the phrase 'new covenant-in-the-land-of-Damascus.'[5]

Now, the fact that 'new covenant' is a gloss on 'covenant in the land of Damascus' at XX,12 shows that at one point the older terminology persisted.[6] This implies that at an early stage the new community continued to regard itself as the *true* community of the (original) Damascus covenant. Only at a secondary stage, and probably as a result of onflict within the parent community, did the new community define itself as the community of the *new* covenant, in order to distinguish itself from the continuing community which clung to the original 'Damascus covenant' and did not accept the Teacher. Exactly the same process is observable in the case of the early church, when it ceased to regard itself as Israel, with a special relationship towards and *within* Judaism, and, acknowledging itself as a distinct entity, came to regard itself as the 'new Israel,' fulfilling but also superseding the 'old covenant' with the 'old Israel.'

The relevance of this deduction for the present text is as follows. If the qualification 'new' was introduced here *after* the condemnation was formulated, then it originally condemned those *who had entered the 'Damascus' covenant*; in other words, it was directed against all those members of the community who refused to accept the Teacher, and only after the Teacher's adherents had acknowledged themselves as members of a 'new covenant' was the word 'new' inserted into the text. If this is the case, those condemned had not 'entered a *new* covenant' at all. As the text now stands, however, the phrase 'new covenant' suggests, and probably wrongly, that *those condemned had once been members of the Teacher's community*. We cannot be certain that this passage was originally a condemnation of those who simply remained in the 'Damascus' covenant and refused to accept the Teacher, but I regard it as probable that such a category of persons must have been addressed by the new community; a specific statement of *their* status *vis-à-vis* the community of the Teacher must have been expressed.

In my opinion, then, those originally condemned here are to be construed as members of the *parent* community, and not as erstwhile members of the *new* community. Only at a secondary stage has the addition of 'new' redirected (possibly unintentionally) the condemnation to those members of the *Teacher's* community who have apostasised, at a time when the original targets of condemnation were no longer in existence or relevant, the split between the two communities having receded into the past.

Membership of the community is emphatically denied to those addressed here; their names are to be struck from the record. 'Excommunication' may be an appropriate description of the procedure. But the situation apparently envisaged is surely so obvious that it does not require to be specifically legislated for. Those who have turned their backs on the (new) covenant have surely already excommunicated themselves, and little would be served by such a formal exclusion; at all events the matter is hardly of sufficient importance to warrant a paragraph in this document. Surely the situation is not as simple as at first sight appears. In speaking of the deletion of names from the register of the community, is this new community claiming to speak with the legitimate voice *of the old one?* Is it the register of names *of the whole 'Damascus' community* (to which the *Admonition* previously referred[7]) which is meant? I believe this makes better sense of the text; it seems to me more likely that the followers of the Teacher are claiming the right to deny membership of the Damascus covenant to those who reject their Teacher rather than merely to those who have left the Teacher's community. In other words, this text claims that *only those who accept the Teacher are truly members of the Damascus covenant.* We are dealing with a divided community in which we hear the voice of one faction, who accept the Teacher, rejecting the other, who do not, as apostate. Their rejection is construed as defection, and represented by the use of the verb שוב. There can only be one 'Damascus' covenant community, and that is the (new) one which the Teacher has established; such is the standpoint of the present section of the *Admonition*.

Consistent with my interpretation is the sectarian claim of continuity with the original Damascus covenant which is implicit in the phrase 'departed from the well of living water,' for this I take to be an allusion to CD III,15-17 and VI,4. Those who reject the Teacher are accused of having thereby rejected the law of the community. But they are nevertheless not condemned in the same terms as 'those who reject the ordinances' at VII,9 (VIII,2) and VIII,19. Their rejection is qualified, and expressed in terms influenced by Ezek. 13,9. The same passage is the source of the phrase 'builders of the wall,' and I have already observed that this phrase earier in the *Admonition* has been glossed so as to refer to a group led by an individual, a Scoffer or Spouter, who is elsewhere (in CD I,14 and the Qumran *pesharim*) identified as an opponent of the Teacher. He is also presumably the איש הכזב to whom the 'men of scoffing' were drawn (XX, 14f.).

The Teacher is here called the מרה היחיד, which is to be translated either as 'unique' or 'beloved' Teacher, or as 'Teacher of the community.' I incline to the last of these because אנשי היחיד in XX,32 seems to mean 'men of the community.' The fact that in 1QS יחד denotes the community lends some support to this preference.[8] The individual in question is called 'teacher of righteousness' in XX,31, and I suggest that this title is to be interpreted in the light of VI,11, where one 'who will teach righteousness' emerges as a figure expected by the 'Damascus' community to appear 'at the end of days.' It is reasonable, then, to conclude that the Teacher mentioned here *claimed to be that figure.* This claim explains the belief of his followers that they represented the original 'Damascus' covenant, and that their Teacher had authority equivalent to—if not greater than—the law originally instituted at the foundation of that covenant by the 'Interpreter of the Law.' As a parallel to this process one may instance the claim of the Church that Jesus was the Messiah, by virtue of which faith in him entailed a revaluation of the Mosaic law. Although this is, I think, one of the more significant parallels to be drawn between the Teacher and Jesus,—and their respective communities[9]—I do not imply that the two figures are to be identified. There are too many problems at present in the way of this suggestion, and although I do not think that we know as much as we think about the origins of the Qumran community, it seems at present unlikely that this identification can plausibly be sustained.

The Ezekiel text (13,9) quoted in this passage carries three component sanctions: exclusion from the 'council of my people,' non-mention in the 'book of the house of Israel' and non-entry into the land. The absence of the last of these in the present passage does not necessarily mean it is overlooked, for any survey of the dominant texts in CD, as well as its ideology, will reveal that the idea of rightful possession of the land lies constantly in the background—when, that is, it is not in the foreground (see for example VIII,14-15). סוד is frequently found in the Qumran literature, and there is ample evidence that, like the parent community of CD, this community did keep a list of names of its members. But סוד occurs elsewhere *in CD* only once, where it means 'secret' (XIV,10). Finally, XX,19 is supporting evidence that this community did have such a list of names, a list which contained only its own members from the time of the Teacher and not those of members of the parent community (see below). Nevertheless, I have already suggested that *originally* the list of members to which the text referred may have been that of members of the 'Damascus' covenant, and not followers of the Teacher.

What is meant by the phrase 'from the day when the teacher . . . was gathered in until the coming of the Messiah of Israel and Aaron'? Stegemann and Murphy-O'Connor agree that the phrase means a second chance for these apostates, though Murphy-O'Connor acknowledges that such a doctrine is at variance with Essene teachings elsewhere, and therefore suspects that the text has been tampered with. With the majority of commentators, I am unable to read this meaning into the text; the sense, as I see it, is that the coming of the Messiah brings the final judgment, by which time it will be too late for these men to join the community, and they will be judged as outsiders. Murphy-O'Connor finds the starting-point of the period of exclusion rather problematic, and assumes that during his lifetime the Teacher would have had the authority to readmit these apostates while after his death his community would not arrogate this authority to itself. A simpler explanation exists: the only chance these men are offered is to accept the authority of the Teacher while he is still alive, and one may assume that the members of the Teacher's community did not believe that his death would predate the coming of the Messiah by any great length of time, since CD VI,11 explains that the 'one who teaches righteousness' will arise 'at the end of days.' Indeed, I suggested earlier that the 'one who teaches righteousness' may have been viewed as the Messiah, a view perhaps modified after his death. According to his followers, this figure had indeed arrived, and his followers are offering to members of the parent community who have refused to accept him the same kind of challenge which the parent community adopted towards would-be converts in IV,10f.: the time for decision is brief! It will be argued that this new community both reapplied and also expanded parts of the original *Admonition*, a process which must be understood as the expression of a claim to be the true representatives of the 'Damascus' covenant. It is on this basis, of course, that the new community of the Teacher continued to use and redact (and perhaps considerably expand if the very limited evidence from the Qumran caves has been correctly interpreted) the 'Damascus Document.' The result, as revealed by the Cairo mss., at any rate, is a new 'Damascus covenant,' a new list of names, and a new eschatological timetable, in which the 'age of wrath' is redefined, and the exilic origin of the community obscured by more recent events in which the appearance of the new community figures. (See the following chapter for an amplification of these remarks.)

The material under review in this chapter, then, spoke originally of members of the parent community who had refused to accept the claims of the Teacher to be the expected eschatological figure, but who remained within the 'Damascus' covenant as they saw it. In the eyes of the new community, only acceptance of the Teacher's authority *during his lifetime* will ensure that these men are counted among the saved at the 'gathering in of the people.' The phrase 'new covenant in the land of Damascus' betrays a consciousness of formal separation, and its use here has the effect of reapplying the warning to erstwhile members of the new community.

How can the excommunication announced in this passage be effective once the Teacher has in fact departed? And what happens to members of the Teacher's community who offend without specifically rejecting the Teacher? The interpolated material which immediately follows answers the second problem, while XX,13b-22a answers the first.

*Discipline within the new community: XX,1b-8*

XX,1b-8a is out of place in many respects, and is to be regarded as an interpolation. Nevertheless, its presence helps to confirm the identity of this new community with the community of 1QS. Murphy-O'Connor has observed that 'nothing similar to the vocabulary of this passage is found elsewhere in CD' and 'had CD XX,1c-8a been found as an isolated fragment it would have been presumed that it belonged to the *Rule*, both because of its vocabulary, and because this attitude of concern for an erring member is found only in this section of the *Rule* [= 1QS VIII].'[10] In regarding this passage as interpolated, Murphy-O'Connor concurs with Denis, Schwarz and Stegemann, and the conclusion is surely a sound one. The passage is to be regarded, then, as later than the surrounding material, and its contents do not contribute to our understanding of the growth of CD except in confirming the identity of the new community. No further comment on it is required in the present study.

### Warning to covert traitors: XX,8b-13a

The following passage is another critique of other apostates, but, as Murphy-O'Connor has perceived, not the same group as XIX,33b-XX,1a. This group consists not of *actual*, but of *potential* apostates, and the fact that they are singled out in this way betrays the insecurity of the new community. The opening redactional formula כמשפט הזה asserts that those who have defected within their hearts are no better than those who have physically left; it can hardly refer back to those mentioned in 1b-8a, which is a major argument for that passage's interpolation. In fact, the connection is explicitly made in 10b-11a: 'they shall receive the same judgment as their companions who turned back (שוב) with the "men of scoffing" . . .'

Those now criticised are כל המואם בראשונים ובאחרונים. מאם is transferred from VII,9 and VIII,19; the important question here is *what* is rejected, for what is rejected tells us more about the character of the new community. There are broadly two alternative translations of בראשונים ובאחרונים, either associating it with the subject of the verb ('among the former and the latter'), or making it the direct object of the verb, namely what is rejected. The first alternative is possible, it seems to me, only if the 'former' are members of the parent community. It can hardly mean a group in the past, as it does elsewhere in the *Admonition*, and the only relevant group who could be plausibly regarded as 'former' would be members of the parent community. But since these have been treated in a preceding warning, there is no point in including them here. Moreover, such men are probably those identified as followers of the 'men of scoffing,' to whom those addressed by the present warning are compared. One must therefore favour the latter translation, as do both Stegemann and Murphy-O'Connor.

However, it is surprising that no commentator who translates in this way has commented upon the identical phrase in Jub. 1,26 (Charles' translation):

And do thou write down for thyself all these words which I

declare unto thee on this mountain, the first and the last,
which shall come to pass in all the divisions of the days in the
law . . . until I descend and dwell with them throughout
eternity.

In Jubilees, the phrase 'the first and the last' may mean either
'totality' or 'from beginning to end,' but also it may mean 'what has
been revealed at first' (Torah) and 'what has been revealed subsequently'
(the teaching of the book of Jubilees). The second interpretation seems
to me more attractive as an explanation of the book of Jubilees itself,
and certainly it makes the best sense of the phrase in our passage, since
we are looking to identify something exclusive to the new community.
Both Jubilees and the new community offer what are in effect new
dispensations, yet both claim the authority of an earlier dispensation.
In both cases the 'former' and the 'latter' are to be *distinguished*, but
not *separated* from each other. I hold, then, that the 'former' are the
teachings of the parent community and the 'latter' those of the
Teacher, agreeing with the view advocated by Murphy-O'Connor,
who points to XX,32 where after the 'former ordinances' the text
mentions the 'voice of the Teacher of Righteousness.'[11]

But what are the 'former'? In IV,8 we met the פרוש התורה אשר התוסרו
בו הראשונים, the 'details of the law in which the founders were
instructed,' where the stress was on the continuity between the rules
by which the founders of the community lived and those to be followed
by 'those who came after them.' But ראשונים is more often used in the
*Admonition* of the members of the first covenant which came to grief at
the Exile, and amid the ruins of which the covenant with the remnant
was instituted. The ambiguous use of the term ראשונים in the
*Admonition* reverberates in our passage. In the first place, the 'former'
are the laws on which the Damascus covenant was founded, by the
ראשונים. But also, building on the other meaning of ראשונים, a
typological possibility has been created: where the original *Admonition*
contrasted the (Mosaic) covenant of the ראשונים with the covenant of
Damascus, the followers of the Teacher can contrast the (Damascus)
covenant of the ראשונים with the *new* 'covenant in the land of
Damascus.' Moreover, this contrast can reflect the same ambiguity of
supersession and continuity which characterised the relationship
between the 'covenant of the ראשונים' and that of the community.[12]
(We may compare the ambiguity to be found in the attitude towards
the Old Testament adopted in the New Testament.) Here, then,

ראשונים applies to the dispensation which governed the original Damascus covenant, which has now been superseded, or perhaps one should say 'fulfilled' by the addition of the 'new' dispensation brought by the Teacher.

A further typological use of the original *Admonition* is exposed in the warning itself, which is expressed with the aid of two allusions, Ezek. 14,3 (note the proximity to Ezek 13!) and CD II,17ff. (specifically III,5.11). These allusions make two points. The Ezekiel text refers to the elders of Israel who come to consult the prophet, and who, the prophet is made to know, are secretly idolaters. The word 'heart' provides a link with the allusion from the *Admonition* where 'stubbornness of their heart' denotes the recurrent sin of pre-exilic Israel (it was also used in VIII,8 of the 'princes of Judah'), as the result of which God's anger caused the desolation of the land and the abrogation of the covenant with the old Israel. Would-be traitors of the new community are therefore being invited to see themselves in this light, and in particular to contemplate their corresponding fate. The reapplication of terms and motifs in the *Admonition* by the new community is an important feature of this part of the *Admonition*, and indeed reveals a fundamental characteristic of the relationship between the 'old' and 'new' communities.

Both Stegemann and Murphy-O'Connor find difficulty with 10b-13a, which opens with a variation of the introductory כמשפט formula in 8b and closes with a threat very similar to that in 10a. Stegemann regards these lines as comprising a separate source; for him 8b-10a concerns outsiders, and only 10b-13a insiders. But he is unduly distracted by the recurrence of כמשפט, or perhaps his exegesis is again too mechanical. In any case, he does not pause to ask why a critique of outsiders should be included at this point. Murphy-O'Connor, on the other hand, observes that the text explicitly equates the judgment of covert with overt apostates. In fact, the two instances of כמשפט in this passages are not identical: the first conforms to the formula with which most of the warnings are introduced, and may be redactional; the second כמשפט has to be construed with the verb שפט: 'they shall be judged by the same judgment.'

However, difficulties remain with Murphy-O'Connor's interpretation of this passage. First, the repetition of 'they have no share in the House of the Law' is awkward if it applies to the same group—especially since the penalty for covert traitors is worse in that their families also incur penalty. Second, the phrase 'for they spoke error'—

תעה is also used as a recurring motif in II,14ff—suggests *overt* and not the *covert* rebellion which Murphy-O'Connor correctly sees as the issue here, highlighted by the word 'heart' in lines 9 and 10. There is an interpretation, however, which resolves both of these difficulties. The punishment of the covert traitors is to relinquish their share in the 'House of the Law' (on this phrase, see below). This penalty is then explained on the basis of an existing judgment: they are to be judged like (כמשפט) those who have physically left. It is *these* who had actually spoken out against the covenant (and are the subject of רבר), as a result of which *they and their whole families* were banned from the community, a sanction which was only possible because they had in fact physically left, and their defection was public. With a *covert* traitor, the treason might or might not be felt to be less and therefore deserving of a more lenient penalty, but the real reason for the reprieve of the families is that families cannot be held to share in the responsibility for covert treason because such an offence is private to the individual, and may be unknown to his family.

'Having a share in the House of the Law' may, on this view, be equated with not being inscribed in the register (XIX,35). But, again obviously, one cannot strike a covert traitor's name from the register until and unless he is discovered! The 'House of the Law' must refer to the community itself, and the word 'house' may be inspired by the 'sure house' of III,19. The use of the word 'law' may be polemical, claiming that only this new community observes the law. Rabin and Murphy-O'Connor have also pointed to eschatological dimensions of this word. Its appearance here may reflect the phrase 'former and latter' in 8b, for the issue in this passage is in fact acceptance of the two components of the community law, without which one cannot be said to be fulfilling Torah.

We need not interpret the accusation of 'rejecting the former and latter' as implying that the *former* laws were ever rejected. The point is surely that of accepting or rejecting both equally. While some members of the community may have abandoned it in favour of the wider Jewish community, it seems more likely that the real danger recognised in this passage is further defection from the community of the Teacher to the original 'Damascus' community, to which some 'defection' has already taken place. The warning is therefore against adhering to the 'former' while secretly rejecting the 'latter.'

This seems to be confirmed by the phrase על חוקי הצדק, 'against the righteous ordinances,' in 11b and the addition of the word ואמנה in 12a.

The use of צדק in this final section of CD is markedly more frequent than in the rest of the *Admonition* and I would suspect that it has a sectarian connotation for the new community: the חוקי הצדק are the teachings of the מורה צדק. אמונה occurs once elsewhere in CD XIII,16 to refer to some kind of commercial agreement. What does it mean here? I think a fairly confident answer can be given. The wording 'rejected the covenant which they established in the land of Damascus' would have been quite acceptable to followers of the Teacher, who regarded themselves as members of the true 'Damascus covenant.' But the original covenant, as presented in the *Admonition*, comprised only the 'former' laws, and not the 'latter.' Such a rejoinder could not be allowed to those here criticised, who privately rejected the 'latter' rules of the new community and believed the 'former' laws to be sufficient. To condemn this attitude it was necessary for some qualification to be introduced to the phrase 'covenant in the land of Damascus,' and hence the reason for the addition of אמונה (or perhaps האמנת).[13] Apparently, however, even this qualification was not accepted as adequate, and the gloss והוא ברית החדשה, to which I alluded earlier, was added. One may speculate that the addition of ואמנה (which, once the point of it has been realised, is preferable to האמנת) issued from a period before the community adopted the usage 'new covenant.'

### Discipline after the death of the Teacher: XX,13b-22a

Both Stegemann and Murphy-O'Connor find it impossible to accept the unity of this passage and regard the first part (13c-15b) as secondary. Murphy-O'Connor adds 15c-17a as a further addition, since ובקץ ההוא must refer to 13c-15b and cannot refer back to the preceding passage. But in actual fact the connection between 15c-17 and 17bff. is extremely strong, and the whole passage provides a continuous and coherent argument. The quotation of Hos. 3,4 אין מוכח בצדק, 'no one to rebuke in righteousness,' is developed in 17b-18: since there will be no one to rebuke, each will have to undertake that responsibility with regard to his brother, to *make him righteous*. In the light of this analysis, the unity of 13b-22a need not be doubted. Its opening lines suggest that the death of the 'teacher of righteousness' is the key to what follows. The period following his demise is one of uncertainty and crisis, a time when the wrath of God is aroused, since we are now in the shadow of the eschaton which the arrival of the Teacher was held to announce, the period during which the 'apostates' of XIX,35-XX,1a could not be admitted to the community. During this period, according to our passage, there will be no guidance, and the community will have to fend for itself, relying on itself and on God. The absence of the Teacher during this period and in this passage is conspicuous.

If the view is correct which sees this material as later than XIX,33-XX,1a, when the Teacher was still alive, we are able to assign certain developments to the interim. In the first place, we now have mentioned a 'Man of the Lie,' to whom the 'men of scoffing' defected (שבו). Stegemann regards the purpose of this 'interpolation' (as he sees it) as the association of the 'men of scoffing' with the 'Man of the Lie.' The latter phrase is actually unique in CD, although ממיף and כזב are conjoined at I,15, VIII,13 and XIX,26. The introduction of this individual into CD is the work of the new community, inasmuch as he is associated, both as the Man of the Lie here and as the Spouter elsewhere, with the Teacher. Moreover, following Stegemann, we have established the secondary nature of references to him in the original *Admonition*. In I,15 'Man of Scoffing' probably reflects another attempt to associate the titles 'Man of the Lie' and 'men of scoffing'; this passage provides us with a clear example of reinterpretation of parts of CD taking place within CD itself (see the next chapter). I agree with Stegemann's conclusions regarding the secondary nature of all the allusions, but distinguish between the interpolations within the original *Admonition* and the present passage which is an integral part of a supplement to that original *Admonition*. For Stegemann, the whole *Admonition* is Qumranic; in the interpretation developed here the Qumran community is responsible only for the present recension. Such an intepretation offers a very much more plausible explanation of the secondary material than Stegemann is able to provide. In conclusion, then, there is no reason why a reference to such figures in this Qumranic appendix to the *Admonition* should be regarded as secondary to the material in which it is embedded.

The calculation of the period of forty years is another new development of the interim. Although, I have suggested, the death of the Teacher was expected to precede by only a short period the arrival of the Messiah, the present calculation may reflect some initial doubt. It can be seen in two ways: some have combined it with the 390 years of I,5 to produce a complete span of 490 years from the time of Nebuchadnezzar, allowing forty years for the activity of the Teacher $(390 + 20 + 40 + 40 = 490)$, giving the ideal ten jubilees or seventy 'weeks of years,' while others suggest that the period of forty years here is dictated by the biblical allusion on which it is based, Deut. 2,14 (cf. 1,35), where the men of the wilderness generation had to expire before entry to Canaan was permitted. There is no reason why both answers cannot be correct. We have already given grounds to suspect a jubilee calendar at work within the CD community,[14] and the figures 390 and 20 glossed into CD I could well be the outcome of such calculations. But it is the typological significance of the 40 years which deserves our attention. The 'men of war' of Deut. 1,26 'rebelled against the commandment of the Lord' and would not go to occupy the land. The application of this biblical context to the situation of the new community is not difficult to appreciate. Those who rebelled and left the community must be allowed to die before the new, purged congregation of Israel can fulfil the divine promise of occupying the land as the rightful Israel. This typology is quite possibly inspired by a passage in the original *Admonition*, III,7ff., where the refusal at Kadesh (Deut 1,19, the same episode) led to the arousal of God's anger. Here the old community/old Israel perspective is reshaped into a new community/old community perspective, at least if the Man of the Lie is a leader of the original community, which seems a reasonable hypothesis for the present. The leading astray of old Israel which produced a previous divine punishment is now repeated in the leading astray of the new Israel (the community of CD) by the Man of the Lie. The new community sees itself re-enacting the rise of the old community. Such observations allow us now to appreciate the intention of the secondary passage in I,13b-18a with its focus on the 'Scoffer' who 'spouted lies.' The difficulty which interpreters have experienced in deciding whether to identify this figure as one of Israel's past or the community's past is resolved if our analysis of the present passage is correct: the ambiguity is deliberate and serves a typological function.

So the death of the Teacher ushers in the 'age of wrath' during which a new roster of names will be kept. 15b introduces what can only be described as a 'targumic' citation of Hos. 3,4 which refers both back to the 'age of wrath' and forward to the status of the leaderless community. The 'king,' 'ruler' and 'judge' can be no other than the Teacher, and once this is seen, the logic of the ensuing quotation from Isaiah is not difficult to follow. The context of this quotation, Is. 59,20, is worth providing:

And the Redeemer shall come to Zion and unto those who

turn from transgression in Jacob, says the Lord. As for me, this is my covenant with them, says the Lord; my spirit which is upon thee, and my words which I have put in thy mouth shall not depart out of thy mouth, nor out of the mouth of thy seed, nor out of the mouth of thy seed's seed, says the Lord, from henceforth and for ever.

The biblical text reinforces what we have seen to be the theme of our passage. Applied to the Teacher of Righteousness, it means that his words are not only in his mouth, but also in the mouth of his descendants, who are his community and also 'those who turn from the transgression of Jacob.' *The words of the Teacher will therefore live within the community for ever.* The new community also hereby acquires for itself a name which is derived from, but also distinct from, a name of its parent community, perhaps another symptom of its estrangement from that parent: it does not refer to itself as שבי ישראל but שבי פשע יעקב.

Another important text quoted is Mal. 3,16-18:

Then those who feared the Lord spoke with one another; the Lord heeded and heard them, and a book of remembrance was written before him of those who feared the Lord and thought on his name. 'They shall be mine,' says the Lord of hosts, 'my special possession on the day when I act, and I will spare them as a man spares his son who serves him. Then once more you shall distinguish between the righteous and the wicked, between one who serves God and one who does not serve him.

Tempting as it might be to extend the context to Mal. 3 as a whole, we should resist it. Murphy-O'Connor errs in this respect by regarding the mention of cultic faults in this chapter as significant. But cultic faults are not the issue with 'apostates' from the new community. The phrase יגלה ישע וצדקה, although probably an intended allusion to Is. 56,1, may have been prompted by Mal. 4,3 'unto them that fear my name shall the sun of righteousness arise with healing in his wings.' We may finally note yet a further example in this last allusion of a reapplication of part of the original *Admonition* which again transfers the old community/old Israel contrast to a new community/old community contrast, namely IV,7: the 'first holy ones' 'justified the righteous and condemned the wicked,' by contrast with the pre-exilic generations who according to I,19 had 'justified the wicked and condemned the righteous.'

A quotation from Ex. 20,6 coupled with one from Deut. 7,9 in which שומרי מצותיו is replaced by שומריו (thus changing the sense) concludes a passage which, although consisting largely of biblical quotation and allusion, is nevertheless a most eloquent profile of a community without its Teacher.

### The status of the 'house of Peleg'(?): XX,22b-34

This section contains statements about the 'house of Peleg' (22b-25a), about those who have entered the covenant and 'broken the bound of the law' (25b-27a), and about the faithful. It is the first two of these, and particularly the relationship between them, which poses the major difficulty for our understanding of the overall sense of this material. It is uncertain whether these two statements refer to the same group, similar groups, or quite different groups. To make matters worse, the 'house of Peleg' cannot easily be identified.

The fact that there is apparently a lacuna preceding this section contributes to our uncertainty on these matters. For it not only obscures our view of the relationship between this material and what precedes, but also calls into question whether the term 'house of Peleg' is actually a correct identification of the group in question. Some commentators accept that בית פלג is preceded by a מ (= 'from'), which may mean that the group are only part of the 'house of Peleg,' and that their relationship to that group is therefore in doubt: are they representative of it, or have they left it because of disagreement with the rest of it?

Both Stegemann and Murphy-O'Connor appeal to 4QpNah IV,1 where there is a mention of the 'house of Peleg.' However, this can hardly help us, for in addition to the fact that we do not know for certain the relationship between the group here and the 'house of Peleg,' it is unwise to use allusions in the *pesharim* to illuminate passages in CD until we are sure that both refer independently to the same historical entity—which must be a conclusion based on exegesis, not a presupposition. The name itself is of little help. Some have suggested that it denotes 'separation' (in Jub. 8,8 Peleg is so named because he separated); but even if this is correct, we are hardly much further forward until we know from whom they separated, and whether from the point of view of the community this was a good or bad thing. For instance, separation could have been from the condemned rump of 'Israel' or from the community itself.

For the sake of simplicity only, I shall refer to this group throughout as the 'house of Peleg'; the inverted commas indicate that it is simply a term of convenience and implies no identification whatsoever. Of the character of this group, we can learn only from what is said of them:

1. they went out from the holy city
2. they leaned on God
3. they defiled the sanctuary (?)
4. they returned (?) . . . the people in a few matters/words.

The last two of these are uncertain. The subject of the verb 'defiled' may be Israel, not the 'house of Peleg,' while the last of these contains a lacuna in a crucial position. Both Stegemann and Murphy-O'Connor divide these four statements into two pairs, the first approving and the second disapproving; leaving the holy city and leaning (depending) on God are good deeds, the other two are bad. However, in defence of this interpretation both scholars are obliged to maintain that the sanctuary which the 'house of Peleg' defiled is the community, and that the text of the fourth item is to be restored, following the suggestion of Vermes,[15] וישבו ע[ו]ר אל [דרך] העם ברברים מעטים. The tense of this last verb is something of a difficulty, for as the last in a series of events in the past it ought to be in the imperfect consecutive. Stegemann suggests that it balances יצאו, 'went out,' in the first item.

Such an interpretation is extremely unlikely. In the first place, it will not suffice to equate the sanctuary with the community with the mere comment that the Qumran community regarded itself as a spiritual temple.[16] Nowhere in CD, nor even in the other scrolls from Qumran, is the word מקרש used absolutely of the community. The nearest to such a usage is in 4QF1 I,9, where מקרש אדם occurs; and this is obviously not a similar case, for the noun is qualified. Moreover, we have already established that the community of the original *Admonition* had not abandoned the use of the Temple in Jerusalem. No more plausible is Cothenet's suggestion that it is the phrase 'holy city' which designates the community.

Other scholars have proposed that ויטמאו את המקרש should be rendered 'declared the sanctuary unclean' or '(when Israel sinned and) defiled the sanctuary.' In all probability, one of these translations is correct, and either of them would connote *approval* of the 'house of Peleg.' If the sanctuary means the Jerusalem Temple, which is the most natural sense, it is difficult to see how it could have been defiled

by the 'house of Peleg' *after* they had left the holy city. An even
weightier objection, in my opinion, is that to accuse the 'house of
Peleg' of defiling the sanctuary and then 'returning to the way of the
people *in small matters*' moves from the sublime to the ridiculous. The
phrase 'in small matters' (or, perhaps more accurately: 'in a few
respects') has to be given proper weight, and it must surely be doubted
whether a condemnation of this group deemed to have defiled the
sanctuary could really culminate in a charge phrased in these terms.
Of the two possible translations, I prefer 'when Israel sinned and
defiled the sanctuary,' since it provides a specific reason for the
departure of the 'house of Peleg' from the holy city, and it seems to me
that the reason for the departure furnishes an important part of the
description.

In fact, the reconstruction of the last item of description is uncertain
and must remain so for the present. We have noted the restoration of
Vermes, 'and returned again to the way of the people . . . '; but
Schechter, Rabin, Dupont-Sommer, Maier and Schwarz read שבו עד אל,
'returned to God.' My view is that דרך is a plausible, but far from
certain, restoration.[17]

The exact nuance of the word שבו, 'returned,' is important also.
Does it connote defection from the community, as many commentators suggest and as it is used elsewhere in this last section of CD?
Murphy-O'Connor has remarked that if this group belonged within
the community, the absence of any statement to that effect is strange.[18]
I think that the opposition 'went out'/'returned' is adequate to explain
the choice of the verb, and that while it represents in the eyes of the
community something of a backward movement, the qualifying
phrase 'in a few respects' shows that this backsliding was only relative.
The use of any qualifying phrase with שוב shows in fact that it cannot
stand here as the technical term for defection unless it is possible to
have *degrees* of defection. More probably, the verb describes movement
away from the community, which is fairly close to the meaning
'defect,' but does not entail that the 'house of Peleg' *was ever fully
within the community.*

It seems to me, therefore, that the 'house of Peleg' are on the whole
approved, but some degree of disapproval is indicated if the proposed
restoration of lines 23-4 is accepted. Subsequently, we find that this
group is to be judged איש לפי רוחו 'each one according to his spirit' in
the עצת הקדש, the 'holy council.' Both these phrases are unique in CD
but paralleled in 1QS,[19] once again supporting my thesis that the

community of the 'new covenant' is the Qumran community. But this statement does not imply, as so many scholars have assumed, that the 'house of Peleg' are members of the community. This interpretation arises from a failure to give weight to every element in the text. It has been too readily assumed that judgment in the 'holy council' is to be understood as a condemnation such as is threatened on other groups in the preceding material.[20] What is significant is that this group is *not* explicitly condemned and indeed that its members are not even treated *as a group*, but 'each one according to his spirit.' When these factors are put alongside the criticism of 'returning to the way of the people in a few respects' there is no problem in understanding the text at all.

In the first place, no question of punishment is raised. The judgment of the 'holy council' pertains not to the ultimate fate of these men but to *their membership of the community*. The difficulties encountered in interpreting the 'holy council' either as the divine court or as acting on its behalf—to which some scholars have resorted—are abolished. The 'house of Peleg' are not initially members of the community, nor have they left (if so, how could they be judged by the community's council? In their absence?). What is said about the 'house of Peleg' is that they have acted in a way which the community sees as sympathetic to itself, but *in a few respects* they have compromised (in the community's view) with practices of non-members. The question is: are the 'house of Peleg' to be admitted to the community in view of their ambivalent qualifications? The answer given is that *as a group* they are to be neither recognised as members nor rejected, but *each one of them* shall be considered on his merits.

If this interpretation is correct, that this paragraph deals with members of the 'house of Peleg' (or whatever) as would-be entrants, we must surely take the following statement as *also applying to these persons*. It has usually been understood as an independent statement applied to any member of the community. But in such a case we would expect וכל אשר פרצו . . . מבאי הברית not וכל אשר באו בברית אשר פרצו. I therefore translate 'all those who have transgressed the limits of the law among those who have entered . . . shall be cut off'. The threat applies to those members *of the 'house of Peleg'* who, as a result of being judged 'each one according to his spirit' are admitted to the community of the covenant. They will receive the same punishment as the 'wicked of Judah.' I would guess that this whole passage confronted a dilemma in which the status of the 'house of Peleg' was disputed: were they to be regarded as insiders or outsiders? An answer is provided which would

satisfy both points of view: as a group they belong neither in nor out;
any worthy members may be admitted, but once admitted, they must
abandon their 'return to the way of the people' and follow the law
perfectly. If they transgress after admission to the community they
will incur the same punishment as if they had never entered.

The whole of 22b–27a taken together fits the context perfectly. This
last group to be considered are not strictly apostates, but in view of
probable misgivings concerning their entry to the community, those of
it who have been permitted to join the community are singled out for
special warning. There is, moreover, on this interpretation no
difficulty with a possible overlap with earlier material, in which
would-be or spiritual defectors from the community were warned.

The 'house of Peleg' paragraph permits us some speculation about
the origins of the community of the 'new covenant' itself. This
community regarded the Temple as having been defiled, and applauded
others who left Jerusalem because they agreed with this view. What
'defiling the Temple' meant we cannot know; nowhere else in CD is
there any hint of a specific single act of Temple defilement, and the
only example we are given of such an act is at V,7 which instances
intercourse with a menstruant. It is hardly likely that the Qumran
community was the direct outcome of a single act of sexual deviation,
or an orgy of ritual Temple defilement. Perhaps the new community
had cut itself off from the Temple in a way which the parent
community had not. Other groups had reacted to a specific act of
'defiling the Temple' in similar ways. Who the groups are, or what the
'defiling' constituted is unanswerable at present, and speculation on
this important question is premature. Stegemann's conclusion that
acceptance of the Teacher of Righteousness entailed a break with the
Temple is very plausible, even if many of the reasons he gives for this
view are incorrect. It is intrinsically unlikely that the new community
was initiated by the arrival of a 'teacher' and by a dispute over the
sanctity of the Temple independently. We must remember, however,
that nothing in either the original *Admonition* nor its Qumran
recension implies that the Teacher was regarded as a High Priest
either within or outside the community.[21]

*Conclusion to the Admonition: XX,27b-34*

Murphy-O'Connor believes that 'sufficient evidence can be adduced
to show that the present section was written by the compiler of the
*Admonition* as the conclusion to his work.'[22] With this assertion, as

will now be clear, I must disagree. I have suggested that the extant material of the original *Admonition* comes to an end with VII,9a. However, I pointed out that VII,9a did not offer us a plausible ending in its present form. We should be looking at the very least for some kind of summary of the *Admonition* and an anticipation of the following *Laws*. These features are to some extent present in this passage, and since it is clear that the *Laws* describe the community of the 'Damascus covenant' and not the Qumran community, it is probable that their connection with the *Admonition* predates the Qumran recension. It seems to me possible, therefore, that underlying this present passage may be material which originally concluded the *Admonition*, and afforded a transition to the following *Laws*. In the present passage, however, we shall be looking for evidence of the way in which the new community sought to present these laws, which it regarded as superseded or supplemented by the rulings of the Teacher.

The passage opens with the statement 'All these who hold fast to these rules (משפטים).' In the present form of the *Admonition* this can only be a reference to the material in IXff. Such 'holding fast,' however, comprises two elements; as well as 'going out and going in according to the law (תורה)' one must 'listen to the voice of the Teacher.' Both Denis and Murphy-O'Connor take this 'teacher' to be God. In view of line 32, however, the reference must be at the very least ambiguous, and given the significance of the Teacher in the whole of the present section, their interpretation must be regarded as improbable. Murphy-O'Connor is impressed by the extent to which the whole of the *Admonition* is recapitulated in this final passage, and it is true that in the first part of it there is little, aside from the mention of the Teacher, which we would regard as peculiar to the new community. But I cannot accept entirely Murphy-O'Connor's conclusion that this passage forms a perfect conclusion to the *Admonition*. An important modification to this view is required. The argument of the passage is best explained by the assumption that it did originally form the conclusion to the pre-Qumranic *Admonition*, but was subsequently reworked. The ideology peculiar to the new community is represented not in the shape of the whole but in a very few phrases, all of which could be extracted from their context to leave a passage in harmony with the original *Admonition*. The phrase in 28b וישמעו לקול מורה is such probable addition; others will be noted presently.

The confession which follows is certainly in keeping with the ideology of the original *Admonition*. Murphy-O'Connor has recognised its kinship with the Day of Atonement prayer,[23] with the prayer of Dan. 9 and I Kings 8,47. Both of the biblical prayers are spoken by exiles. Rather surprisingly, he fails to cite 4QDibHam, which contains a very striking example of this prayer, and which impressed its editor, who has been followed by other commentators, with its lack of sectarian ideology, prompting him to dub it as 'pre-Essene.'[24] In the terminology of Murphy-O'Connor, we should call it 'pre-Qumranic Essene'; and in my own terminology it would be regarded as a product of the community of the covenant of Damascus which was responsible for the *Admonition*. 4QDibHam contains an explicit statement of its exilic origin, and of the 'exilic ideology' expressed in CD. It regards the exile as a continuing punishment, prays for the continuing anger of God to be turned away, accepts the Temple, concentrates on the theme of covenant. It ends:

> let your anger and wrath turn away from us. Look on our . . . trouble and distress and deliver your people Israel [from all] the lands, near and far, every man who is inscribed in the book of life . . .

A fuller treatment of the relationship between this document and CD will have to be undertaken elsewhere; for the present I wish only to draw attention to the importance of the parallel, as well as drawing attention to the fact that the ideology of the Damascus covenant, as distinct from its developments within the Qumran community, finds its expression also outside CD.

The first part of this final passage, then, demands three requirements; observing the law, obeying the Teacher and confessing. With the possible exception of the second of these, there is complete coherence with the ideology of the original *Admonition*. The second part of the passage contains more specific evidence of the new community. It begins at 30b with . . . ולא ירימו יד על, 'and do not lift a hand against . . . ,' which follows from כל המחזיקים 'all who hold fast' in line 27, not from the immediately preceding confession couched in the first person plural. The correctness of this demarcation becomes evident when it is realised that the confession cannot be held to continue to the end of the *Admonition*, but must be located elsewhere. In fact, we have a quotation not of the entire prayer, but only *of its opening lines, by way of identification*. But the recitation of the whole prayer, not merely the opening lines, is implied.

The righteous are now described as those who 'have been instructed in the former rules by which the men of the community are judged,' and who 'obey the Teacher of Righteousness' and do not 'reject (ישיבו) the righteous ordinances (חקי הצדק) when they hear them.' The reference is to rules which *were once operative, but have been superseded.* The אנשי היחד, 'men of the community' who are bound to the Teacher can only be members of the *new* community, and the 'former rules' must therefore be those which pertained in the parent 'Damascus' community. The חקי הצדק are, accordingly, from the מורה הצדק, the Teacher. Whereas in the original *Admonition* (IV,7f.), the rules by which the first members were instructed are identical to those in which new members live, for the new community there exists an additional body of teaching, namely the 'righteous ordinances.'

Reference to the 'former rules' explains, or perhaps is explained by, the presence of the following *Laws*. What were originally the rules given to, or established by, the 'first ones' (ראשונים) have now become the 'former rules' (המשפטים הראשונים) in which members were, or are, originally instructed, but are now superseded or supplemented by the instructions of the Teacher. The continued presence of the original laws in the Qumranic recension shows that they were regarded as still theoretically, or partially, valid. We may presume that sooner or later the instructions of the Teacher were expressed in a literary form also, perhaps comparable to the *Laws* of CD. Quite probably this is how the document 1QS originated, namely as the 'latter ordinances.' The analysis of 1QS by Murphy-O'Connor is consistent with such a suggestion.[25]

I conclude with an observation in a more light-hearted vein. The very last phrase of this *Admonition* runs כי חסו בשם קרשו. The verb חסה is a *hapax legomenon* in CD, and indeed also in the entire Qumran corpus. Nor can its use here be plausibly explained from the context; there is no thematic or verbal connection that I can see. There is continuing uncertainty of the etymology of the term 'Essene.' Although the verb does not necessarily provide us with that etymology, may its use here at the conclusion of the *Admonition* be a conscious and punning allusion to the name with which this community, or its parent, had come to be dubbed . . . ?

## VI  THE REDACTION OF THE *ADMONITION*

It has emerged from the preceding study that the history of the *Admonition* is represented in the Cairo manuscripts by three successive layers of material. The first is what I regard as the original work, whose contents terminate at VII,9, and traces of which may be detected at the end of XX. This original composition also contained the present *Laws*. The second layer comprises two passages of what I have labelled *Warnings*, and the third layer a substantial supplement reflecting the ideology of a new covenant community identified as that which came to live at Qumran.

It is now appropriate to conclude our analysis by reviewing some of the other secondary material which has been found embedded in the earlier layers of the *Admonition*. If the view is correct that our Cairo manuscripts represent a Qumranic recension, it will be expected that the interests of that community have been reflected throughout the material and not confined to the concluding section of the *Admonition*. It can now be suggested, in the light of what we have learnt from the preceding chapter, the glosses and minor expansions presented here are all to be ascribed to the Qumran community. This secondary material falls into four categories:

1. allusions to an individual opponent of the Qumran community.
2. a Qumran community *Heilsgeschichte*.
3. warnings originally uttered in respect of outsiders now redirected towards members of the Qumran community.
4. hostile references to the Temple.
(The last of these I regard as the least certain.)

1.  IV,19f. elaborates a reference to 'the צו'; 'the צו is a spouter, as it says: 'they shall indeed spout.' VIII,12f. contains an expansion within an expansion: 'because a raiser of wind and spouter of lies spouted to them, against all of whose congregation the anger of God is aroused' (the B text expands in a slightly different way). In I,14ff. we also found a secondary expansion which includes a reference to a 'Man of Scoffing' who 'spouted waters of deceit to Israel.' These references can

be grouped together as identifying an individual figure on whom is laid the responsibility of leading others astray. This figure appears in the Qumran *pesharim* as an opponent of the Teacher of Righteousness, but Stegemann has shown that in CD references to this figure are secondary; his argument have already been reviewed in the Introduction. Stegemann was able to see that the removal of these references left the opponents of the community in CD rather shadowy, but because of his presumption that CD was a Qumranic composition, he assumed that the original references which these secondary expansions clarified were nevertheless to historical participants in the drama of Qumran origins. That is to say, in Stegemann's view the secondary material was (at least largely) correct in its identifications.

But even a cursory glance at the passages in which this figure has been introduced (that is, outside XIX,33-XX,34), shows that their context is not at all sectarian. In IV,19 and VIII,12 the 'builders of the wall' are outsiders, and in I,13 the wickedness of Israel which was originally in view was that which led to the Exile. With regard to the historical relationship between this figure and the community of CD the evidence of the *pesharim* has been given priority over strict literary-critical considerations within CD itself, a critical methodological error. A possible direction of enquiry into the problem may be to follow the observation that the *pesharim* prefer individual figures, while CD does not. Not only do we have no Wicked Priest in CD, but even in XX,11 we have 'men of scoffing' only in the plural. It must not be assumed that XIX,33-XX,34 and all of the glosses in which this individual figure appears belong to the same hand or the same period. It is probable that more than one level might ultimately be distinguishable within the Qumran reworking of the *Admonition*.

2.   The most important single revision *within* the original *Admonition* by the Qumran community has undoubtedly taken place in I,1-II,1. Here an original *Heilsgeschichte* contained in a *rîb*-discourse has been distorted by means of chronological and other insertions. The birth of the saved community is now placed not in the Exile, but 390 years after; it is not the original remnant which is saved, but a 'root for planting'; and the creation of this saved community is attributed to a figure called the 'Teacher of Righteousness.' The wickedness of pre-exilic Israel which brought about the divine punishment, desolation of the land, now becomes more a more recent phenomenon, and is seen as a wickedness prevalent in the time of the Teacher, and instigated by an individual called the 'Man of Scoffing' (see above). The *rîb* on which

the discourse reflects also acquires a different aspect. While the basic ideology of the prolonged divine wrath is not necessarily abandoned, the arrival of the Teacher is taken as a sign of the eschaton; the horizon contracts, and the *present time* becomes the new 'age of wrath' which will inaugurate the salvation for which the Teacher's community waits. This temporal contraction corresponds to the spatial contraction which took place when the Qumran community ceased to concern itself with the nation as a whole, and became obsessed with the remainder of the parent community—for it is only to this community that any large-scale defection from the Qumran community could be envisaged. The implication that the development reflected by the history of CD is one of increasing sectarianism with a correspondingly sharpened focus on external enemies is extremely important for the future progress of Qumran research, inviting as it does a re-appraisal of the historical value of the *pesharim* in particular.[1]

Now, in the light of what has been discovered about the Qumranic contribution to CD, I feel justified in returning briefly to the question I left open towards the beginning of my analysis; is the reference to the 'Teacher' in I,1ff. original? Unable previously to answer the question satisfactorily on source-critical or metrical grounds alone, I am now prepared to suggest, in the light of all that has emerged from the analysis, that to view the presence of the Teacher at I,11 as a product of Qumranic recension is most consistent with the widest body of evidence in CD. In particular, it is in keeping with the overall Qumranic reinterpretation of the opening discourse which has undoubtedly taken place. Even so, I cannot regard this question as closed; nor, do I suspect, will others for whom a literal interpretation of the final form of this discourse offers a preferable explanation of Qumran origins.

3.   The original *Admonition* addresses itself to Israelites, concerns itself with the nation, and betrays no absorption with internal squabbling or apostasy. Even in the *Warnings* of VII,9-VIII,19, where wavering members of the community are addressed, it is not these who are made direct objects of criticism, but the outsiders to whose authority they may feel drawn. By contrast, the Qumranic material betrays an insecure community, obsessed with the fear of apostasy, directing its hostility equally towards those of the parent community who reject it, and those within it who, though still physically members, may be secretly renegades.

The clearest example of a re-application of criticism of outsiders to insiders is found in the B text of VIII,2-19 where additions such as the phrases 'entered a covenant of repentance' and 'and against those who walk after them' suggest that a new target is in sight, namely apostates. We have also suggested that the phrase 'builders of the wall' which in the original *Admonition* designated outsiders, possibly the Jewish establishment, has been applied to the community led by the 'Man of Scoffing,' צו, the 'Spouter of Lies,' to whom the Qumran community was so vehemently opposed.

4.   Finally, I have called attention to a group of possible secondary phrases which reflect or imply a hostile attitude towards the Temple; I,4; VI,12b-14a and VI,18b-19. It would be consistent with the clue given at XX,23 to regard these also as products of the Qumran community, although it is unfortunate that we cannot deduce from CD anything specific about the attitude of the Qumran community towards the Temple. There is in fact no suggestion in CD that the attitude towards the Temple constituted a primary issue between the Qumran community and its parent, although if a boycott of the Temple was one of the central doctrines of the Teacher of Righteousness it would be subsumed under the charge of rejecting the Teacher and his 'latter' rulings, which figures as the major issue.

What these additions demonstrate most eloquently is that *the Damascus Document existed in very nearly its present shape before the Qumran community received it*. An originally Qumranic composition would not have taken this form, nor required these expansions.

# CONCLUSIONS AND REFLECTIONS

The following *conclusions* emerge from the study:

1.   The original *Damascus Document* is a coherent composition. This demonstration, if accepted, clears away several misgivings which have expressed as to the validity of any conclusions derived from it, and offers a basis for more detailed and more confident research.

2.   The document achieved its outline and substantially its present form before the foundation of the Qumran community, and betrays an organised, well-developed community with a clearly-expressed ideology and historical traditions.

3.   This community did not boycott the Temple, but did not believe the Temple could be used except under the terms of its own halachah.

4.   This community regarded the 364-day (solar) calendar as divinely revealed to it in exile. Whether this exile is geographically to be taken literally, it is certainly no mere symbol and its origin is firmly assigned to the conquest of Nebuchadnezzar.

5.   There are no specific predominant points of disagreement between this community and Judaism outside it; the community regarded those outside as rejected by God since the Babylonian devastation, and as left by God to stray in error, misled by Belial, until the predestined period of time should be fulfilled, at which time the community, as the true remnant, would occupy the land and inherit all the promises of God. Although outside the community a different calendar was used, and possibly unacceptable cultic practices, the document does not make specific criticisms on these points.

The following *reflections* are offered:

1.   The ideology of CD has powerful roots in priestly Exilic literature, especially the Holiness Code and Ezekiel. There is no doubt, therefore, of the exilic origin of its ideology. However, such an ideology does not necessarily imply a sixth-century BCE origin for the community itself. It is perhaps unlikely that we shall ever be able to define precisely the point of origin, although the correspondences

between CD and ideological strands found in Ezra and Nehemiah certainly permit one to suggest that the foundations of the ideology of CD, and of its community, may antedate the middle of the fifth century BCE.

2.   The presence of this community in Palestine is presupposed at some stage by the evidence of the Qumran community. However, although a Palestinian setting for the composition of the *Admonition* has been hitherto taken for granted, there is nothing specifically to contradict the view that it was *composed* in the Diaspora, especially since some of the *Laws* appear to imply such a context. It is worth considering whether the second level of the *Admonition*, the *Warnings* of VII,9-VIII,19, is not in some way connected with a return to Palestine, a move which led directly or indirectly to conflict with political and religious authorities to whom the ideology of the community was unacceptable.

3.   The date of composition of the *Admonition* must lie before the occupation of Qumran by the Qumran community and it would appear to come after the composition of the book of Jubilees. These termini are not, in my opinion, as helpful as might at first appear, for I consider that the date of occupation of Qumran on archaeological grounds need not predate the beginning of the 1st century BCE, while the possibility that Jubilees existed in a earlier form before the 2nd century BCE cannot be discounted. (Nor can we be certain that the reference to Jubilees in CD XIV is not secondary.[1]) We can only say that both works come from the same circles, which probably produced parts of Enoch as well. The theory of an Eastern Diaspora origin is individually plausible for each of these compositions (and, incidentally, for the narratives of the book of Daniel); collectively, such indications further support the probability that CD's 'Damascus' community originated in the Diaspora, and may invite investigation of a common background to all of this literature.

4.   The Qumran community arose out of this earlier community, prompted by the arrival of a person who claimed to be (or was accepted as) a figure expected by the original community to appear 'at the end of days.' Whatever external causes may have provoked the creation of the Qumran community—and an act seen as defilement of the Temple seems to be indicated—an understanding of the character of this community will probably depend very much more upon the ideological roots which the Damascus covenant community provided than on external historical events. In other words, the Qumran community is

only incidentally a product of political and social events in Palestine, and certainly no positive traces of a 'Hellenistic crisis' are to be perceived.

5.	The use of historical traditions in the *Admonition* by the Qumran community, their emendation and reinterpretation, compel us to undertake a long-overdue critical reappraisal of the historical value of the exegeses of the *pesharim*. One can only suspect, pending such an inquiry, that their previous treatment as documents of primary historical value has been a hindrance rather than a help in the elucidation of the origins, and hence of the identity and ideology, of the Qumran community.

# NOTES TO INTRODUCTION

1 To date, three volumes of the Cave IV fragments have appeared in *DJD(J)*: J.M. Allegro, *Qumran Cave 4*, I, 1968 (DJDJ V); J.T. Milik, *Qumrân Grotte 4*, II, 1977 (DJD VI); M. Baillet, *Qumrân Grotte 4*, III, 1982 (DJD VII).

2 Prolegomenon to S. Schechter, *Documents of Jewish Sectaries*, repr. New York, 1970, 24.

3 Details of the Qumran fragments of the work are most conveniently found in J.A. Fitzmyer, *The Dead Sea Scrolls: Major Publications and Tools for Study*, Missoula, 1977,[2] 20 [= 5QD], 21 [= 6QD]; 31 [= 4QD[a,b,e]]. Cf. also 90-92 for a reconstruction of the 'original' *Damascus Document* based on the suggestions of J.T. Milik, *Ten Years of Discovery in the Wilderness of Judaea*, London, 1959, 151-152.

4 S. Schechter, *Documents of Jewish Sectaries*, Cambridge, 1910 (repr. New York, 1970), V-LXIX, 1-20.

5 L. Rost, *Die Damaskusschrift neu bearbeitet* (Kleine Texte, 167), Berlin, 1933.

6 C. Rabin, *The Zadokite Document*, Oxford, 1954, 1958.[2]

7 Schechter, XXII; but somehow he calculates 390 years from the Exile to 'within a generation of Simon the Just, who flourished about 290 B.C.'

8 I. Lévi, 'Un écrit sadducéen antérieur à la destruction du Temple,' *REJ* 61 (1911), 161-205; 63 (1912), 1-19.

9 Lévi, 173. For details of the reference and the chronology, see on Margoliouth.

10 G. Margoliouth, 'The Calendar, the Sabbath and the Marriage Law in the Geniza-Zadokite Document,' *ET* 23 (1911-12), 362-365; 24 (1912-13), 553-558; 25 (1913-14), 560-564. Cf. also 'The Sadducean Christians of Damascus,' *Expositor* 8 (1911), 499-517; (1912), 213-235.

11 J.L. Teicher, 'The Damascus Fragments and the Origin of the Jewish Christian Sect,' *JJS* 2 (1951), 115-143; B.E. Thiering, *Redating the Teacher of Righteousness*, Sydney, 1979; *The Gospels and Qumran*, Sydney, 1981.

12 R.H. Charles, 'Fragments of a Zadokite Work,' *Apocrypha and Pseudepigrapha of the Old Testament*, Oxford, 1913, II, 785-834.

13 The following comment from G.F. Moore in Foakes Jackson and Kirsopp Lake, eds., *The Beginnings of Christianity*, I, 97f. n.2, is worth recalling: 'Dr. R.H. Charles . . . naïvely works out the sum with the aid of a modern handbook of dates, and comes to the year 196.'

14　M.-J. Lagrange, 'La secte juive de la Nouvelle Alliance au pays de Damas,' *RB* 9 (1912), 213-240, 321-360.

15　G.F. Moore, 'The Covenanters of Damascus: A Hitherto Unknown Jewish Sect,' *HTR* 4 (1911), 330-377.

16　See above, n.5.

17　E. Meyer, 'Die Gemeinde des neuen Bundes im Lande Damaskus: Eine jüdische Schrift aus der Seleukidenzeit,' *Abhandlungen der preussischen Akademie der Wissenschaften* (Berlin), Phil.-hist. Klasse, 1919, 9, 1-65.

18　L. Ginzberg, *Eine unbekannte jüdische Sekte*, New York, 1922; E.T. *An Unknown Jewish Sect*, New York, 1970 (including a preface by Eli Ginzberg).

19　C. Rabin, *Qumran Studies*, Oxford, 1957, offered a detailed comparison of the Qumran community with Pharisaic חבורות.

20　A. Büchler, 'Schechter's "Jewish Sectaries",' *JQR* 3 (1912-13), 429-485.

21　A. Marmorstein, 'Eine unbekannte jüdische Sekte,' *Theologisch Tijdschrift* 52 (1918), 92-122; S. Zeitlin in *JQR*; from 1949 this journal carries Zeitlin's similar view on the Qumran scrolls. His edition of CD (in less than perfect facsimile) contains an introduction restating his views (S. Zeitlin, *The Zadokite Fragments*, Philadelphia, 1952).

22　Studies of the Qumran scrolls are so well documented that copious reference is superfluous. For a convenient review of the comparisons between CD and 1QS see M. Burrows, *The Dead Sea Scrolls*, New York, 1955 (repr. Grand Rapids, 1979), 187-194; in more detail, H.H. Rowley, *The Zadokite Fragments and the Dead Sea Scrolls*, Oxford, 1952; P. Wernberg-Møller, 'Some Passages in the "Zadokite Fragments" and their Parallels in the "Manual of Discipline",' *JSS* 1 (1956), 110-128.

23　Recent reviews on Qumran studies include: M. Delcor, 'Où en sont les études qumraniennes?,' *Qumran. Sa piété, sa théologie et son milieu*, ed. M. Delcor, Paris/Leuven, 1978, 11-46; M.A. Knibb, 'The Dead Sea Scrolls: Reflections on some Recent Publications,' *ET* 90 (1978-9), 294-300; J. Charlesworth, 'The Origin and Subsequent History of the Authors of the Dead Sea Scrolls: Four Transitional Phases among the Qumran Essenes,' *RQ* 10 (1980), 213-233; and G. Vermes, 'The Essenes and History,' *JJS* 32 (1981), 18-31.

24　G. Jeremias, *Der Lehrer der Gerechtigkeit*, Göttingen, 1963.

25　A convenient recent summary of alternative identifications, together with bibliography, is to be found in G. Vermes, *The Dead Sea Scrolls. Qumran in Perspective*, London, 1977, 142-62. Vermes is among those scholars who currently identify the 'Wicked Priest' and the 'Man of the Lie.' Another is B.E. Thiering, but she regards the individual concerned as a sectarian leader; see her *Redating the Teacher of Righteousness* (n. 11 above).

26　H. H. Rowley, 'The 390 Years of the Zadokite Work,' *Mélanges bibliques rédigés en l'honneur de André Robert*, Paris, 1957, 341-347.

27 Milik, *Ten Years*, 87-93; Fitzmyer, 'Prolegomenon' to Schechter, 16.

28 Both possibilities are raised by R. de Vaux, *Archaeology and the Dead Sea Scrolls*, London, 1973, 112, and refuted.

29 For a critique of Stegemann's theses, see below.

30 F.M. Cross, *The Ancient Library of Qumran*, London, 1958, 81f.; cf. also R. North, 'The Damascus of Qumran Geography,' *PEQ* 87 (1955), 34-48, who suggests that Qumran may have been within the territory of the Nabatean kingdom which included Damascus.

31 Josephus, *War* II,119-161; Pliny, *Natural History*, V,17.

32 Philo, *Quod Omnis Probus Liber Sit*, 75-91.

33 To my knowledge, the book has been reviewed only once, in *RQ* 8 (1973), 277-281, by J. Carmignac. However, a summary may be found by H. Bardtke in *Theologische Rundschau* 41 (1976), 100-119.

34 'Methodisch ist vielmehr zu fordern, dass sämtliche erreichbare Aussagen *eines bestimmten Bereiches* mit historisch fixierbaren Aspekten zueinander in Beziehung gesetzt, auf sachliche Zusammenhänge und notwendige Differenzierungen hin untersucht, dann in ihrem chronologischen Verhältnis zueinander bestimmt und schliesslich nach Möglichkeit zu anderweitigen historischen Aussagen in Beziehung gesetzt werden.' (12)

35 'Andererseits kehren gewisse stereotype Aussagen über solche Gegner unter Verwendung uniformer Terminologie ständig in den verschiedenen, formal ganz unterschiedlich zu charakterisierenden und auch sicher nicht gleichzeitig entstandenen Qumrantexten wieder; und einzelnen Personen auf der Gegenseite werden mit so markanten Zügen gezeichnet, dass die Folgerung, es handele sich dabei um ganz bestimmte historische Individuen, unvermeidlich ist und sich in Literatur nach anfänglichen Schwankungen in der Meinungsäusserung nicht zuletzt wegen ständiger Vermehrung des Textmaterials hierfür mit Recht fast allgemein durchgesetzt hat.' (13)

36 'Die der Zahl nach meisten, am weitesten ins Detail gehenden und ihren historischen Bezugspunkten nach differenzierten Aussagen über die Qumrangemeinde und ihre geschichtliche Umwelt bietet die Textgruppe der *pešarim*. Diese stehen deshalb mit Recht allgemein im Mittelpunkt der Diskussion über die Geschichte der Qumrangemeinde.'

37 Stegemann is by no means blind to data which embarrass his reconstruction. The absence of the Wicked Priest in 1QH as well as CD he finds 'remarkable' (196) and he acknowledges puzzlement at the lack of references to specific enemies. But his method offers him no means of evaluating such data.

38 The first scholar to propose this identification was G. Vermes, *Les Manuscrits du Désert de Juda*, Tournai, 1954.

39    Cf. J. Murphy-O'Connor, 'Demetrius and the Teacher of Righteousness,'
      *RB* 83 (1976), 400-420; H. Burgmann, 'Das umstrittene Intersacerdotium
      in Jerusalem 159-152 v. Chr.,' *JSJ* 11 (1980), 135-176, has criticised in
      detail Stegemann's thesis that the 'teacher of righteousness' was the
      Zadokite predecessor of Jonathan.

40    The argument offered by Stegemann is as curious as it is improbable. The
      term 'Pharisee' is taken to represent the Aramaic פרישיא, 'separators,' and
      their existence as a party is attested by Josephus at least as early as the
      time of Jonathan. They acquired their name because they separated from
      the Teacher; the term 'Pharisee' is derogatory. The reason why there is
      no reference to פרישיא in the Scrolls is because the scrolls are in Hebrew. It
      is difficult not to comment on the implausibility: even allowing that there
      is no Hebrew equivalent for the Aramaic, such as פרושים, are we to
      suppose that the Teacher's group was larger than that of the 'Man of the
      Lie'? If not, as seems to be the case according to the hypothesis, it ought to
      have been the *Teacher's* community who were dubbed the 'separators.'

41    I. Rabinowitz, 'A Reconsideration of "Damascus" and "390 Years" in the
      "Damascus" ("Zadokite") Fragments,' *JBL* 73 (1954), 11-35.

42    Rabinowitz, 15, prompted by the mention of 'twenty years' in Neh. 1,1.

43    Rabinowitz's 'basic admonition' is I,1-III,20; V,13-17; VIII,3-9; XX,32-
      33: his glosses are III,21-V,12; V,18-VII,12b; VIII,9-19; XIX,34-XX,31;
      XX,34. There are also further additions such as VII,12c-VIII,2.

44    In addition to Denis and Schwarz (see below), Stegemann and Murphy-
      O'Connor, see A. Rubinstein, 'Urban Halachah and Camp Rules in the
      "Cairo Fragments of a Damascene Covenant",' *Sefarad* 12 (1952), 283-
      96, whose contribution, of course, preceded that of Rabinowitz. He found
      three portions in the document, each of a different date. The first is
      'historical-admonitory' (I-VIII); the second is in two sections, 'camp-
      rules,' and the third, inserted between the two (VII,6b-9a) contains
      'urban laws.'

45    E. Wiesenberg, 'Chronological Data in the Zadokite Fragments,' *VT* 5
      (1955), 284-308.

46    A. Jaubert, 'Le pays de Damas,' *RB* 65 (1958), 214-248.

47    As additional indications of a Babylonian connection, Jaubert cites the
      book of Baruch's affinities with both Babylon and Qumran (see *RB* 63,
      1956; 65-66), פרתיה in CD XIII,8 (= Parthia?), and baptism, which is a
      Babylonian practice.

48    O.J.R. Schwarz, *Der erste Teil der Damaskusschrift und das Alte
      Testament*, Diest, 1965.

49    S. Iwry, 'Was There a Migration to Damascus? The Problem of שבי ישראל,'
      *W.F. Albright Volume, Eretz-Israel* 9 (1969), 80-88.

50    M.H. Segal, 'The Habakkuk "Commentary" and the Damascus Frag-
      ments,' JBL 70 (1951), 131-147.

51    A.-M. Denis, *Les thèmes de connaissance dans le Document de Damas*, Louvain, 1967.

52    'Evolution de structures dans le secte de Qumran,' *Aux origines de l'Eglise*, Bruges, 1964, 23-49.

53    W.F. Albright, *From the Stone Age to Christianity*, Baltimore, 1940, 2nd ed. 1946, reprinted with a new introduction, New York, 1957. The discussion of the Essenes is found in 288-289 of the second edition, and 374-378 of the 1957 reprint, which also contains in its introduction (19-22) an assessment of the Qumran material, claimed to comprise 'very significant new evidence' in support of his 1940-1946 opinions.

54    W.F. Albright and C.S. Mann, 'Qumran and the Essenes: Geography, Chronology and Identification of the Sect,' *The Scrolls and Christianity*, ed. M. Black, London, 1969, 11-25.

55    W.D. Davies, *The Gospel and the Land*, Berkeley, 1974, 103f. But Davies nevertheless identifies 'Damascus' with Qumran (100).

56    Morton Smith, 'The Dead Sea Sect in Relation to Ancient Judaism,' *NTS* 7 (1961), 347-360.

57    J. Blenkinsopp, 'Interpretation and the Tendency to Sectarianism: An Aspect of Second Temple History,' *Jewish and Christian Self-Definition, II*, ed. E.P. Sanders *et al.*, London, 1981, 1-26.

58    P.D. Hanson, *The Dawn of Apocalyptic*, Philadelphia, 1975.

59    Cf. H.-P. Müller, 'Mantische Weisheit und Apokalyptik,' *VTSupp.* 22, Leiden, 1972, 269-293; W. Lee Humphreys, 'A Lifestyle for Diaspora: A Study of the Tales of Esther and Daniel,' *JBL* 92 (1973), 211-223; J.J. Collins, *The Apocalyptic Vision of the Book of Daniel*, Missoula, 1977, esp. 58.

60    P. Garnet, *Salvation and Atonement in the Qumran Scrolls*, Tübingen, 1977. A useful survey of the Exile motif in 'intertestamental' Judaism is contained in M.A. Knibb, 'The Exile in the Literature of the Intertestamental Period,' *Heythrop Journal* 17 (1976), 253-272.

61    J. Starcky, 'Les quatre étapes du messianisme à Qumrân,' *RB* 70 (1963), 481-505.

62    J. Murphy-O'Connor, 'La génèse littéraire de la *Règle de la Communauté*,' *RB* 76 (1969), 528-549. This analysis has been developed by J. Pouilly, *La Règle de la Communauté de Qumrân: son évolution littéraire*, Paris, 1976, in what is in my opinion a less than satisfactory manner, despite Murphy-O'Connor's approving 'avant-propos' (7-8).

63    J. Murphy-O'Connor, 'The Essenes and their History' *RB* 81 (1974), 215-244.

64    J. Murphy-O'Connor, 'An Essene Missonary Document? CD II,14-VI,1,' *RB* 77 (1970), 201-229.

65    J. Murphy-O'Connor, 'A Literary Analysis of Damascus Document VI,2-VIII,3,' *RB* 78 (1971), 210-232.

66 J. Murphy-O'Connor, 'The Critique of the Princes of Judah (CD VIII,3-19),' *RB* 79 (1972), 200-216.

67 J. Murphy-O'Connor, 'A Literary Analysis of Damascus Document XIX,33-XX,34,' *RB* 79 (1972), 544-564.

68 EH, 237, n.90: 'it is true that the legal section of CD contains regulations regarding sacrifice . . . but they are surprisingly few in number and the supportive citation from the OT in each case gives the impression of a theoretical point rather than a practical ordinance. This harmonises with the general character of the legislation which, as we have seen, belongs to the stage when the Essenes were out of contact with the Temple.' But if they were theoretically developed outside Palestine—which may be accepted as a perfectly plausible suggestion—it remains problematical that they were not abrogated after the return to Palestine, especially if a boycott of the Temple was such a fundamental commitment of the community, as Murphy-O'Connor argues. The *Laws* of CD appear, in fact, to be a *selection* from community legislation rather than the whole of it (much of which may have been esoteric), in which case the retention of laws permitting use of the Temple is even more unlikely. For a treatment of this problem, see my article forthcoming in the Festschrift Volume for Yigael Yadin, *JJS* 33 (1982).

## NOTES TO CHAPTER I, STRUCTURE AND PLOT

1 Schechter, X.

2 Rost, 1. For a convenient review of opinions, cf. Schwarz, 69ff. Murphy-O'Connor, EMD, 201ff. takes a different view, but the commentators he has in mind have mostly not even considered the question of literary unity or complexity.

3 Milik, *Ten Years*, 151f. For a 'tentative outline' based on the Qumran evidence, see Fitzmyer, *DSS*, 90ff. It is still unclear to me how one decides where fragments may have fitted into the whole, and we continue to await, with decreasing patience, the publication of all the fragments. Those edited by Baillet have already appeared in *DJD 3*.

4 K.G. Kuhn, 'Der gegenwärtige Stand der Erforschung der in Palästina neu gefundenen hebräischen Handschriften,' *TLZ* 85 (1960), 651-652; J. Becker, *Das Heil Gottes*, 57. Cf. the criticism of this view in Murphy-O'Connor, EMD, 203.

5 Qumran fragments of the *Laws* apparently include the form of the ritual for the Feast of the Renewal of the Covenant. From this, some have deduced (e.g. Vermes, *DSSE*, 97) that 'the entire Damascus Rule was originally connected with that festival.'

6   Baltzer, 112ff.; cf. 99ff. for analysis of 1QS.
7   Cf. the convenient summary 89-93 and the remarks on 97.
8   Baltzer, 112.
9   By 'catechetical' I mean in this instance formal instruction whose basis is both revelation and tradition and whose contents comprise the beliefs of a religious community into which the audience wish to enter. I should make it clear that I use the term descriptively, and do not imply any formal, or form-critical judgment.
10  Hartman, 11.
11  E.g. Rabin, 1ff.

## NOTES TO CHAPTER II, HISTORY

1   Cf. Prov. 1,8.15; 2,1; 3,1.11, etc., and 4,1.10 especially; Sirach 2,1.7;3,1.8. 12.17.
2   Cf. Murphy-O'Connor, EMD, 204.
3   E.g. I Enoch 92.
4   Hartman, 62.
5   Hartman, 60-61; for a description of the *rîb* in the Old Testament, Hartman relies on the work of J. Harvey, 'Le "rîb-pattern," réquisitoire prophétique sur la rupture de l'alliance,' *Biblica* 43 (1962), 172-196; *Le plaidoyer prophétique contre Israel après la rupture de l'alliance. Etude d'une formule littéraire de l'Ancien Testament*, Bruges/Paris, 1967. A more recent examination and appraisal is found in K. Nielsen, *Yahweh as Prosecutor and Judge*, JSOTS 9, Sheffield, 1978.
6   Denis, 81: 'annoncent toutes trois le proche châtiment des impies revoltes, héritiers de tous les apostats de l'histoire . . . révèlent . . . à ceux qui "tiennent ferme" à l'alliance les volontés divines, grâce à quoi ils pourront comprendre la malice des impies et, à l'oppose, la conduite parfaite à tenir en ce temps de jugement.'
7   On this material, Stegemann, 131-145.
8   I retain the traditional English translation of the phrase, but in quotation marks. In my Translation I omit these wherever it is clearly a specific individual who is referred to; the distinction is not always easy, although it is important if, as I shall maintain, the office preceded, as it were, the historical figure who claimed it.
9   Ginzberg, 259f., argued that שנים . . . . נבוכדנאצר was in fact a second gloss, dependent on שנים . . . . תשעים, which in turn defined the קץ חרון, for only on the supposition of two glosses could the solecism שנים be explained.
10  Rabinowitz, 13.
11  Jeremias, 151f; for discussion of the 'teacher of righteousness' in CD, 151-

166.

12    Ginzberg (110, n.4) had already suspected this word because it was
      absent from the biblical text from which the Sirach phrase was taken,
      Ezek. 39, 23.

13    Jeremias, 151, n.3; R.A. Soloff, 'Toward Uncovering Original Texts in
      the Zadokite Fragments,' *NTS* 5 (1958-59), 62-67.

14    Murphy-O'Connor's historical reconstruction is embarrassed by the fact
      that 'twenty years' will not fit. He therefore argues that the figure may be
      intended to indicate half a generation, and, since in reality a generation is
      twenty rather than the traditional forty years, may represent ten years
      (EH, 224).

15    Jeremias, *ibid.*, n. 13, recognises that the added וממקרשו may have to do
      with the atttiude towards the Temple of the Qumran sect. This seems to
      be correct, although he regards both the original text and the gloss as
      emanating from the Qumran community, unlike the view to be presented
      here. The addition of '20 years' signifies much the same as that of 390
      years, namely a telescoping of the timespan of the original text into more
      recent history. Whether either of the figures has any evidential historical
      value can hardly be determined without external evidence; intrinsically,
      any assumption of reliability seems hazardous, as the majority of scholars
      allow.

16    The fullest recent debate on the question is in Schwarz, 83ff. In
      particular, one may mention the contributions of Ginzberg, Rabinowitz,
      Wiesenberg and Rowley as representing the best advocacy of respective
      possibilities.

17    Cf. Jeremias, 52.

18    Is.51,7 (שמעו אלי יודעי צדק) is probably the biblical source of CD I,1. See
      also in the same chapter שמעו אלי רדפי צדק (v. 1); הקשיבו אלי . . . אלי האזינו (v. 4).

19    Further comments on צדק and the Qumran community in CD will be
      found in Chapter V.

20    Cf. V,15; VII,9; VIII,2.3 (=XIX,6.14.15). In the *Laws*, פקד is used not of
      divine activity, but of mustering, appointing, or assessing members of the
      community (X,2; XIII,11; XIV,3.6; XV,6.8).

21    See especially VI,2, but also X,5; XII,23, XIV,19, XIX,11 and XX,1 speak
      of the 'Messiah of Aaron and Israel'

22    For further discussion, see Chapter VI.

23    The phrase 'when he remembered the covenant of the first ones' was
      recognised by Schechter as an allusion to Lev. 26,45, which itself refers to
      the Exile. In a note on this citation ('Une citation de Lévitique 26, 45 dans
      le *Document de Damas*, I,4; VI,2,' *RQ* 6 (1967-8), 289-291), R. Le Déaut
      has suggested that, as in the Neofiti Targum, CD combines an allusion to
      Lev. 26,42 and 45, implying a double remembrance of a covenant in

Egypt and with the patriarchs. I am not convinced by his assertion that 'dans le document de Damas, l'expression "alliance des premiers" est également une allusion, au moins directe, à la geste patriarcale et ne s'applique plus à la génération de l'Exode' (290) since I do not think that Lev. 26,45 actually means to say that the 'ancestors' here are the Egypt-wilderness generation. The sense of the biblical text seems to me rather as follows: 'the covenant I made with the ancestors, which I demonstrated especially in my bringing them out of Egypt.' That is to say, the Exodus is not an occasion of the (new) covenant, but an outcome of the old (patriarchal) one. The importance of this allusion in the context of the Holiness Code is that the Exodus is portrayed as the prototype of another event—the leading out of exile—which will also be in remembrance of this same original covenant. CD at any rate does not seem to know of more than one 'first' covenant, the one which ended at the Exile, and from the perspective of the document, it is irrelevant whether it was first made with Noah, Abraham or Moses; it is essentially the same covenant. להם in Lev. 26,45 means: 'I will do *for them* what I did . . . ' i.e. the remembering of the original covenant will take a concrete form. We can confirm this interpretation from the text of Ezek. 20,18ff where there is a wilderness-exodus typology. See especially vv. 36-38. The Deuteronomic-type language of Ez. 20,42 points to typology between conquest and re-entry after the Exile.

24  Denis, 13: 'l'objet de la pénétration est l'action eschatologique de Dieu, du moins ses prodromes.'

25  Stegemann, 132: 'Wie der Streit Gottes mit den Menschen in einem bestimmten Zeitraum, als der hier die Entstehungszeit der Qumran-gemeinde erscheint.'

26  There is an interesting parallel in the case of the tales of the book of Daniel. While the exilic situation of the hero is being typologically applied to the Maccabean period, the Exile and the diaspora retain their historical value. Indeed, the visions of the book, following a hint from the second chapter, present the whole of history from the Exile to the time of Antiochus as an epoch of ever-increasing royal arrogance and rebellion against God. The typology is, in this scheme of world-history, obliterated, for Nebuchadnezzar is not an *archetype* of Antiochus but the *ancestor of all successive emperors*. See my article, 'Eschatology in the Book of Daniel,' *JSOT* 17 (1980), 33-53. Denis, 43f. argues for especially close links between the CD discourses and the book of Daniel, but in my opinion overemphasises the connection by failing to take adequate account of other related literature, both biblical and extra-biblical.

27  It should be remarked that the ideology of CD emphasises not the Exile but the desolation of the land. However, the idea of 'exile' is not absent from CD, and I retain the term in a historical rather than theological

sense. The two are, of course, basically inseparable; the destruction of Israel and the banishing of the remnant are part of the 'desolation of the land.' On 'exilic soteriology' and CD, see Garnet, 87-97.

28 The meaning of the 'period of wickedness' is established below in Chapter III.

29 For a discussion of this problem, see Schwarz, 75-76.

30 Ginzberg, 5f.

30 Jeremias 81ff. for a detailed discussion of the phrase. He comments that it is 'sicher umfassend und schliesst auch die vergangenen Geschlechter mit ein.'

31 Rabin emends to יעשׂה; Bardtke, *Die Handschriftenfunde am Toten Meer. Die Sekte von Qumran*, Berlin, 1961,[2] 259, has suggested reading the participle; most commentators translate as future without comment. Excellent discussion is provided by Schwarz, 76f.

32 Jaubert, 236; 'faisait connaître aux dernières générations—celles d'après l'éxil—ce que Dieu avait fait dans une dernière génération—celle de 587—à une congrégation de traîtres—les traîtres de l'alliance qu'avait frappés la ruine de Jérusalem.' (She identifies the 'teacher of righteousness' with Ezra).

33 In CD VIII,5 (=XIX,17) and in XIX,34 בוגדים is perhaps used in a general sense as a description of those with whom whe community is contrasted. In XIX,34, on the other hand, it is used of defectors from the (Qumran) community. But the use of עדה at II,1 suggests that דור אחרון is the more likely gloss, together with the fact that as part of this original text this phrase could only have created confusion. It is probably a comment intended, like 12bff., to identify the 'faithless' with the contemporary generation.

34 Schwarz, 76: 'inhaltlich gesehen, könnte man ihn einen Exkurs oder besser auch einen Kommentar zum Begriff des "letzten Geschlechtes" nennen.'

35 At the beginning of 12 הם refers back to the בוגדים עדת and העתהיא refers to that of the biblical citation, not back to that of the 'congregation of traitors.' What follows thus has no direct link at all with the preceding material. For the detailed argumentation, see Stegemann, 132ff.

36 Murphy-O'Connor. LADDXIX, 63, n.61.

37 Murphy-O'Connor, EH, 234.

38 Murphy-O'Connor in fact concurs with such observations elsewhere; in CPJ, 210, n. 31 he accepts that references to 'builders of the wall' at IV,19 and VIII,13 have been glossed because these were 'understood to designate a group particularly hostile to the community and under the leadership of a false teacher who is perhaps to be identified with the "Man of Lies" of the pesharim.'

39 On the meaning of the phrase in the Qumran texts, see van der Woude,

*Die messianischen Vorstellungen der Gemeinde von Qumran*, Assen, 1957, 9f.; he agrees with Rabin that it means 'members,' not 'entrants.' Cothenet translates 'initiates.'

40 There has a wide difference of opinion over the reading of this. Schechter took it to be a relic of להשמידם 'to destroy them,' Charles read ארצם 'their land,' Hvidberg (cited by Rabin: I have unfortunately been unable to secure Hvidberg's dissertation, which is in Danish) emended to מיעמדם [sic] 'from their arising,' and this suggestion was adopted by Rabin who also suggested מישׂראל 'from Israel.'

41 Schwarz, 80.

42 Cf. I,11 ויודע, and see above, n.17. The translation of Rabin here, 'make them known,' is based on a statistical assessment of OT usage without regard to the internal evidence of CD.

43 For this meaning, see van der Woude, 16ff.

44 Schiffmann, *The Halachah at Qumran*, Leiden, 1975, 65ff.

45 Murphy-O'Connor, EMD, 219, argues that the similarity of structure, midrash, interpretation and application, confirms the *unity* of source, but this is no argument in favour of the same source; V,17b actually begins with a כי which suggests to me that it was once a discourse of the same kind as the first three in CD, but now without its introductory summons.

46 See Chapter IV.

47 Schiffmann, 47ff.

48 Talmon, 'Calendrical Reckoning,' 65.

49 On the dating of Jubilees, see VanderKam, *Textual and Historical Studies in the Book of Jubilees*, Missoula, 1977. One reservation I have with his careful dating is that *Jubilees* may be a composite document. Several scholars, including J.B. Segal (*The Hebrew Passover*, London, 1963), G.L. Davenport (*The Eschatology of the Book of Jubilees*, Leiden, 1971) and P. von der Osten-Sacken (*Gott und Belial*, Göttingen, 1969), have suspected this, and it does not seem to me that VanderKam is sufficiently cautious. But see his discussion of *Jubilees* and the Qumran Scrolls (including CD), 255-285.

50 Charles nevertheless regards the phrase 'who were left over of them' as an interpolation (is it because it contradicts his interpretation of the passage as apppying to the Hasidim?)

51 Denis, 28ff.

52 Schiffmann, 22-32. His conclusion is (32) that 'the *nigleh*, then, is nothing more than scripture, while the *nistar* is sectarian interpretation of it.' VanderKam accepts this view, arguing in '2 Maccabees 6,7A and Calendrical Change in Jerusalem,' *JSJ* 11 (1981), 52-74 (a proof of which the author kindly supplied in advance of publication) that the 'covenanters believed their 364-day calendar was revealed in biblical literature' (3f.).

53 See above, n. 23.

54 E.g. Deut. 28,12; Is. 41,18; Ps. 105,41.

55 A possibly significant parallel is the halachic activity of Nehemiah and Ezra. See most recently, D.J.A. Clines, 'Nehemiah 10 as an Example of Early Jewish Biblical Exegesis,' *JSOT* 21 (1981), 111-117.

56 Denis (39) is an exception: he contrasts the well here with that in VI,3-9. But it is the similarity, especially of context, which tells against him.

57 Murphy-O'Connor, EMD, 208.

58 Jaubert has established that this calendar is reflected in Priestly writings, generally dated to the period of the Babylonian Exile. It is probably much older (see Morgenstern, 'The Calendar of Jubilees, its Origin and its Character,' *VT* 5 (1955), 43-76). Jaubert's thesis has been attacked, but reviewed and defended by VanderKam, 'The Origin, Character and Early History of the 364-Day Calendar: A Reassessment of Jaubert's Hypothesis,' *CBQ* 41 (1979), 390-411. Jaubert's thesis was originally set out in her 'Le Calendrier des Jubilés et de la secte de Qumran. Ses origines bibliques,' *VT* 3 (1953), 250-264, and 'Le calendrier des Jubilés et les jours liturgiques de la semaine,' *VT* 7 (1957), 35-61.

59 Murphy-O'Connor, EMD, 209.

60 E.g. O. Betz, *Offenbarung und Schriftforschung in der Qumransekte*, Tübingen, 1960, 180ff.

61 Schwarz, 155ff., whose discussion is based on a number of passages from CD; besides IV,2c-4c she considers VI,4c-11b; VII,14b-21a and XIX, 9c-13b. She also suggests that the earliest stage of the community should probably be sought in the Babylonian Exile.

62 CD I,14; II,19; V,5.17.20; VI,10; VII,20. Charles is wrong to translate 'holding office' here, for the verb never has that meaning in CD. Cf. also the occurrences of מעמד in II,9 and IV,5 which bear most directly on the meaning of עמד here; the echoes of predestination are not to be missed.

63 The fullest discussions of the meaning of the term are by Iwry and Murphy-O'Connor, EMD 211ff. (='returnees'); Rabinowitz 16, n.20 (='captivity'); and Schwarz 117f. (='penitents'). Cf. also Cross, *ALQ*, London, 1958, 81, n.46.

64 See W.L. Holladay, *The Root* שוב *in the Old Testament*, Leiden, 1958; H.-J. Fabry, *Die Wurzel* שוב *in der Qumran-literatur. Zur Semantik eines Grundbegriffes*, Bonn, 1975, whose conclusions support Stegemann's translation 'repent.' Observations made below (Chapter V) concerning the use of this verb in CD XIX-XX suggest that its meanings in CD and in the Qumran literature may need to be differentiated.

65 Iwry, 86f.

66 We must not compare this categorisation with the present one; they are not intended to be compatible at all. Few scholars, however, appear able to reconcile their view of the CD community (usually the Qumran community) with the admission of non-Israelites, but it may be relevant

that Ezekiel, whose influence on this community is considerable, proposes that non-Jews in the land should be regarded not as aliens, but as equal to Israelites (47, 21-23); 'among the children of Israel.' As for the Qumran community, the well-known description of Pliny (*Natural History* V,17ff.) implies constant and successful recruitment from outside; was this *necessarily* restricted to Jews?

67 Schiffman, 40 for פרוש=list. He cites 1QM IV,7.8.11.
68 On the meaning of 'Damascus', see below on VI,11.
69 Schechter, curiously, did not emend at all, translating 'the holy they alter which God made atonement for them,' which makes no more sense in English than in Hebrew.
70 See above, n.23.
71 Denis, 85.
72 For a discussion of such a 'timetable' at Qumran, see Milik, '*Melki-ṣedeq et Melki-reša*ᶜ,' *JJS* 23 (1972), 96-109.
73 Murphy-O'Connor, EH, 224. See above, n.14.
74 Murphy-O'Connor, EH, 225. His basis for the claim, however, is an interpretation of CD XIX,33-34 which I do not accept (see below, *ad loc.*).
75 Garnet, 91f., nn. 3 and 4 has the most detailed discussion; but he reads להסתפח 'pouring out.' A recent discussion of the phrase is found in D. Schwarz, ' "To Join Oneself to the House of Judah," (Damascus Document IV,11),' *RQ* 10 (1981), 435-446.
76 Cf. Chapter IV below on VII,9ff.
77 Discussion in Schwarz, 139-40.


## NOTES TO CHAPTER III, LAWS

1 Murphy-O'Connor, EMD 219ff.
2 Stegemann analyses II,14ff. to the end of the *Admonition* in terms of an original *Grundschrift* with extensive interpolation, but, unlike Murphy-O'Connor, makes little or no attempt to account for the structure of the whole document or explain its purpose.
3 On the material covered in this chapter, Stegemann, 150-165.
4 Jeremias, 96ff.
5 Rabin thinks the gap between בזה and בוני, together with the change of subject, indicates a lacuna, but it seems rather to be the scribe's method of indicating a new subject or section—there is a gap between הארץ and פשרו in line 14. The change of subject is also a change of sentence. There is absolutely no break in the argument, unless one identifies the 'builders of the wall' with those who escape one net and succumb to another. But this is not the case.

6   At first it seems that Murphy-O'Connor regarded the whole phrase
    ימיפון . . . . יני בוני as a gloss (EMD 220) but in a later article (CPJ 210, n.31) he
    seems to imply that the first part of it may be original.

7   Further discussion of the phrase 'builders of the wall' below on VIII,12
    (Chapter IV).

8   Stegemann, of course, while arguing that the reference is secondary,
    regards the original text as a Qumran product and also accepts the
    historical reliability of the reference to the 'spouter.' Note should also be
    taken of the contrast between 'house of Judah' in IV,11 and 'house of
    Israel' in Ezek. 14. The presence of גדר in both cases may betray a
    conscious device on the part of the redactor.

9   Dupont-Sommer regards the omission as accidental. It is a precarious
    hypothesis. Yet possibly the accusation of riches *was* the original second
    net; such an accusation is reflected in VIII,5 (see below, *ad loc.*) and
    VI,15. Conceivably its accidental omission could have necessitated the
    clumsy manufacture of 'defiling of the sanctuary' out of originally sexual
    offences as a replacement.

10  So Rabin, Dupont-Sommer, Maier, Cothenet and Murphy-O'Connor.

11  E.g. M. Burrows, *The Dead Sea Scrolls*, New York, 1955, 353; Schwarz,
    142.

12  E.g. Jeremias, Stegemann and Murphy-O'Connor. Schwarz, 142, offers a
    full discussion. She moves the passage describing the sanctuary defile-
    ment and also regards the 'sanctuary' as the community. Murphy-
    O'Connor agrees that the phrase is misplaced, but refuses to identify
    sanctuary and community here (unlike XX,23, with no better pretext; see
    below, Chapter V, *ad loc.*).

13  Murphy-O'Connor, EMD, 222.

14  Murphy-O'Connor, EMD, 223, says there were 'very definite social
    pressures that demanded participation in the Temple ritual'; a good
    example of the extent to which the view that the CD community
    'rejected' the Temple has infected exegesis. Surely it is the halachah as a
    whole which is at issue and not the Temple cult (which is not
    condemned); 'approaching' must be seen in the light of VI,14b 'keeping
    apart from the children of the Pit' (see below).

15  Note the same feature in IV,11b.12a. Could these quotations also be
    redactional?

16  This is incidentally another clue that V,11-15a is secondary; the כי must
    refer back to the *practices* and not the rejection of the community's
    covenant and the abusive epithets thereby incurred.

17  Murphy-O'Connor, EMD, 224.

18  *Ibid.*

19  In a similar vein, Dupont-Sommer also assigns the desolation of land to
    recent times, and thinks of events in the reigns of Hyrcanus II and

Aristobulus II, preceding the intervention of the Romans.

20 Jeremias, 89, providing a typical instance of a major weakness of his thesis. He tends to ignore literary-critical problems and the context of individual words, phrases and passages, treating recurrent instances univocally, and apparently believing that the problems of Qumran origins can be reduced to a set of stereotyped terms. Despite his much more sensitive approach, Stegemann is often guilty of the same charge to some extent also.

21 Why he does this is difficult to see; I think the dominant consideration may have been his view of the unity of the 'well-midrash' which, he says, is self-contained in that 'neither the antecedent nor the subsequent context make any contribution to its intelligibility (LADDVI2, 228ff.). But even if this were the case, the criterion is a dubious one in isolation. At all events, he does at least concede that the midrash 'dovetails with the end of the Missionary Document' and suggests that it may have been composed precisely to function as a link between that document and VI,11ff.

22 The common tradition of the three accounts is also to be traced in Jubilees 1. But an evaluation of this goes beyond the immediate concerns of the present study. It is, however, another extremely important avenue of further research.

23 The exact phrase is דורש בתורה, which may have nothing to do with the דורש התורה of CD. On the other hand, the Qumran community believed that the laws instigated by the 'Interpreter of the Law' were superseded or perhaps 'fulfilled' by those of the 'teacher of righteousness' and, after the teacher's death by the community itself (see below on XX,13bff.). Consequently the title דורש התורה may be especially significant for the attitude of the Qumran community to the basis of its own laws.

24 These are the candidates of Jaubert and Rabinowitz respectively; like nearly all scholars, they identify the 'interpreter of the law' with the 'teacher of righteousness.'

25 See the sensible comment of Garnet, 93, n.1, and the useful discussion of Carmignac, 'Le retour du Docteur de Justice à la fin des jours?,' *RQ* 1 (1958-59), 235-248. Carmignac's discussion proceeds plausibly until he seeks a solution of his own. Bizarre though this conclusion is, it is no more so than the view of Dupont-Sommer that the 'teacher of righteousness' was to be resurrected (see his translation *ad loc.*).

26 Apart from the probable meaning of the phrase in Hosea, which speaks of a divine act and not a human, the lawgiving role of the Messiah is amply attested throughout Jewish literature from the Exile to the rabbis.

27 On פרוש = list, see above, Chapter II, n.74.

28 Schiffman, 36.

29 J. Myers, *Ezra-Nehemiah* [Anchor Bible], New York, 1965, 151. Cf. also

Ezra 4,8 (with different pointing).

30 Murphy-O'Connor (LADDVI2) and Garnet (113) had independently recognised the connections between CD and the Holiness Code, but the former noticed only the legal parallels in CD's 'injunctions,' while the latter applied the insight to Qumran literature generally

31 Cf. Mark 7,11-13.

32 LADDVI2, 214.

33 The meaning of תענית is not certain. To my knowledge, all the commentators understand it to mean the Day of Atonement, for in Lev. 16,31 and 23,27 the *verb* ענה is used in connection with *Kippurim*. The fast is also, perhaps significantly, called the 'sabbath of rest' (cp. 1QpHab 11,8). In Ezekiel, as in Ezra and Nehemiah, the Day of Atonement is absent; and, as Rabin notes, in Ezek. 9,5 תענית refers to fast-days *other* than *Kippurim*.

34 A discussion of this passage will also be found in my paper in the Yadin Festschrift, *JJS* 33 (1982).

35 Murphy-O'Connor, LADDVI12, 214, 218.

36 Murphy-O'Connor, EH 223; here he follows the lead of Iwry, 85. It can hardly be retorted that the laws about the Temple are theoretical or ideal, for as a whole the laws of CD are certainly not so, and one cannot wish away laws awkward to one's viewpoint in this way.

37 See especially Stegemann, 225.

38 Murphy-O'Connor, 'The Translation of Damascus Document VI,11-14,' *RQ* 7(1971), 553-556.

39 For an discussion of the process see Murphy-O'Connor, CPJ, 200-206.

40 See Chapter II, n.37.

41 Cf. the quotation from Talmon, 'Aspects of the Dead Sea Scrolls,' *Scripta Hierosolymitana* IV, 163-4 in VanderKam, *THSBJ*, 271. Yet, as Vanderkam himself stresses, Jubilees (he cites 49,6-21) presupposes continuing use of the Temple while adopting a calendar not observed there. Perhaps not too much weight should be laid on Jub. 49, since Segal has argued in an article unremarked by VanderKam ('The Hebrew Festivals and the Calendar,' *JSS* 6 (1961), 74-94; cf. his *The Hebrew Passover*, London, 1963) that this chapter is secondary. On the attitude toward the Temple of Jubilees, see also G.L. Davenport, *The Eschatology of the Book of Jubilees*, Leiden, 1971.

42 For a further discussion of further evidence bearing on this questions, see below, Chapter IV on VII,9bff. and Chapter V on XX,22bff.

43 On this translation, see below, Chapter V, *ad loc.*

44 See above, Chapter II on II,13 and IV,5b.

## NOTES TO CHAPTER IV, WARNINGS

1   On this section, see Murphy-O'Connor has three articles: CPJ, LADDVI2 and 'The Original Text of CD 7:9-8:2 + 19:5-14,' *HTR* 64 (1971), 379-386. The last-mentioned deals specifically with the problem under discussion.

2   'The Amos-Numbers Midrash (CD 7,13b-8,1a) and Messianic Expectation,' *ZAW* 92 (1980), 397-404.

3   For discussion of the meaning of this passage, see Van der Woude, *MV*, 49f. Jaubert, PD, 230, suggests that the Tabernacle itself was transferred to 'Damascus.'

4   The despising of the books of the prophets may have some historical significance, although it is impossible to be sure. In VI,1 those who 'prophesy falsehood' are blamed for Israel's departure from God, while numerous biblical texts used in the *Admonition* deal with false prophecy—notably Ezek. 13 which lies behind VIII,12. It is also as a false prophet that the 'Scoffer' is portrayed (using the verb נטף; I,14; VIII,13).

5   Cf. discussion of פקד in I,7 (above, Chapter II).

6   CD XIII,23-XIV,2 also combines the threat with the Isaiah quotation, but rather than confirming the literary unity of promise and warning, as Murphy-O'Connor claims (LADDVI2,224), the text has probably been expanded through a gloss prompted by the present passage. Nevertheless, the literary unity of promise and threat is not in doubt.

7   E.g. Schechter, Charles, Maier, Cothenet, Jeremias, Murphy-O'Connor.

8   See above, Chapter II, on IV,11.

9   Schwarz, 118, in the context of a lengthy discussion of the possible historical reference of this material, 115ff.

10   Cf. Schwarz, 114f., 127.

11   Murphy-O'Connor, LADDVI2, 225f.

12   Not 'consistently,' as Murphy-O'Connor states (LADDXIX, 417), for I have argued above that in IV,6.8.9 ראשונים means the founders of the community. However, there it is used as an adjective with the noun קדושים, as we have reconstructed it) and it does have the meaning Murphy-O'Connor claims for it at I,4.16; III,10; VI,2.

13   Murphy-O'Connor, *ibid*. Rabinowitz also speaks of the 'Assyro-Babylonian captivity'; and, of course, the merging of the two is as early as the book of Ezekiel.

14   See above, Chapter II, n.37 and Chapter III, n.35.

15   CPJ, 200-206.

16   Jeremias, 110ff.

17   On this passage, Stegemann,166ff.

18   Jeremias, 89.

19   The suggestion is taken up by Murphy-O'Connor, CPJ, 206.

20   The comparison with VI,14ff. was made by Dupont-Sommer 135, n.2:
     'The description of the conduct of the wicked . . . is a sort of counterpart
     of the description given a little earlier of the conduct of the perfect
     sectary.'

21   The text is here again curious. A follows with הבא לעשות נקמה, 'who comes
     (or: 'will come') to do vengeance,' while B has הבא עליהם לנקם נקמה. There
     is also the question whether ראש before 'kings' means 'head' or 'poison' (as
     in the biblical quotation). Commentators are divided, and some who opt
     for the former are tempted to identify this 'king' (e.g. Pompey, according
     to Dupont-Sommer). The idea of 'poison' wreaking vengeance is not
     impossible if Deut. 32,33 and 35 are associated. See the discussion by
     Murphy-O'Connor, CPJ, 208. My guess is that the B text may have been
     accommodated to VIII,1.

22   Schwarz, 136, again provides a full discussion.

23   This accusation (clarified in the B text) is difficult to interpret. It may
     imply that the target is the religious authorities who ought to have been
     setting standards instead of following them. Were they felt by the
     community to be reacting to popular opinion? Even if this inference were
     correct, can we deduce anything further?

24   CPJ, 211.

25   Reading שבי ישראל for his שרי ישראל.

26   Ms. A actually has בשונאי, which could invite a further set of complications.

27   Murphy-O'Connor, CPJ, 212ff. refers first to the critique of the ruling
     classes in Sirach. He notes the phrases 'leaders of Judah' (ἄρχοντες Ιουδα
     [ but a superior reading is ἄνδρες Ιουδα!]) and 'covenant of our fathers'
     (διαθήκη πατέρων ἡμῶν) in I Macc. 2,15-20. He notes that the LXX
     renders שר by ἄρχων, and that in the same I Macc. passage occurs
     ἀπόστασις, which the LXX uses to render מעל and מרד. His conclusive
     parallel, he argues, is the critique of the Wicked Priest in 1QpHab VIII,9-
     13. Both that critique and this have as their target political authority.
     Finally, Murphy-O'Connor compares terms in this passage with their
     occurrence in the so-called 'Teacher hymns,' Community Hymns, the
     1QS 'Manifesto' and the 1QS 'Discourse on the Two Spirits.' Parallels
     with the 'Teacher hymns' are the most extensive, for ten of the twelve
     terms he lists occur in both our passage and these hymns; two of them
     occur in the Manifesto which Murphy-O'Connor regards as also a
     product of the Teacher of Righteousness; and also, quotation of Deut. 32
     is used, he claims, only here and in the 'Teacher hymn,' 1QH V,10.27.
     The evidence is not as impressive as it seems. The Discourse on the Two
     Spirits has three of the chosen terms, one more than the Manifesto, but
     Murphy-O'Connor does not regard it as a product of the Teacher of
     Righteousness, but a relatively late composition. A key term, בגד, is found
     outside CD twice in 1QS, four times in 1QpHab and once in 1QH, but

nowhere in the passages he chooses for comparison. נבר occurs three times in our passage and three times in so-called 'Teacher hymns,' but fourteen times altogether in 1QH—more frequently outside the 'Teacher hymns.' This is no way to present a statistical argument. What Murphy-O'Connor is really saying is that his historical reconstruction of the origins of the Qumran community, which depend on a precise identification of the 'Wicked Priest' and the 'Teacher,' do provide a plausible setting for the critique of the 'princes of Judah.' This is true, but such a claim does not amount to much, given the variety of plausible alternatives. In the case of the I Macc. parallels, too, one requires to establish whether the linguistic evidence reflects the Maccabean period to which it refers or the late Hasmonean era in which it was written, in which case one could use the same evidence to place this critique in the early first century BCE. The fact is that there is nothing specifically to associate this passage with the Qumran community rather than the 'Damascus' community responsible for the original *Admonition*.

28   See the discussion in Schwarz, 93.

29   Segal, cited by Rabin, *ad loc.*, regarded it as a gloss, and Cothenet echoes the suggestion.

## NOTES TO CHAPTER V, THE NEW COVENANT

1   Stegemann, 172-183, covers the material dealt with in this chapter.

2   Murphy-O'Connor, LADDXIX, analyses the material dealt with in this chapter.

3   See the discussion above, Chapter II, on I,1ff. and the Conclusions below.

4   On the possible translations of שוב here, cf. A. Rubinstein, *VT* 7 (1957), 358.

5   Attempts to equate Damascus uniformly with Qumran are misguided, as we have already demonstrated. One might consider the possibility that the new community understood its settlement at Qumran as a new 'Damascus,' except that 'Damascus' is used in none of the Qumran scrolls. The choice of the term would, even in this case, be best accounted for on the supposition that 'Damascus' was already in currency as a symbol of the place of covenant. Stegemann's view that 'Damascus' is not even a geographical symbol is incomprehensible, while Vermes' discussion of the symbolism Damascus-Jerusalem-Qumran (*Scripture and Tradition in Judaism*, Leiden, 1973, 43-49) assumes the equation Damascus = Qumran.

6   It is true that the phrase 'covenant in the land of Damascus' does not occur in the *Admonition* outside the 'New Covenant' material. However,

the components are are all present; Damascus is unquestionably presented as the place where the community's covenant was established. I think it is legitimate to infer that the phrase was in currency, for otherwise it becomes impossible to account for the present form of XX,12.

7   See above, Chapter II, on IV,5bff.

8   On the translation, see van der Woude, *MV*, 37f.; Murphy-O'Connor, LADDXIX, 546, n.6, thinks that originally יחיד stood alone.

9   For a detailed and sober comparison of the two figures, see Jeremias, 319ff.

10   Murphy-O'Connor, LADDXIX, 554f.

11   Murphy-O'Connor regards 'the former and the latter' as the title of a code of laws, just as he regards אלה החקים in XIX,14 as the title of a body of legislation (LADDVI). The suggestion in this case at any rate is not implausible, although in view of the Jubilees usage, unnecessary.

12   God 'remembered' the 'covenant of the ראשונים' in I,4 and VI,2, but 'established' (חקים: or does it mean 'confirmed'?) a (new?) covenant in III,13. Murphy-O'Connor, LADDVI, 229 has drawn attention to this difference.

13   ואמנה is read by Rabin, Dupont-Sommer, Schwarz, Jeremias and Lohse; האמנת by Maier, Denis, Stegemann and Murphy-O'Connor.

14   See above, Chapter II, on III,21ff.

15   Vermes, *Les manuscrits du désert de Juda,*173. His restoration is inspired by VIII,16 and XIX,29, and actually concludes ברברים רעים, which is now agreed to be incorrect, while מעטים is widely accepted.

16   Murphy-O'Connor, LADDXIX, 558, appeals to the arguments of Klinzing, *Die Umdeutung der Kultus,* for the view that the Qumran community regarded itself as a spiritual Temple. This may or may not be the case; at all events, Klinzing in fact regards opponents of the sect as those who defiled the sanctuary, and consequently accepts that the Temple is meant here (18, n.57). A recent discussion of the question is found in D. Schwarz, *RQ* 10 (1981), 442.

17   My view is based on a study of the original at the Cambridge University Library, and I am grateful to Dr. S.C. Reif for his comments on the reading of the text. There is certainly a vertical mark over the word עד, which suggests either that the scribe accidentally omitted a ו, or that he indicated that in his opinion it should be read as עוד, not עד. After the word אל there is a lacuna followed immediately by a mark which most resembles a ר, but if such must be an unusual one.

18   Murphy-O'Connor, LADDXIX, 557; 'those who went out of the Holy City and leaned on God are understood to be converts to the community, but it would be surprising if this were not stated more clearly.' Their status is in fact described clearly in 25-27a which therefore belongs with

22b-24. The first premise is not strictly valid, nor is the second, which misses the point of the phrase כל מבאי הברית. The conclusion is nevertheless correct.

19  לפי רוח in 1QS II,20; IV,26: עצת קדש in 1QS II,25; VIII,21.

20  Cf. Denis, 174, who perceives the problem. He observes that שפט in the sense of 'condemn' is unique here. Murphy-O'Connor comments that eschatological punishment is certainly implied, and that the condemnation of the community and the punishment of God are presented as mutual.

21  Both Stegemann and Murphy-O'Connor make much of the fact that the 'teacher of righteousness' was a High Priest; Stegemann in particular understands the Teacher's rôle within the community as high-priestly. The lack of any such hint in CD adds to the discrepancy between the Qumran *pesharim* and CD, and reminds one also that the Wicked Priest is absent from the latter.

22  Murphy-O'Connor, LADDXIX, 556.

23  Murphy-O'Connor, 559f., citing J. Baumgarten, 'Sacrifice and Worship among the Jewish Sectaries of the Dead Sea (Qumran) Scrolls,' *HTR* 46 (1958), 158-9.

24  M. Baillet, 'Un receuil liturgique de Qumrân, Grotte 4: "Les Paroles des Luminaires",' *RB* 68 (1961), 195-250; 'Ce n'est pas encore la période proprement essénienne.' Cf. also Garnet, 9-11, who deals with this text as his first under the rubric 'pre-Essenian literature.' His interpretation of the document is essentially sound.

25  Murphy-O'Connor, 'La génèse littéraire de la "Règle de la Communauté",' *RB* 76, 528-549; developed by J. Pouilly, *La Règle de la Communauté de Qumrân*, Paris, 1976.


NOTE TO CHAPTER VI, REDACTION OF THE *ADMONITION*

1  A similar development in sectarian attitude may be plotted in the traditions and the documents which have been compiled into the *War Scroll*. See my *1QM, The War Scroll from Qumran*, Rome, 1976.


NOTE TO CONCLUSIONS AND REFLECTIONS

1  This possibility is mooted by P. von der Osten-Sacken, *Gott und Belial*,

198f., in the interests of a highly dubious theory of the development of Qumran dualism; his suggestion has been rejected by VanderKam, *THSBJ*, 257 n. 91. However, if it is acknowledged that CD itself is the product of some considerable literary development, the reference it apparently contains to Jubilees becomes impossible to date and the question of the literary relationship one which cannot necessarily be solved in terms of simple dependence of one upon the other.

# SELECT BIBLIOGRAPHY

For a very extensive bibliography on CD up to 1969, see J.A. Fitzmyer in Schechter, *Documents of Jewish Sectaries*, 25-34. Fuller information on works since 1947 can be obtained from the standard Qumran bibliographies, for which see J.A. Fitzmyer, *The Dead Sea Scrolls. Major Publications and Tools for Study*, Missoula, 1975, 1977, 57-58.

An asterisk beside the author's name indicates that his or her views have been discussed in the *Introduction*; beside the title, it means that the work has been referred to in the book by the author's name alone.

*Albright, W.F. and Mann, C.S. 'Qumran and the Essenes: Geography, Chronology and Identification of the Sect,' *The Scrolls and Christianity*, ed. M. Black, London, 1969, 11-25.

Baltzer, K. *Das Bundesformular*, Neukirchen, 1960, 1964[2]: E.T., *The Covenant Formulary*, Philadelphia, 1971.

Becker, J. *Das Heil Gottes*, Göttingen, 1964.

Beckwith, R. 'The Significance of the Calendar for Interpreting Essene Chronology and Eschatology,' *RQ* 10 (1980), 167-202.

Brown, R. 'The Teacher of Righteousness and the Messiah(s)' in *The Scrolls and Christianity*, ed. M. Black, London, 1969.

Carmignac, J. 'Le Retour du Docteur de Justice à la fin des jours?' *RQ* 1 (1958-9), 235-248.

'Comparaison entre les manuscrits "A" et "B" du Document de Damas,' *RQ* (1959-60), 53-67.

*Charles, R.H. *'The Zadokite Fragments,' in *Apocrypha and Pseudepigrapha of the Old Testament*, Oxford, 1913, II, 785-834.

Charlesworth, J. 'The Origin and Subsequent History of the Authors of the Dead Sea Scrolls: Four Transitional Phases among the Qumran Essenes,' *RQ* 10 (1980), 213-233.

Cothenet, E. *'Le Document de Damas,' in *Les Textes de Qumran*, ed. J. Carmignac and P. Guilbert, Paris, 1963,[2] II, 129-204.

Cross, F.M. *The Ancient Library of Qumran*, London, 1958.

Davies, P.R. 'The Ideology of the Temple in the Damascus Document,' *Essays in Honour of Y. Yadin*, *JJS* 33 (1982), 287-301.

Deichgräber, R. 'Zur Messiaserwartung der Damaskusschrift,' *ZAW* 78 (1966), 333-343.

De Vaux, R. *Archaeology and the Dead Sea Scrolls*, London, 1973.

Delcor, M. 'Contribution à l'étude de la legislation des sectaires de Damas et de Qumran,' *RB* 61 (1954), 533-553; 62 (1955), 68-75.
'Où en sont les études qumraniennes?,' in *Qumran. Sa piéte, sa théologie et son milieu*, ed, M. Delcor, Paris/Leuven, 1978.

*Denis, A.-M. *Les thèmes de connaissance dans le Document de Damas*, Louvain, 1967.

Dupont-Sommer, A. *Les écrits esséniens découverts près de la Mer Morte*, Paris, 1959: *E.T., *The Essene Writings from Qumran*, Oxford, 1961 (esp. 114-163).

Fabry, H.-J. *Die Würzel* שוב *in der Qumran-Literatur. Zur Semantik eines Grundbegriffes*, Bonn 1975.

Fitzmyer, J. 'The Use of Explicit Old Testament Quotations in Qumran literature and in the New Testament,' *NTS* 7 (1960-1), 297-333 [=*Essays on the Semitic Background of the New Testament*, London, 1971/ Missoula, 1974,[2] 3-58.

*Garnet, P. *Salvation and Atonement in the Qumran Scrolls*, Tübingen, 1977.

*Ginzberg, L. *Eine unbekannte jüdische Sekte*, New York, 1922: *E.T. revised and updated, *An Unknown Jewish Sect*, New York, 1970.

Hartman, L. *Asking for a Meaning*, Lund, 1979.

Huppenbauer, H. 'Zur Eschatologie der Damaskusschrift,' *RQ* 4 (1963-4), 567-573.

*Iwry, S. *'Was There a Migration to Damascus? The Problem of שבי ישראל,' *W.F. Albright Volume, Eretz Israel* 9 (1969), 80-88.

*Jaubert, A. 'Le Calendrier des Jubilés et de la Secte de Qumran: ses Origines bibliques,' *VT* 3 (1953), 250-264.
*'Le pays de Damas,' *RB* 65 (1958), 214-248.
*La notion de l'Alliance dans le Judaïsme*, Paris, 1963.

Knibb, M. 'The Exile in the Literature of the Intertestamental Period,' *Heythrop Journal* 17 (1976), 253-272.
'The Dead Sea Scrolls: Reflections on some Recent Publications,' *ET* 90 (1979), 294-300.

Kuhn, K.G. *Konkordanz zu den Qumrantexten*, Göttingen, 1960.
'Nachträge zur *Konkordanz zu den Qumrantexten*,' *RQ* 4 (1963-4), 163-234.

*Lagrange, *'La secte juive de la Nouvelle Alliance au pays de

Damas,' *RB* 9 (1912), 213-240.

Le Déaut, R. 'Une citation de Lévitique 26,45 dans le *Document de Damas* I,4;VI,2,' *RQ* 6 (1967-8), 289-291.

*Lévi, I. *'Un écrit sadducéen antérieur à la destruction du Temple,' *REJ* 61 (1911), 161-205; 63 (1912), 1-19.

    'Document rélatif à la Communauté des Fils de Sadoc,' *REJ* 65 (1913), 24-31.

Lohse, E. *Die Texte aus Qumran hebräisch und deutsch*, Munich, 1974, 63-107.

Maier, J. *Die Texte vom Toten Meer*, Munich, 1960, I,46-70; II,40-62.

Mann, C.S. see Albright, W.F.

*Margoliouth, G. 'The Calendar, The Sabbath and the Marriage Law in the Geniza-Zadokite Document,' *ET* 23 (1911-2), 362-365; 24 (1912-3), 553-558; 25 (1913-4), 560-564.

*Meyer, E. 'Die Gemeinde des neues Bundes im Lande Damaskus: eine jüdische Schrift aus der Seleukidenzeit,' *Abhandlung der preussischen Akademie der Wissenschaften*, Phil.-hist. Klass 9, Berlin, 1919, 1-65.

Milik, J.T. *Ten Years of Discovery in the Wilderness of Judaea*, London, 1959.

Moore, G.F. 'The Covenanters of Damascus: A Hitherto Unknown Jewish Sect,' *HTR* 4 (1911), 330-377.

Morgenstern, J. 'The Calendar of Jubilees, its Origins and its Character,' *VT* 5 (1955), 43-76.

*Murphy-O'Connor, J. *[=EMD] 'An Essene Missionary Document? CD II,14-VI,1,' *RB* 77 (1970), 201-229.

    *[=LADDVI] 'A Literary Analysis of Damascus Document VI,2-VIII,3,' *RB* 78 (1971), 210-232.

    'The Original Text of CD 7:9-8:2 4 19:5-14,' *HTR* 64 (1971), 379-386.

    'The Translation of Damascus Document VI,11-14,' *RQ* 7 (1971), 553-556.

    *[=CPJ] 'The Critique of the Princes of Judah (CD VIII,3-19),' *RB* 79 (1972), 200-216.

    *[=LADDXIX] 'A Literary Analysis of Damascus Document XIX,33-XX,34,' *RB* 79 (1972), 544-564.

North, R. 'The Damascus of Qumran Geography,' *PEQ* 87 (1955), 34-48.

Rabin, C. *The Zadokite Documents*, Oxford, 1954, 1958.[2]

*Qumran Studies*, Oxford, 1957.

*Rabinowitz, I. *"A Reconsideration of "Damascus" and "390 Years" in the "Damascus" ("Zadokite") Fragments,' *JBL* 73 (1954), 11-35.

'The Guides of Righteousness,' *VT* 8 (1958), 391-404.

Rost, L. *Die Damaskusschrift neu bearbeitet*, Berlin, 1933.

'Zur Struktur der Gemeinde des neuen Bundes im Lande Damaskus,' *VT* 9 (1959), 393-398.

Rowley, H.H. *The Zadokite Fragments and the Dead Sea Scrolls*, Oxford, 1952.

'The 390 Years of the Zadokite Work,' in *Mélanges bibliques rédigés en l'honneur de André Robert*, Paris, 1957, 341-347.

Rubinstein, A. 'Urban Halachah and Camp Rules in the "Cairo Fragments of a Damascene Covenant",' *Sefarad* 12 (1952), 283-96.

'Notes on Some Syntactical Irregularities in text B of the Zadokite Documents,' *VT* 7 (1957), 356-361.

*Schechter, S. *Documents of Jewish Sectaries*, Cambridge, 1910, IX-LXIX,1-20. Reprinted New York, 1970 with a Prolegomenon by J.A. Fitzmyer.

Schiffmann, L. *The Halachah at Qumran*, Leiden, 1975.

Schwarz, D. 'To Join Oneself to the House of Judah (Damascus Document IV,11)' *RQ* 10 (1981), 435-446.

*Schwarz, O. *Der erste Teil der Damaskusschrifte und das AT*, Diest, 1965.

Segal, M.H. 'The Habakkuk "Commentary" and the Damascus Fragments,' *JBL* 70 (1951), 131-147.

*Smith, Morton 'The Dead Sea Sect in Relation to Ancient Judaism,' *NTS* 7 (1961), 347-360.

Soloff, R.A. 'Toward Uncovering Original Texts in the Zadokite Documents,' *NTS* 5 (1958-9), 62-67.

Starcky, J. 'Les Maîtres de Justice et la chronologie de Qumran,' in *Qumran. Sa piété, sa théologie et son milieu*, ed. M. Delcor, Paris/Leuven, 1978, 249-256.

*Stegemann, H. *Die Entstehung der Qumrangemeinde*, Bonn, 1971.

Talmon, S. 'The Calendrical Reckoning of the Sect from the Judaean Desert,' *Aspects of the Dead Sea Scrolls, Scripta Hierosolymitana* 4, 1958.

Thiering, B. *Redating the Teacher of Righteousness*, Sydney, 1979.

VanderKam, J. *Textual and Historical Studies in the Book of Jubilees*,

Missoula, 1977.

'The Origin, Character, and Early History of the 364-Day Calendar: A Re-Assessment of Jaubert's Hypotheses,' *CBQ* 41 (1979), 390-411.

'2 Maccabees 6,7a and Calendrical Change in Jerusalem,' *JSJ* 11 (1981), 52-74.

Vermes, G. *Les manuscrits du Désert de Juda*, Tournai, 1954.

'Lion-Damascus-Mehokek-Man—Symbolical Traditions in the Dead Sea Scrolls,' in *Scripture and Tradition in Judaism*, Leiden, 1961, 40-66.

'Sectarian Matrimonial Halakhah in the Damascus Rule,' in *Post-Biblical Jewish Studies*, Leiden, 1975, 50-56.

'The Essenes and History,' *JJS* 32 (1981), 18-31.

Weinert, F. '4Q159: Legislation for an Essene Community outside of Qumran?,' *JSJ* 5 (1974), 179-207.

'A Note on 4Q159 and a New Theory of Essene Origins,' *RQ* 9 (1977), 223-230.

Wernberg-Møller, P. 'צדק, צדיק, and צדוק in the Zadokite Fragments (CDC), the Manual of Discipline (DSD) and the Habakkuk Commentary (DSH),' *VT* 3 (1953), 310-315.

*Wiesenberg, E. 'Chronological Data in the Zadokite Fragments,' *VT* 5 (1955), 284-308.

Winter, P. 'Sadoqite Fragments IV 20,21 and the Exegesis of Genesis 1:27 in Late Judaism,' *ZAW* 68 (1956), 71-84.

Zeitlin, S. *The Zadokite Fragments. Facsimile of the Manuscripts in the Cairo Genizah Collection in the Possession of the University Library, Cambridge, England*, Philadelphia, 1952.

## TEXT

[This text is not intended as a critical edition, for which those
of Rabin and Rost are recommended. In the main it follows
the readings of Rabin: crucial readings are referred to in the
notes accompanying the translation.]

## I

ועתה שמעו כל יודעי צדק ובינו במעשי

אל כי ריב לו עם כל בשר ומשפט יעשה בכל מנאציו

כי במועלם אשר עזבוהו הסתיר פניו מישראל וממקדשו

ויתנם לחרב ובזכרו ברית ראשנים השאיר שארית

5 לישראל ולא נתנם לכלה ובקץ חרון שנים שלוש מאות

ותשעים לתיתו אותם ביד נבוכדנאצר מלך בבל

פקדם ויצמה מישראל ומאהרן שורש מטעת לירוש

את ארצו ולדשן בטוב אדמתו ויבינו בעונם וידעו כי

אנשים אשמים הם ויהיו כעורים וכימגששים דרך

10 שנים עשרים ובן אל אל מעשיהם כי בלב שלם דרשוהו

ויקם להם מורה צדק להדריכם בדרך לבו ויודע

## TRANSLATION

### *Sigla*

< > gloss or secondary expansion
[ ] lacuna in the text: restored
( ) words supplied to clarify the sense

## MS A

## HISTORY

### I

1 And now listen, all who know righteousness, and understand the dealings of
2 God. For He has a dispute with all flesh and executes judgment with all who despise Him.
3 For when they sinned in forsaking Him, He hid His face from Israel <and from His sanctuary >
4 and delivered them to the sword. But when He remembered the covenant of the fathers He preserved a remnant
5 for Israel and did not bring them to total destruction. And in the period of wrath <three hundred and
6 ninety years from delivering them into the hand of Nebuchad-nezzar king of Babylon>
7 He punished them, but He made a root for planting grow from Israel <and from Aaron> to occupy
8 His (or: its) land and to flourish on the goodness of His (or: its) soil. And they recognised their iniquity and knew that
9 they were guilty men, and they were like the blind and those who grope (their) way
10 <for twenty years>. But God understood their deeds, that they sought Him with a perfect heart
11 <and He raised for them a teacher of righteousness to lead them in the way of His heart>. And He made known

לדורות אחרונים את אשר עשה בדור אחרון בעדת בוגדים

הם סרי דרך היא העת אשר היה כתוב עליה כפרה סוררה

כן סרר ישראל בעמוד איש הלצון אשר הטיף לישראל

15 מימי כזב ויתעם בתוהו לא דרך להשח גבהות עולם ולסור

מנתיבות צדק ולסיע גבול אשר גבלו ראשנים בנחלתם למען

הדבק בהם את אלות בריתו להסגירם לחרב נקמת נקם

ברית בעבור אשר דרשו בחלקות ויבחרו במהתלות ויצפו

לפרצות ויבחרו בטוב הצואר ויצדיקו רשע וירשיעו צדיק

20 ויעבירו ברית ויפירו חוק ויגודו על נפש צדיק ובכל הולכי

תמים תעבה נפשם וירדפום לחרב ויסיסו לריב עם ויחר אף

## II

אל בעדתם להשם את כל המונם ומעשיהם לנדה לפניו

ועתה שמעו אלי כל באי ברית ואגלה אזנכם בדרכי

רשעים     אל אהב דעת הכמה ותושיה הציב לפניו

12 to later generations what He had done to <the last generation> a congregation of traitors.

13 <They are the 'turners from the way.' That was the time about which was written: 'like a wandering heifer

14 so did Israel stray'—when the 'man of scoffing' arose who spouted waters of deceit to Israel

15 and led them astray in a wilderness without way, to bring low the everlasting heights and to turn aside

16 from the paths of righteousness and to remove the boundary which the fathers had set up on their inheritance, in order that

17 the curses of His covenant should apply to them, delivering them to the sword which executes the vengeance of the

18 covenant.> For they sought the easy way and chose illusion and looked out for loopholes

19 and chose the 'fair neck' and acquitted the guilty and condemned the innocent

20 and broke the covenant and violated the ordinance and banded together against the life of the righteous man,

21 and their soul abhorred all who lived uprightly, and they persecuted them with the sword, and *fomented public strife. And God's

## II

1 anger was aroused against their congregation to destroy their whole multitude, for their deeds were a defilement in His presence.

*Note*

21 *The verb may mean 'incite,' 'exult' or possibly 'oppress.' Unlike most of the other phrases, this is not apparently a biblical quotation;* מריבי עם *is found in Ps. 18,44* = *II Sam. 22,44:*עמי.

## II

2 And now listen to me, all who enter the covenant, and I will open your ear to the ways of

3 the wicked. God loves knowledge; wisdom and counsel He has appointed in His presence;

עָרְמָה וְדַעַת הֵם יְשָׁרְתֻהוּ אֶרֶךְ אפים עמו ורוב סליחות

5 לכפר בעד שבי פשע וכוח וגבורה והמה גדולה בלהבי אש

בי כל מלאכי הבל על סררי דרך ומתעבי חק לאין שארית

ופליטה למו כי לא בחר אל בהם מקדם עולם ובטרם נוסדו ידע

את מעשיהם ויתעב את דורות מדם ויסתר את פניו מן הארץ

מי עד תומם וידע את שני מעמד ומספר ופרוש קציהם לכל

10 הוי עולמים ונהיית עד מה יבוא בקציהם לכל שני עולם

ובכולם הקים לו קריאי שם למען התיר פליטה לארץ ולמלא

פני תבל מזרעם     ויודיעם ביד משיחו רוח קדשו והוזי

אמת ובפרוש שמו שמותיהם ואת אשר שנא התעה

ועתה בנים שמעו לי ואגלה עיניכם לראות ולהבין במעשי

15 אל ולבחור את אשר רצה ולמאוס כאשר שנא להתהלך תמים

בכל דרכיו ולא לתור במחשבות יצר אשמה ועני זנות כי רבים

תעו בם וגבורי חיל נכשלו בם מלפנים ועד הנה בלכתם בשרירות

4   prudence and knowledge serve Him as ministers; patience is beside Him and abundance of pardon

5   to forgive those who repent of sin, but power and might and great wrath with fiery flames

6   by all the angels of destruction against those who turn from the way and abhor the ordinance, without remnant

7   or survivor of them. For from the beginning of the world God did not choose them, and before they came into being He knew

8   their deeds and abhorred their generations from the beginning*, and hid His face from the land

9   until *their annihilation. And He knew (or: knows) the years of their existence and the number and details of their (allotted) periods for all

10   beings in eternity, and all that happens, even to all things that will transpire in their (allotted) periods for all the years of eternity (or: of the world).

11   And in all of them He has established for Himself 'men called by name' in order to leave a remnant for the land and to fill

12   the surface of the earth with their seed. And He teaches them through those anointed by His holy spirit and those who see

13   the truth; and their names He has placed* in a list, but those whom He hates He has allowed to go astray (or: allows to go astray).

*Notes*

8   *Reading* מקדם *for* מדם.

9   *The translation ignores the problematic* מי *of the Hebrew.*

13   *Reading* שם *for* שמו.

### II

14   And now, children, listen to me and I will open your eyes to see and understand the dealings of

15   God, and to choose what He likes and reject what He hates; and to walk uprightly

16   in all His ways and not to be drawn by (the) thoughts of a guilty nature or by lustful eyes. For many

17   have gone astray because of them; powerful men have come to grief because of them, in the past and up to the present. By walking in the stubbornness of their

לבם נפלו עירי השמים בה נאחזו אשר לא שמרו מצות אל

ובניהם אשר כרום ארזים גבהם וכהרים גויותיהם כי נפלו

20 כל בשר היה בחרבה כי גוע ויהיו כלא היו בעשותם את

רצונם ולא שמרו את מצות עשיהם עד אשר חרה אפו בם

## III

בה תעי בני נח ומשפחהותיהם בה הם נכרתים

אברהם לא הלך בה ויע[ן]ל א[ו]הב בשמרו מצות אל ולא בחר

ברצון רוחו וימסור לישחק וליעקב וישמרו ויכתבו אוהבים

לאל ובעלי ברית לעולם　　　בני יעקב תעו בם ויענשו לפני

5 משגותם ובניהם במצרים הלכו בשרירות לבם להיעץ על

מצות אל ולעשות איש הישר בעיניו ויאכלו את הדם ויכרת

זכורם במדבר להם בקדש עלו ורשו את רוחם ולא שמעו

לקול עשיהם מצות יוריהם וירגנו באהליהם ויחר אף אל

בעדתם ובניהם בו אבדו ומלכיהם בו נכרתו וגיבוריהם בו

10 אבדו וארצם בו שממה בו חבו באי הברית הראשנים ויסגרו

לחרב בעזבם את ברית אל ויבחרו ברצונם ויתורו אחרי שרירות

לבם לעשות איש את רצונו　　　ובמחזיקים במצות אל

אשר נותרו מהם הקם אל את בריתו לישראל עד עולם לגלות

להם נסתרות אשר תעו בם כל ישראל　　　שבתות קדשו ומועדי

18 heart the Watchers* of heaven fell; because of it those who did not keep the commandments of God were caught

19 as were their children, who were as tall as cedars and whose corpses were like mountains when they fell, because

20 all flesh which was on dry land perished and became as if they had not been—because they did

21 as they wanted and did not keep the commandments of their Maker until His anger was aroused against them.

## III

1 Because of it the children of Noah went astray* as did their families; through it they were cut off.

2 Noah did not follow it, and he was accoun[ted* a Fri]end (of God) because he kept the commandments of God and did not choose

3 what he himself wanted. And he passed on (the commandments) to Isaac and Jacob, and they kept (them) and were written down as Friends

4 of God and covenant partners for ever. The children of Jacob went astray because of them and were punished according to their

5 error. And their children in Egypt walked in the stubbornness of their heart in taking counsel against

6 the commandments of God and doing each one as he thought right. They ate blood, and their males were cut off

7 in the desert. (And He spoke*) to them at Kadesh: 'Go up and possess the land,' but they chose what they themselves wanted* and did not listen

8 to the voice of their Maker, the commandment of their Teacher, but murmured in their tents. And the anger of God was aroused

9 against their congregation. By it their children perished; by it their kings were cut off; by it their warriors

10 perished, and by it their land was made desolate. By it* the first covenant members incurred guilt and were delivered up

11 to the sword—because they had forsaken the covenant of God and chosen what they wanted and been drawn after the stubbornness

12 of their heart to do each one as he wanted. But with those who adhered to the commandments of God,

13 who were left over of them, God established (or: confirmed) His covenant with Israel by revealing

14 to them the hidden things in which all Israel had gone astray—His

15 כבודו עידות צדקו ודרכי אמתו וחפצי רצונו אשר יעשה

האדם וחיה בהם          פתח לפניהם ויחפרו באר למים רבים

ומואסיהם לא יחיה והם התגוללו בפשע אנוש ובדרכי נדה

ויאמרו כי לנו היא ואל ברוי פלאו כפר בעד עונם וישא לפשעם

ויבן להם בית נאמן בישראל אשר לא עמד כמהו למלפנים ועד

20 הנה המחזיקים בו לחיי נצח וכל כבוד אדם להם הוא כאשר

הקים אל להם ביד יחזקאל הנביא לאמר הכהנים והלוים ובני

## IV

צדוק אשר שמרו את משמרת מקדשי בתעות בני ישראל

מעלי הם יגישו לי הלב ודם          הכהנים הם שבי ישראל

היוצאים מארץ יהודה והנלוים עמהם    ובני צדוק הם בחירי

ישראל קריאי השם העמדים באחרית הימים הנה פרוש

5 שמותיהם לתולדותם וקץ מעמדם ומספר צרותיהם ושני

התגוררם ופירוש מעשיהם     הקודש שונים אשר כפר

אל בעדם ויצדיקו צדיק וירשיעו רשע וכל הבאים אחריהם

לעשות כפרוש התורה אשר התוסרו בו הראשנים עד שלים

הקץ השנים האלה כברית אשר הקים אל לראשנים לכפר

10 על עונותיהם כן יכפר אל בעדם ובשלים הקץ למספר השנים

האלה אין עוד להשתפח לבית יהודה כי אם לעמוד איש על

holy sabbaths and His glorious

15 festivals, His righteous testimonies and His true ways, and the desires of His will, which a man should do

16 and live by. He opened to them and they dug a well of copious water.

17 <And those who despise it shall not live.> For they had been defiling themselves with human sinfulness and unclean practices

18 and had said, 'but this is ours.' Yet God in His wonderful mysteries forgave their iniquity and removed their sin

19 and built for them a sure house in Israel whose like has not stood from past times until

20 now. Those who adhere to it will live for ever and all the glory of Adam shall be theirs. This is as

21 God established for them in the words of Ezekiel the prophet, saying: 'The priests and the levites and the sons of

## IV

1 Zadok who kept charge of My sanctuary when the children of Israel went astray

2 from Me shall approach Me with* fat and blood.' The priests are the 'captivity of Israel'

3 who went out from the land of Judah; (the levites are*) those who joined them, and the sons of Zadok are the chosen ones of

4 Israel, those 'called by name' who arise at the end of days. Here is a list

5 of their names, in their generations, the period of their lifespan, the number of their afflictions, the years of

6 their residence (in exile) and a list of their deeds: [ . . . These are] the holy [founders] whom God

7 forgave; they acquitted the righteous and condemned the guilty. And (as for) all who have entered (the covenant) after them,

8 to behave in accordance with the details of the law in which the founders were instructed, until the completion of the

9 period of these years, God will, according to the covenant which He established (or: confirmed) with the founders, to forgive

10 their iniquities, forgive them also. And at the completion of the period, according to the number of these

11 years, there will be no (further) joining the House of Judah, but rather 'each man must stand upon

מצודו נבנתה הגדר רחק החוק ובכל השנים האלה יהיה
בליעל משולח בישראל כאשר דבר אל ביד ישעיה הנביא בן
אמוץ לאמר פחד ופחת ופה עליך יושב הארץ     פשרו
15 שלושת מצודות בליעל אשר אמר עליהם לוי בן יעקב
אשר הוא תפש בהם בישראל ויתנם פניהם לשלושת מיני
הצדק הראשונה היא הזנות השנית ההון השלישית
טמא המקדש העולה מזה יתפש בזה והניצל מזה יתפש
בזה     בוני החוין אשר הלכו אחרי צו הצו הוא מטיף
20 אשר אמר הטף יטיפון הם ניתפשים בשתים בזנות לקחת
שתי נשים בחייהם ויסוד הבריאה זכר ונקבה ברא אותם

12 his watchtower.' 'The wall is built, the boundary is extended . . . '

*Notes*

## II

18 *Reading* עירי *for* עידי.

## III

1 *Reading* תעו *for* תעי.
2 *Reading* ויע]ל או[הב.
7 *Supplying* וידבר, *omitted accidentally after* במדבר.
  *Supplying* ארץ ויבחרו ברצון *before* רוחם.
10 *Supplying* בו *before* חבו *and emending* חבו *to* הבו.

## IV

2 *The MT has been abridged in this quotation, and has* קרב *instead of*
  נגש.
3 *Restoring* הלוים, *omitted accidentally before* והנלוים.

## LAW

## IV

12 And during all those years
13 Belial is let loose on Israel, as God spoke through Isaiah the
   prophet, the son of
14 Amoz, saying: 'Terror and the pit and the snare are upon you,
   inhabitant of the land.' Its meaning is
15 the three nets of Belial about which Levi the son of Jacob spoke, in
   which he traps Israel and presents them in the guise of three kinds
   of
16 righteousness. The first is lust, the second wealth and the third
18 defiling the sanctuary. Whoever escapes one is trapped in another,
   and whoever is rescued from this one is trapped in (yet)
19 another. The 'builders of the wall' who have 'followed after
   Zaw'<the Zaw is a spouter,
20 as it says: 'they shall indeed spout'> are trapped in two: in lust by

## V

ובאי התבה שנים שנים באו אל התבה     ועל הנשיא כתוב

לא ירבה לו נשים ודויד לא קרא בספר התורה החתום אשר

היה בארון כי לא נפתח בישראל מיום מות אלעזר

ויהושע ויושע והזקנים אשר עבדו את העשתרת ויטמן

5 נגלה עד עמוד צדוק ויעלו מעשי דויד מלבד דם אוריה

ויעזבם לו אל וגם מטמאים הם את המקדש אשר אין הם

מבדיל כתורה ושוכבים עם הרואה את דם זובה ולוקחים

איש את בת אחיהֻ ואת בת אחותו     ומשה אמר אל

אחות אמך לא תקרב שאר אמך היא ומשפט העריות לזכרים

10 הוא כתוב וכהם הנשים ואם תגלה בת האח את ערות אחי

אביה והיא שאר     וגם את רוח קדשיהם טמאו ובלשון

גדופים פתחו פה על חוקי ברית אל לאמר לא נכונו ותועבה

הם מדברים בם כלם קדחי אש ומבערי זיקות קורי

עכביש קוריהם וביצי צפעונים ביציהם הקרוב אליהם

15 לא ינקה כהר ביתו יאשם כי אם נלחץ כי אם למילפנים פקד

אל את מעשיהם ויחר אפו בעלילותיהם כי לא עם בינות הוא

הם גוי אבד עצות מאשר אין בהם בינה כי מלפנים עמד

משה ואהרן ביד שר האורים ויקם בליעל את יחנה ואת

taking
21 two wives during their lifetime, whereas the principle of creation
is 'male and female He created them,'

V

1 and those who went into the ark 'two by two they went into the
ark.' <And concerning the prince, it is written:
2 'He shall not multiply wives for himself'; but David had not read
the sealed book of the law which
3 was in the ark (of the covenant), for it had not been opened in
Israel since the deaths of Eleazar,
4 Joshua* and the Elders, because (during this time) they were
worshipping Ashtoreth; so it was hidden
5 (and not*) revealed until Zadok arose. Hence the deeds of David
were overlooked, except the blood of Uriah,
6 and God allowed them to him.> Also they defile the sanctuary in
not
7 separating according to the law, but sleeping with a menstruating
woman or marrying
8 the daughter of brother or sister. Yet Moses said: 'You shall not
9 approach your mother's sister, for she is akin to your mother.' The
law of incest is written in terms
10 of males, but it is the same for women, so that a brother's daughter
should not have intercourse with the brother of
11 her father, for he* is akin (to her father). Also, they have defiled
their holy spirits and with a blasphemous
12 tongue have opened their mouths against the ordinances of God's
covenant, saying that they are not established; it is an abomination
13 they are speaking against them. They are 'all of them kindlers of
fire and lighters of firebrands.' 'Their webs
14 are spiders' webs and their eggs adders' eggs.' He who associates
with them
15 will not be held innocent; the more he does it the guiltier he is, if he
is not compelled. For* in earlier times God
16 punished their deeds and His anger was aroused against their
doings, for 'it is not a people of understanding';
17 'they are a nation devoid of counsel, because there is no
understanding in them.' For in earlier times Moses
18 and Aaron arose with the help of the Prince of Lights, while Belial

אהיהו במזמתו בהושע ישראל את הראשונה

20　　　ובקץ הרבן הארץ עמדו מסיגי הגבול ויתעו את ישראל

ותישם הארץ כי דברו סרה על מצות אל ביד משה וגם

## VI

במשיחו הקודש וינבאו שקר להשיב את ישראל מאחר

אל ויזכר אל ברית ראשנים　　　ויקם מאהרן נבונים ומישראל

חכמים וישמעם ויחפורו את הבאר באר חפרוה שרים כרוה

נדיבי העם במחוקק הבאר היא התורה וחופריה הם

5　שבי ישראל היוצאים מארץ יהודה ויגורו בארץ דמשק

אשר קרא אל את כולם שרים כי דרשוהו ולא הושבה

פארתם בפי אחד　　　והמחוקק הוא דורש התורה אשר

אמר ישעיה מוציא כלי למעשיהו　　　ונדיבי העם הם

הבאים לכרות את הבאר במחוקקות אשר חקק המחוקק

10　להתהלך במה בכל קץ הרשיע וזולתם לא ישינו עד עמד

יורה הצדק באחרית הימים

raised up Jannes and
19 his brother in his cunning, when Israel was saved the first time.
20 And at the time of the destruction of the land, there arose those
who 'moved the boundary' and led Israel astray,
21 and the land became desolate because they spoke rebellion against
the commandments of God given through Moses and through

## VI

1 those anointed with holiness*, and prophesied falsely to turn
Israel from
2 God. But God remembered the covenant of the fathers and he
raised from Aaron men of understanding and from Israel
3 men of wisdom, and He let them hear (His voice), and they dug the
well, 'a well which princes dug, which nobles of
4 the people dug with a staff.' The well is the law, and those who dug
it are
5 the 'captivity of Israel' who went out from the land of Judah and
settled in the land of Damascus,
6 all of whom God called 'princes' because they sought Him and
because their
7 renown* was not denied by anyone. And the Staff is the
Interpreter of the Law of whom
8 Isaiah spoke (when he said): 'He produces a tool for His work.'
And the nobles of the people are
9 those who have entered (the covenant) to dig the well with the
staves (rules) which the Staff (legislator) fashioned (legislated)
10 to walk in during all the period of wickedness <and without them
they will not succeed> until there shall arise
11 one who will 'teach righteousness' at the end of days.

*Notes*

4 *In error, 'Joshua' is written twice, with a slight variation of spelling.*
5 *Supplying* ולא *omitted at the beginning of the line in error; cf. the
same feature at VII,12.*
11 *Reading* הוא *for* היא, *an understandable scribal error or possibly
alteration.*
15 *Omitting* אם *as an error after the preceding* כי אם.

וכל אשר הובאו בברית

לבלתי בוא אל המקדש להאיר מזבחו ויהיו מסגירי

הדלת אשר אמר אל מי בכם יסגיר דלתו     ולא תאירו מזבחי

חנם אם לא ישמרו לעשות כפרוש התורה לקץ הרשע ולהבדל

<sup></sup>15 מבני השחת ולהנזר מהון הרשעה הטמא בנדר ובחרם

ובהון המקדש ולגזול את עניי עמו להיות אלמנות שללם

ואת יתומים ירצחו ולהבדיל בין הטמא לטהור ולהודיע בין

הקודש לחול ולשמור את יום השבת כפרושה ואת המועדות

ואת יום התענית כמצאת   באי הברית החדשה בארץ דמשק

<sup></sup>20 להרים את הקדשים כפירושיהם לאהוב איש את אחיהו

כמהו ולהחזיק ביד עני ואביון וגר     ולדרוש איש את שלום

## VII

אחיהו ולא ימעל איש בשאר בשרו להזיר מן הזונות

כמשפט להוכיח איש את אחיהו כמצוה ולא לנטור

מיום ליום ולהבדל מכל הטמאות כמשפטם ולא ישקץ

איש את רוח קדשיו כאשר הבדיל אל להם כל המתהלכים

## VI

1   *Reading* משיחי *for* משיחו *cf. II,6.*
7   *Reading* תפארתם *for* פארתם.

## VI

11  And all who have been admitted into the covenant
12  (are not) to enter the sanctuary 'to light His altar in vain,' <and become 'closers of the door,
13  as God said: 'Who among you will close its door, and you shall not light my altar
14  in vain'> unless they are observant in doing according to the law as detailed for the period of wickedness: to separate
15  from the children of the Pit; to refrain from unjust wealth which defiles, (whether) in vowing, or devoting,
16  or in respect of Temple property; <this is to 'rob the poor of His people, that widows become their spoil
17  and that they might murder the orphans'> to separate the unclean from the clean and to make clear the difference between
18  the holy and the profane; to keep the Sabbath day according to the details; <and the festival days
19  and the Fast Day according to the finding of the members of the new covenant in the land of Damascus>
20  to offer the holy things according to their details; to love each one his brother
21  as himself; to support the poor, the needy and the stranger; to seek each one the well-being of

## VII

1   his brother; <and not to sin each one against his kinsman;> to keep away from lust
2   according to the regulation; to reprove each man his brother according to the commandment and not bear a grudge
3   from one day to the next; to keep away from all uncleanness according to their rules, <and for each man not
4   to defile his holy spirit> as God has taught them to distinguish

באלה בתמים קדש על פי כל יסורו ברית אל נאמנות להם 5
להיותם אלף דור    ואם מחנות ישבו כסרך הארץ ולקחו
נשים והולידו בנים והתהלכו על פי התורה    וכמשפט
היסורים כסרך התורה כאשר אמר בין איש לאשתו ובין אב
לבנו וכל המואסים בפקד אל את הארץ להשיב גמול רשעים
עליהם בבוא הדבר אשר כתוב בדברי ישעיה בן אמוץ הנביא 10
אשר אמר יבוא עליך ועל עמך ועל בית אביך ימים אשר
באו מיום סור אפרים מעל יהודה בהפרד שני בתי ישראל
שר אפרים מעל יהודה וכל הנסוגים הסגרו לחרב והמחזיקים
נמלטו לארץ צפון    כאשר אמר והגליתי את סכות מלככם
ואת כיון צלמיכם מאהלי דמשק    ספרי התורה הם סוכת 15
המלך כאשר אמר והקימותי את סוכת דוד הנפלת המלך
הוא הקהל וכיניי הצלמים וכיון הצלמים הם ספרי הנביאים
אשר בזה ישראל את דבריהם    והכוכב הוא דורש התורה
הבא דמשק כאשר כתוב דרך כוכב מיעקב וקם שבט
מישראל השבט הוא נשיא כל העדה ובעמדו וקרקר 20
את כל בני שת    אלה מלטו בקץ הפקודה הראשון

(them). (As for) all who walk

5  according to these injunctions, in perfect holiness, following all His instruction—the covenant of God is established* for them

6  that they may live for a thousand generations. And if they live in camps, following the order of the land, and take

7  wives and have children, these (sc. the wives and children) shall walk according to the law and according to the rules of

8  the Instructions, by order of the law which says: 'for a man and his wife, and for a father and his

9  son.' And (as for) all who reject—when God shall visit the earth to repay the reward of the wicked

10  upon them,

## WARNINGS

10  when there shall come to pass the word which is written in the words of Isaiah, son of Amoz, the prophet,

11  who said: 'There shall come upon you and upon your people and upon your father's house days which

12  have (not*) come since the day when Ephraim departed from Judah.' When the two houses of Israel separated,

13  Ephraim ruled over Judah, and all who turned back were delivered to the sword, while those who held fast

14  escaped <to the land of the north, as it says: 'And I will exile the booth* of your king

15  and the "kiyyun"* of your images from my tent to Damascus.' The books of the law are the booth of

16  the king, as He said: 'And I will raise up the booth of David which is falling.' The king is

17  the assembly, and the 'kiyyun' of the images* are the books of the prophets

18  whose words Israel despised. And the star is the Interpreter of the Law

19  who came to Damascus, as it is written: 'A star shall come forth from Jacob and a sceptre shall arise

20  from Israel.' The sceptre is the prince of all the congregation and when he arises he shall 'destroy

21  all the children of Seth.' These escaped at the time of the first* visitation

## VIII

והנסוגים הסגירו לחרב וכן משפט כל באי בריתו אשר
לא יחזיקו באלה לפוקדם לכלה ביד בליעל הוא היום
אשר יפקד אל היו שרי יהודה אשר תשפוך עליהם העברה
כי יחלו למרפא וידקמום כל מורדים מאשר לא סרו מדרך
5 בוגדים ויתגוללו בדרכי זונות ובהון רשעה ונקום וניטור
איש לאחיו ושנוא איש את רעהו ויתעלמו איש בשאר בשרו
ויגשו לזמה ויתגברו להון ולבצע ויעשו איש הישר בעיניו
ויבחרו איש בשרירות לבו ולא נזרו מעם ויפרעו ביד רמה

## VIII

1 while those who turned back were delivered to the sword>. And thus is the judgment on all members of His covenant who
2 have not held fast to these (Injunctions), being visited to destruction by the hand of Belial.

## Notes

### VII

5 Here the B text opens.
Reading נאמן for נאמנות; but see XIV,5 which also gives נאמנות.
12 Supplying ולא omitted at the beginning of the line in error; cf. the same feature at V,5.
14 Reading סוכת for סכות, as in line 15.
15 This is better left untranslated; its meaning in Amos is disputed.
17 The text reads וכיני הצלמים וכיון הצלמים. Most probably one of these word-pairs is a gloss, but it is impossible to tell which. I have translated the latter pair and omitted the former.
21 Reading הראשונה for הראשונים.

### VIII

2 This is the day
3 when God shall visit 'the princes of Judah <have become> upon whom Thou wilt pour wrath.'
4 For they hoped for healing, but the blemish shall stick. All are rebellious, because they did not depart from the way
5 of traitors but defiled themselves in the ways of lust and ill-gotten wealth, revenge and grudge-bearing
6 one with another, and hating each one his neighbour. They despised each one his kinsman
7 and they indulged in unchastity and behaved arrogantly for the sake of wealth and profit and did each one as he pleased
8 and chose each one in accordance with the stubbornness of his heart. They did not separate from the people and rebelled with a high hand

ללכת בדרך רשעים אשר אמר אל עליהם חמת תנינים יינם

10 וראש פתנים אכזר    התנינים הם מלכי העמים וינם הוא

דרכיהם וראש הפתנים הוא ראש מלכי יון הבא לעשות בהם

בהם נקמה ובכל אלה לא הבינו בוני החוץ וטחי התפל כי

שוקל רוח ומטיף כזב הטיף להם אשר חרה אף אל בכל עדתו

ואשר אמר משה לא בצדקתך ובישר לבבך אתה בא לרשת את הגוים

15 האלה כי מאהבתו את אבותך ומשמרו את השבועה

וכן המשפט לשבי ישראל סרו מדרך העם באהבת אל את

הראשנים אשר העירו אחריו אהב את הבאים אחריהם כי להם

ברית האבות    ובשונאי את בוני החוץ חרה אפו    וכמשפט

הזה לכל המואס במצות אל ויעזבם ויפנו בשרירות לבם

20    הוא הדבר אשר אמר ירמיה לברוך בן נרייה ואלישע

לגהזי נערו    כל האנשים אשר באו בברית החדשה בארץ דמשק

9   to walk in the way of the wicked, about whom God said: 'Serpents' venom is their wine

10  and cruel poison of asps.' The serpents are the kings of the nations and their wine is

11  their ways and the poison of asps is the head (or: poison*) of the kings of Greece who will come to wreak

12  vengeance on them. <But all these things they do not understand, (these) 'builders of the wall' and 'daubers of plaster' because

13  a raiser of wind and spouter of lies spouted to them, against all of whose congregation the anger of God is aroused.>

14  But, as Moses said: 'Not because of your righteousness nor the uprightness of your heart are you going to dispossess these

15  nations, but because (God) loved your fathers and kept His promise.'

16  And this is the judgment of the 'captivity of Israel' who departed* from the way of the people: because of God's love for

17  the founders who walked* after him, He loves those who come after them, for theirs is

18  the 'covenant of the fathers.' But against <those who hate>* the 'builders of the wall' His anger is aroused. And like this

19  judgment (it will be) for everyone who rejects the commandments of God and forsakes them and turns* in the stubbornness of his heart.

20  *This is the word which Jeremiah spoke to Baruch the son of Neraiah and Elisha

21  to Gehazi his servant. All the men who entered the new covenant in the land of Damascus...

## Notes

### VIII

*11*  ראש *can mean either 'head' or 'poison.' It means 'poison' in the OT text quoted, and probably 'head' in the interpretation.*

*16*  *Reading* סרי *for* סרו.

*17*  *The B text makes sense, but perhaps by emending a corrupt reading* הועירו *to* העירו *(after an erasure). The A text is impossible, and my proposal is to emend it to read* הלכו, *which occurs with* אחר *at IV,19; XIX,32 and XI,15. But I cannot explain the corruption.*

## XIX

נאמנות להם לחיותם לאלפי דורות :    כב שומר הברית והחסד
לאהב ולשמרי מצותי לאף דור :    ואם מחנות ישבו כחוקי
הארץ אשר היה מקדם ולקחו נשים כמנהג התורה והולידו בנים
ויתהלכו על פי התורה :    וכמשפט היסודים כסרך התורה
כאשר אמר ב"איש לאשתו ובין אב לבנו וכל המאסים במצות ⁵
ובחקים להשיב גמול רשעים עליהם בפקד אל את הארץ
בבוא הדבר אשר כתוב ביד זכריה הנביא חרב עורי על
רועי ועל גבר עמיתי נאם אל הך את הרעה ותפוצינה הצאן
והשיבותי ידי על הצוערים :    והשומרים אותו הם עניי הצאן
אלה ימלטו בקץ הפקדה והנשארים ימסרו לחרב בבוא משיח ¹⁰
אהרן וישראל :    כאשר היה בקץ פקרת הראשון אשר אמר יחזקאל
ביד יחזקאל והתוו להתות התיו על מצחות נאנחים ונאנקים
והנשארים הסגרו לחרב נוקמת נקם ברית :    וכן משפט לכל באי

18 *The A text makes perfect grammatical sense, but is obviously incorrect. I have restored the intended sense by bracketing a gloss, but I am not sure that the present text came about in this manner. The purpose of such a gloss, if deliberate, eludes me.*

20 *20-21 is peculiar to the A text, and may suggest a further and possibly substantial deviation from the B text.*
*With this verb the text switches from singular to plural. I have retained the singular for elegance.*

## MS. B

### XIX

1  ... established for them that they may live for thousands of generations; as it is written: 'Who keeps the covenant and loyalty

2  to those who love Him* and keep His commandments* for a thousand generations.' And if they live in camps, following the order

3  of the land, as it was from of old, and take wives as directed by the law, and have children,

4  these (sc. the wives and children) shall walk according to the law and according to the rules of the Instructions*, by order of the law

5  which says: 'for a man and his wife, and for a father and his son.' And (as for) all who reject the commandments

6  and the ordinances, to bring the reward of the wicked upon themselves when God shall visit the earth,

7  when there shall come to pass the word which was written by the hand of Zechariah the prophet: 'Awake, O sword, against

8  my shepherd and against the man who is near to me, says God; smite the shepherd and the sheep will be scattered

9  and I will turn my hand to the little ones.' Those who keep (the commandments and the ordinances)* are the 'poor of the flock.'

10  These shall escape at the time of the visitation, and those who are left shall be delivered to the sword when the Messiah of

11  Israel and Aaron comes. (It will be) as it was in the time of the first* visitation, as He said

12  by the hand of Ezekiel: 'to make a mark upon the foreheads of those who sigh and groan.'

13  But those who were left were handed over to the sword which

בריתו אשר לא יחזיקו באלה ההקים לפקדם לכלה ביד בליעל

15 הוא היום אשר יפקד ל כאשר דבר היו שרי יהודה כמשיגי

גבול עליהם אשפך כמים עברה :　כי באו בברית תשובה

ולא סרו מדרך בוגדים ויתעללו בדרכי זנות ובהון הרשעה

ונקום ונטור איש לאחיהו ושנא איש את רעהו ויתעלמו איש

בשאר בשרו ויגשו לזמה ויתגברו להון ולבצע ויעשו ~~את~~

20 איש הישר בעיניו ויבהרו איש בשרירות לבו ולא נזרו מעם

ומחטאתם :　ויפרעו ביד רמה ללכת בדרכי רשעים :　אשר

אמר ל עליהם חמת תנינים יינם וראש פתנים אכזר :　התנינים

מלכי העמים ויינם הוא דרכיהם וראש פתנים הוא ראש

מלכי יון הבא עליהם לנקם נקמה ובכל אלה לא הבינו בוני

25 החיץ וטחי תפל כי הולך רוח ושקל ~~סופח~~ סופות ומטיף אדם

wreaked the vengeance of the covenant. And thus is the judgment on all members of

14 His covenant who have not held fast to these the ordinances, being visited to destruction by the hand of Belial.

*Notes:*

### XIX

2 *Reading* לאהבהו *with the MT of Deut. 7,9.*
  *Reading* מצותיו.
4 *Reading* יסורים *with the A text for* אסורים.
9 *Reading* אותם *for* אותו.
11 *Reading* הראשונה, *a corruption common to both texts; see on VII,21.*

### XIX

15 This is the day when God shall visit, as He has spoken: 'The princes of Judah have become like those who remove

16 the boundary, upon whom I will pour out wrath like wa[ter]. For they entered a covenant of repentance,

17 but did not depart from the way of traitors but defiled themselves in lustful ways and ill-gotten wealth,

18 revenge and grudge-bearing one with another, and hating each one his neighbour. They despised each one

19 his kinsman and they indulged in unchastity and behaved arrogantly for the sake of wealth and profit and did

20 each one as he pleas[ed] and chose each one in accordance with the stubbornness of his heart and did not separate from the people

21 and their sin, and re[bel]led with a high hand to walk in the way of the wicked, about

22 whom God said: 'serpents' venom is their wine and the cruel poison of asps.' The serpents are

23 the kings of the nations and their wine is their ways and the poison of asps is the head (or: poison*) of

24 the kings of Greece who will come upon them to wreak vengeance. <But all these things they do not understand, (these) 'builders of the

25 wall' and 'daubers of plaster,' because a walker in wind and raiser

לכזב אשר חרה אף אל בכל עדתו :    ואשר אמר משה
לישראל לא בצדקתך וביושר לבבך אתה בא לרשת את הגוים
האלה כי מאהבתו את אבותיך ומשמרו את השבועה :    כן
משפט לשבי ישראל סרו מדרך העם באהבת אל: את הראשנים
30 אשר העידו על העם אחרי אל ואהב את הבאים אחריהם כי להם
ברית אבות    ושונא ומתעב אל את בוני החיץ וחרה אף אפו בם ובכל
ההלכים אחריהם וכמשפט הזה לכל המאס במצות אל
ויעזבם ויפנו בשרירות לבם וכן כל האנשים אשר באו בברית
החדשה בארץ דמשק ושבו ויבגדו ויסורו מבאר מים החיים :

of storms and spouter to men

26 of lies* (spouted to them), against all of whose congregation the anger of God is aroused.> But, as Moses said

27 to Israel: 'Not because of your righteousness nor the uprightness of your heart are you going to dispossess these

28 nations, but because (God) loved your fathers and kept His promise.' This

29 is the judgment of the 'captivity of Israel' who departed* from the way of the people: because of God's love for the founders

30 who testified against the people in God's favour*, He loves those who come after them, because theirs is

31 the 'covenant of the fathers.' But God hates and abhors the 'builders of the wall' and his anger is aroused against them and against all

32 who follow them. And like this judgment (it will be) for everyone who re[je]cts the commandments of God

33 and forsakes them and turns* in the stubbornness of his heart.

*Notes:*

### XIX

23 ראש *can mean either 'head' or 'poison.' It means 'poison' in the OT text quoted, and probably 'head' in the interpretation, though whether an individual figure is meant is uncertain because of the pun.*

26 *Literally 'a spouter of men to lies.'*

29 *Reading* סרי *for* סרו.

30 *The B text makes sense, but perhaps by emending a corrupt reading* הועירו *to* העירו *(after an erasure). See on VIII,17.*

33 *With this verb the text switches from singular to plural, in both A and B texts. I have retained the singular for elegance.*

### XIX

33 [And] thus all the men who entered the new

34 covenant in the land of Damascus* and have turned back and acted treacherously and departed from the well of living water

35 לא יחשבו בסוד עם ובכתבו לא יכתבו מיום האסף יער מורה

## XX

מורה היחיד עד עמוד משיח מאהרן ומישראל    וכן המשפט

לכל באי עדת אנשי תמים הקדש ויקוץ מעשות פקודי ישרים

הוא האיש הנתך בתוך כור ‏‎‎‎:ה‎ בהופע מעשיו ישלח מעדה

כמו שלא נפל גורלו בתוך למודי אל כפי מעלו ‏זה‎ יוכיחוהו אנשי

5 דעות עד יום ישוב לעמד במעמד אנשי תמים קדש אשר אין

גורלו בתוך ובהופע מעשיו כפי מדרש התורה אשר יתהלכו

בו אנשי תמים הקדש אל ‏זה‎ יאות איש עמו בהון ובעבודה

כי אררוהו כל קדושי עליון וכמשפט הזה לכל המאס בראשונים

ובאחרונים אשר שמו גלולים על לבם וישימו וילכו בשרירות

10 לבם אין להם חלק בבית התורה :    כמשפט רעיהם אשר שבו

עם אנשי הלצון ישפטו כי דברו תועה על חקי הצדק ומאסו

בברית ואמנה אשר קימו בארץ דמשק והוא ברית החדשה :

ולא יהיה להם ולמשפחותיהם חלק בבית התורה    ומיום

האסף יוריה היחיד עד תם כל אנשי המלחמה אשר הלכו

15 עם איש הכזב כשנים ארבעים :    ובקץ ההוא יחרה

35 shall not be reckoned in the 'council of the people' and shall not be
written in their rec[ords] from the time the Teacher

## XX

1 of the community is gathered in until the arrival of the Messiah
from Aaron and from Israel
<And thus is the judgment (also)

2 for all who have entered the congregation of the men of perfect
holiness and is loth to do what is stipulated for upright men.

3 He is the man who is 'melted in the middle of a furnace.' When his
deeds become apparent, he shall be dismissed from the congregation

4 as one whose lot has not fallen among those 'taught by God.'
According to his offence shall the men of knowledge rebuke him

5 until the day when he shall return to take his place in the ranks of
the men of perfect holiness.

6 Once his deeds have become clear in the light of the study of the
law by which

7 the men of perfect holiness walk, no man may have dealings with
him in respect of property or work,

8 for all the holy ones of the Most High have cursed him.>
And the same judgment applies to everyone who rejects the
former

9 and the latter (ordinances), who have placed idols on their heart
and walked in the stubbornness

10 of their heart. They have no share in the House of the Law. They
shall receive the same judgment as their companions who turned
back

11 with the 'men of scoffing,' for *they* spoke heresy against the
ordinances of righteousness and rejected

12 the covenant and bond which they affirmed in the land of
Damascus <that is, the new covenant>.

13 There i[s]* no share for those or for their families in the House of
the Law.
From the day

14 when the Teacher of the community was gathered in until the
'disappearance of all the men of war' who turned back

15 with the Man of the Lie is about forty years. And during that
period the anger of God will be aroused

אף אל בישראל כאשר אמר אין מלך ואין שר ואין שופט ואין מוכיח בצדק ושבי פשע י[ע]ק[ב] שמרו ברית אל אז [י]ד[ב]רו איש אל רעהו להצדיק איש את אחיו לתמך צעדם בדרך אל ויקשב אל אל דבריהם וישמע ויכתב ספר זכרון ליראי אל ולחושבי שמו עד יגלה ישע וצדקה ליראי אל ושבתם וראיתם בין צדיק ורשע בין עבד [א]ל לאשר לא עבדו : ועשה חסד ל[אלפים] לאוהביו ולשמריו לאלף דור :[ ]מבית פלג אשר יצאו מעיר הקדש : וישענו על אל בקץ מעל ישראל וטמאו את המקדש ושבו עד אל [ ] העם בדברים מעט[י]ם ב[כ]לם איש לפי רוחו ישפטו בעצת הקודש : וכל אשר פרצו את גבול התורה מבאי הברית בהופע כבוד אל לישראל יכרתו מקרב המחנה ועמהם כל מרשיעי יהודה בימי מצרפותיו וכל המחזיקים במשפטים האלה לצאת ולבוא על פי התורה וישמעו לקול מורה ויתודו לפני אל כי אנו רשענו גם אנחנו גם אבותינו בלכתנו קרי בחקי הברית ואמת משפטיך בנו : ולא ירימו יד על חקי קדשו ומשפט צדקו ועדוות אמתו : והתיסרו במשפטים הראשונים אשר נשפטו בני אנשי היחיד והאזינו לקול מורה צדק : ולא ישיבו

16 against Israel, as He said: 'No king, no ruler and no judge, n[o-on]e
17 to rebuke in righteousness.'* But those who have turned from the
sin of [Ja]cob, who have kept* the covenant of God, they shall
then speak one
18 to another in order that each one may keep his brother righteous,
that their steps may be secure in the way of God and God may
heed
19 their words. 'And He shall hear and a book of remembrance shall
be written (before Him) of those who fear God and think upon
20 His name,' until deliverance and righteousness are revealed to
those who fear [God. 'And you shall again] discern between the
innocent and
21 the guilty (or: the righteous and the wicked), between one who
serves God and one who does not serve Him.' 'And He will show
mercy to [thousands],' 'to those who love Him,'
22 and those who wait for Him 'for a thousand generations.'
. . . of the house of Peleg who went out from the Holy City
23 and leaned upon God at the time when Israel sinned and defiled
the sanctuary, but returned again
24 [to the wa]y of the people in a few respec[ts. Ea]ch of them is to be
judged individually, according to his spirit in the holy council.
25 And all who have transgressed the limits of the law among those
who have entered the covenant; when the glory of God appears
26 to Israel, they shall be cut off 'from the mid[st] of the camp,' and
with them all the evildoers of (or: who do evil to)
27 Judah in the days of its trials. But all who hold fast to these rules, to
go out
28 and come in according to the law, and obey (the) Teacher, and
confess before God, 'We
29 have done wickedly, both we and our fathers, in walking contrary
to the ordinances of the covenant.
30 Thy judgments against us are righteous and correct . . . ,' and do
not lift a hand against His holy ordinances and righteous
judgments
31 and true testimonies and have been instructed by the former rules
by which
32 the men of the community are judged, and obey the Teacher of
Righteousness, and do not reject
33 the righteous ordinances when they hear them—(these men) shall

אל חקי הצדק בשמעם אתם ישישו וישמחו ויעז לבם ויתגברו
על כל בני תבל וכפר אל בעדם וראו בישועתו כי חסו בשם קדשו

'rejoice and be glad,' their heart shall be strong, and they shall prevail
34 over all the inhabitants of the world; God shall pardon them and they shall see His deliverance, for they have taken refuge in His holy name.

*Notes:*

## XIX

34 *Here the A text finishes.*

## XX

13 *Restoring* היה *(not* יהיה *as some commentators).*
17 *This is a paraphrastic and interpretative rendering of the MT. See* Rabin, *ad loc.*
  *Reading* שמרי *for* שמרו.